T0354996

by R. Gordon Zyne

Novels
Degrees of Desire
Shiners
Malchus One Ear

Poetry and Spiritual Writings
Messiah Works
Meditations on the Ultimate Concern
The Eternal Source
Spirit Care
Hold the Darkness Close

Art and Creative Design
RichardGordonZyne.com

GIVE BIRTH
TO A
DANCING STAR

THEOPOETIC MEDITATIONS

R. GORDON ZYNE

GIVE BIRTH TO A DANCING STAR
THEOPOETIC MEDITATIONS

iUniverse books may be ordered through booksellers or by contacting:

iUniverse
1663 Liberty Drive
Bloomington, IN 47403
www.iuniverse.com
844-349-9409

ISBN: 978-1-6632-7047-4 (sc)
ISBN: 978-1-6632-7048-1 (e)

Library of Congress Control Number: 2025901497

Print information available on the last page.

iUniverse rev. date: 02/06/2025

For
Paula
Danny, Nick, Jessica
Maddie and Tuna
and
All the Lovers of Life and Living Things on the Earth

"One must still have chaos in oneself to be able to give birth to a dancing star."
—*Friedrich Nietzche, Thus Spoke Zarathustra*

Introduction

Theopoetry is a literary and spiritual expression that bridges the gap between doctrinal or systematic theology and poetry. It is an approach to articulating the Divine and the human experience of God through poetic language. Unlike traditional theological discourse, which relies on analytical and doctrinal precision, Theopoetry embraces metaphor, emotion, and imagination to delve into the mysteries of existence and transcendence.

Theopoetry uses the evocative and symbolic power of poetry to engage with theological themes such as creation, redemption, grace, faith, and the ineffable nature of God. It may not provide clear-cut answers but instead invites the reader into a contemplative or experiential encounter with the Divine.

Theopoetry oscillates between the transcendence of God (beyond human comprehension) and the immanence of God (present and near in creation and human experience). It emphasizes mystery and awe, portraying the Divine as both deeply personal—incarnate—and profoundly cosmic.

By tapping into the emotional and imaginative aspects of human experience, both serious and humorous, theopoetry transcends intellectual boundaries and appeals to the heart and spirit. It often speaks to universal human longings, such as the desire for connection, meaning, and hope.

Theopoetry draws inspiration from sacred texts, liturgy, and religious tradition, reinterpreting them in ways that resonate with contemporary life. It can also incorporate modern philosophical and cultural influences, blending ancient truths with modern sensibilities. Theopoetry focuses on poetic exploration, such as the interplay of human suffering and Divine grace, as a way to engage with Divine mystery. It is less concerned with doctrinal precision and more with evoking a sense of the sacred. Theopoetry invites readers to experience theology as a living, dynamic encounter rather than a rigid framework. It seeks to move beyond dogma into the realm of shared human and Divine mystery, offering space for wonder, doubt, and the sacred imagination.

In a world where theological language can feel abstract or inaccessible, these daily theopoetic meditations provide a way to connect deeply and personally with spiritual truths. It honors the complexity of faith, the beauty of the Divine Spirit, and the richness of human experience, creating a space where imagination and theology meet.

THE MEDITATIONS

1
Give Birth to a Dancing Star

Growth is not tender, nor kind. It is a rupture, a breaking apart. The seed does not bloom gently—it splits, its fragile skin tearing as roots push into the dark, searching, claiming space where there was none.

Growth is destruction, and destruction is life clawing forward. When life falls apart, it feels like a forest fire—air thick with smoke, ground left black and empty. Silence follows, heavy and raw.

But from the charred remains, green rises. It always rises. The earth shifts, and we stumble, clinging to the fragile scaffolding of what we once called normal. It crumbles anyway, collapsing into the dust of yesterday. Yet chaos, cruel as it seems, is a midwife. Its hands are rough, its voice sharp, but its purpose unyielding.

The storm rolls in, the sky splits open, and we are torn loose, unmoored, spinning in violent winds. But this storm, this destruction, is not the end.

It is the tearing down of walls too small to hold the vastness we are becoming, walls that must fall to make way for more. *One must have chaos in oneself to give birth to a dancing star. —Nietzsche*

And so, from the wreckage, something begins. The star does not arrive quietly. It bursts into existence, wild and radiant, spinning into the vastness, born from the ruins of what was.

Let the ground tremble. Let the walls fall. Let the storm rage. For in every shattered piece, there is space being made, space for something luminous, something infinite, something new.

Growth is not gentle. It is destruction. But from the chaos, a new dancing star is born.

2
Awakening

You who dwell in the quiet winds, and in the stillness of my heart, kindle within me a faith that is not borrowed, not handed down like a relic, but alive—alive as the dew upon the morning grass, as the river flowing to the sea.

May my soul rise to meet You as the sun meets the sky, not out of habit, but with the wonder of first light. May my steps find their way to You, not along paths paved by others, but through the wild, untamed fields of discovery and surrender.

Teach me, Breath of Life, that faith is not a fortress, but an open sky. Not a chain, but the rhythm of waves returning again and again to their source.

Let my heart be a vessel, emptied of noise, filled with the sound of Your whisper. Let my doubts and questions be as stones in the stream, their edges smoothed by Your grace.

God of the Present Moment, break me free from the weight of ritual devoid of meaning. Help me to see You not only in the sanctuary, but in the unfolding of each day—in the rustling leaves, the laughter of a stranger, the silence between breaths.

Grant me the courage to let go of what I think You are, so that I may encounter what You truly are. For You are not confined to the walls of my understanding, but move freely, calling me to do the same.

May this faith grow, not like a towering oak, but as a wildflower—fragile, unexpected, and infinitely alive. And in its blossoming, may I come to know You not as a distant God, but as the pulse of all that is.

3
The Quiet Dawn

He will not come riding the clouds, nor will trumpets tear the sky. Instead, He comes as a whisper, soft as the breath that stirs the soul, calling us to wake.

The second coming is not a step, not a footfall breaking silence. It is the veil lifting from our eyes, the scales of fear falling, so we see what was always there: the Christ within, the dawn of our becoming.

The heavens do not split; the earth does not quake. It is we who tremble—our minds unmade, our hearts remade. The kingdom grows where once only walls stood.

This is the birth of love unbound. This is the breaking of the old world. Not the end, but the opening. Not a person, but the transformation of all.

He comes as a light we did not know we already carried.

4
Resurrection

Resurrection is not a whisper at the edge of the grave—it is a shout that rattles the bones of history. To restore life to the dead is to spit in the eye of darkness, to pull breath from beyond the veil of endings. It is the echo of the third day—the stone rolled back, the linen left folded, the gardener speaking your name.

Resurrection is the rise of a nation, sinews knitting dry bones into marching flesh—hope with a pulse. It is the caterpillar becoming a chrysalis becoming a butterfly.

Resurrection says to death, you are not the end of the story. It is victory carved from grief's stubborn soil, a blooming of new beginnings from the carcass of despair. But resurrection isn't a rewind—it isn't the same song played twice. It is new skin stretched over old wounds, a glorified body that carries its scars like medals. It's hope with hands—still torn, still holy.

Resurrection is not something final. It is a man broken by failure, rising from his ruin, and calling it grace. A woman stitched from sorrow lifting her head to the light after the long night. A child, weeping, believing again after someone speaks a truth that does not betray.

Resurrection is cosmic rebellion—all Creation remade, dust spun into galaxies, heaven kissing earth until they blur. "Behold," says the voice in Revelation, "I make all things new." Not some things. All.

Resurrection is not reincarnation, not the endless wheel of return. It is a doorway, not a loop. It is not the soul wearing new faces to pay off its debts. It is not repetition—it is a metamorphosis—it is the epitome of transformation.

Resurrection rises in the silence after you've surrendered to despair—and find yourself still breathing. It lifts you when the world says you cannot rise. It turns water into wine, weeping into dance, graves into gardens. Pain into healing.

Resurrection is never quiet. It breaks the lock. It calls your name. It says: You were dead—but now you live.

5

The Soft Voice Within the Silence

When sadness folds into anger, anger twists into fear, or doubles back into itself—a circle without an end—what then?

The wind rises, howling through the cracks. The flame wavers, its light fragile, its edges softening.

It dims, but it does not go out. And so, we ask, *What now? What should we do?* The questions gather like stones, stacked high, pressing heavily against the silence.

Does God help? The trees do not answer. They stand still, their roots tangled in the quiet. The river flows, endless and indifferent.

A bird cries out in the distance, its voice carrying no solutions, only the echo of its wings beating against the sky. And yet, we respond. Not with certainty, but with breath.

Not with answers, but with movement, the slow unfolding of action. The heart rises, though it aches. The hands stretch forward, though they tremble.

The world keeps turning, even when we cannot feel it shift beneath us. God is not the fire, but the space it fills.

Not the light, but the shadow it casts. Not the answer, but the soft voice within the silence.

Sadness collapses into anger, anger falls into fear, and the circle begins to spin again. But through it all, the flame remains—steady, small, alive. Its heat is faint, but enough.

Enough to remind us of what we carry. Enough to say we are still here. Still alive.

6

Grace Waits at Every Turn

Hands clasped, yet they move, fingers weaving silent prayers into the fabric of the earth. The path takes shape, not through perfection, but through each uncertain, uneven step pressing forward through the dust.

Grace waits at every turn— not in fanfare or blazing trumpets, but in the quiet touch of a hand brushing against our shoulders, in the whisper that says, *This way. Keep going.*

We stumble; our knees scrape against the stones of regret, and our hearts grow heavy with the weight of trying. But even then, we rise. Again. And again.

Heaven does not remain distant. It bends low, humble, and gentle, meeting us in broken places, lifting what cannot lift itself. Heaven does not carry us, but it steadies us, holds us long enough to take another step.

Each fall etches a map of where we've been. Each rise becomes a quiet promise of where we might go.

The path is not easy. It was never meant to be. But beneath the bruises, the torn hands, and the weary feet, something glows.

Soft, eternal, steady— a flame that refuses to die.

Faith walks with us. Grace meets us. And heaven bends, not to judge, but to walk beside us, step by step.

7
Faith

Faith is a flame, small and trembling, yet unyielding. It moves with the winds of doubt, its light fragile but steady, its warmth enough to touch a trembling heart.

The storm arrives, wild and unrelenting, tearing through the trees, bending their branches, stripping leaves from their homes. Yet the roots hold fast, quiet and unseen, their strength murmured deep through the dark earth.

What is it to trust in what the eye cannot see? To stretch trembling fingers into the void and find not emptiness, but the steady pulse of something vast, something unbroken?

Faith is not the absence of fear. It is the step taken despite fear's shadow. It is the voice that whispers in the silence. It is the hand that rises, slow but certain, to light the flame again, and again, and again.

Even as the night presses close, even as the winds howl and rage, the flame remains. It burns.

8
Edge of Truth

Truth cuts deeper than the surgeon's blade— no clean incision, no practiced hand stitching the wound shut. Instead, it comes to us jagged, its edge raw and rusted, ripping through sinew and marrow, leaving us undone, exposed, bleeding in the silence of what we thought we knew.

It does not ask permission. It does not wait for us to be ready. Truth falls, sudden and relentless, like a guillotine at dawn, its shadow looming long before the strike.

And when it lands, what remains? Fragments. A hand groping for what isn't there. A face fractured in shards of broken glass. The sound of a name we cannot speak without trembling.

The wounds truth leaves do not heal, not in the way we hope. It marks us, alters us. Scar tissue forms, thick and unyielding, mapping what was lost, what was torn away, and what we still carry.

Truth does not soothe. It offers no comfort. It stands, stark and unrelenting, pressing its weight into the hollow spaces where lies once lived.

And yet— within the ache of its clarity, something begins. Slowly. Painfully. We rise, not unbroken, but whole in a way we hadn't known before. Not untouched, but real.

9
Seed of Life

In the quiet of my heart, love stirs like a hidden seed. It is not mine to claim, not mine to contain—it belongs to the wind, to the rain, to the light that bids it grow.

It does not bloom for my glory, but for the good of the other. Its roots drink the waters of selflessness, its petals stretch to the warmth of compassion. It is no longer I who lives but love that lives in me.

I watch it break open the ground, crack the hard shell of my ego, and rise in delicate strength, teaching me the weightlessness of surrender, the abundance of giving, the holiness of seeking another's good.

This is life: to let love flower freely, to let its fragrance fill the space between souls, to let its seeds scatter in the winds of grace, planting eternity in the soil of the present.

10
I Am Still Here

The room has no windows. The walls press in, gray and blank, as if they've seen too much and decided they don't care anymore. Machines hum their tired song—a funeral march for no one, played for an audience that never came.

Life and death sit together in the corner, sharing a cigarette, their fingers tangled like lovers who can't stop fighting. The air thickens, heavy with ghosts too stubborn to leave.

Wires crawl under the floor like veins, pumping nothing into nowhere. The lights flicker, hesitant, like they can't decide if the fight is worth it.

Outside, the city screams. People run, chasing things they'll never hold, their faces smudged like scraps of paper blowing down an alley. But here, the clocks are tired.

The seconds stretch, sticky and slow. Everything drags. Even death seems bored. The machines don't feel pain, don't care about hope. They just hum, droning on and on like a drunk uncle who won't leave the table. But somewhere, beneath the hum and the buzz, something whispers: *I'm still here.*

It isn't a victory. It isn't a prayer. It's just a fact.

The walls lean in, listening. The machines stutter, their rhythm softening for a moment. Life and death pause, the cigarette burning between their fingers, watching— waiting— to see if that voice will speak again.

11
Flood

The road shimmered, washed clean by the morning, as we walked. Her steps were steady but worn, each one carrying the weight of a year drowned in sorrow.

7

The river had come like a thief, its hands wide and merciless. It took the dogs, the business, the home, the work of a thousand days. It left her standing in the brittle silence of an emptied life.

Grief surged behind her eyes— a tide that rose and fell, never fully receding. Yet she kept walking, through the rubble of weeks, through the shifting sands of months. She held her daughter close, as if the weight of the world could be balanced in the curve of a small, hopeful smile.

Papers piled high on tables, forms without mercy. The language of insurance was a gray, foreign fog, dense and unkind. Each phone call was a fresh wound. Each night was a ledger of survival.

But today, the air felt softer, as if the earth itself had exhaled. The flood, relentless and cold, had washed something loose.

The fears she had carried for years— hidden beneath the surface like jagged stones— had been smoothed in its wake.

She did not speak of triumph. There were no banners, no proclamations of joy. But her steps, lighter now, hummed with a quiet hymn. The wind moved gently through the trees, and in its soft, careful song, something in her had been saved.

12
The Grace of Forward Motion

Strength blooms in the heart, slow and quiet, like wildflowers in forgotten fields. Its roots dig deeper than fear, casting shadows to the past.

Forward steps begin— hesitant, uneven, yet each one a small victory over the weight of yesterday.

Imperfect yet whole, we walk—not because the path is easy, but because grace whispers, "You are ready."

Through forgiveness, light as dawn, the burdens unravel—softening in the warmth of morning. What was once heavy becomes something we no longer have to carry.

13
Metamorphosis

Metamorphosis—it's not some magic trick, not a Houdini act to wow the crowd, not some Divine applause line that rolls back the stone for a standing ovation.

It's quieter than that, sharper than that, like the voice of a stranger saying your name when you thought no one was looking, when you thought no one even knew you had a name.

It's the hand that shows up just before you fall— not to save you, but to remind you that you're still alive. It's the eyes of a child on a subway train, wide with questions you stopped asking years ago.

It's the way the sun slips through the blinds on a morning when you swore there was no point in getting out of bed.

Metamorphosis isn't a show; it's a breath— just one more than you thought you had left. It's a stranger's coat wrapped around your shoulders on a freezing night. And it's nothing— just a flicker, a whisper of something better before the dark comes back.

14
Follow Him!

God isn't in the clouds. He's in the sweat of two bodies colliding in the night, in the trembling hands of a man offering his last dollar to the homeless kid outside the bar. God's not a cosmic puppeteer, no king in the sky. He's just love— raw, unfiltered, human, and utterly reckless.

Jesus didn't sit in stained glass. He kicked over tables, shook the dust from his feet, and called out the fat cats feeding on the backs of the poor. His compassion wasn't soft; it had fists, it had fire. It burned through the lies of every system that sold power dressed as peace.

The kingdom of God? It's a conspiracy of love, a street-level revolt against every machine that grinds men into dust and calls it profit. It's not golden gates. It's soup kitchens, it's protest lines, it's the woman handing out sandwiches to workers on strike.

The Way of Jesus? It's no quiet stroll; it's the blistered feet of a man marching away from the seduction of empire, away from the easy lies of Sunday sermons that sell comfort instead of justice. It's blood under your fingernails from clawing at the chains wrapped around your neighbor's neck.

The Cross? That's no symbol of glory. It's an execution, a warning shot from the empire to anyone who dares to say no. But Jesus carried it anyway, walked straight into the teeth of the machine, and told it to choke on him.

And the Resurrection? It's not some magic trick. It's the voice of a stranger saying your name when you thought no one was looking. It's the hand of a nurse lifting you from your knees when you swore you couldn't go on.

This whole thing— it's not about waiting for heaven. It's about making it here. Now!

Go! Follow Him!

15
Dear Friend, Just Go!

He cried out for Mary, his voice cracking like the spine of an old Bible, fingers crooked, pointing at the ceiling— a desperate map to somewhere he thought she'd be waiting. For an hour, maybe more, he kept calling her name. Come on, Mary. Full of grace. Come on.

His body, stripped down to bone and a diaper, looked like the ruins of a place no one dared rebuild. Emaciated, collapsed into the hollow of his hospital bed, he was the wreckage of a man holding out for heaven.

I told him to go. Please, my Dear Friend, just go. They're waiting for you. They don't care about the way you look now. You don't have to stand, don't have to dress, don't have to say you're sorry anymore. Just go.

But he wouldn't listen. He kept crying out for her. Hail Mary. Hail Mary. Like she was the only one who'd hear

I sat there, watching his hands stiffen, his lips trembling like prayers that didn't know how to end. I think she hears you, Dear Friend. I whispered it, my voice too small for the room. I know she hears you. She's coming. She has to be coming.

I stayed with him, waiting for her too. Waiting for that sigh, the moment his breath would let go and float to wherever Mary's hands were waiting to catch him.

But he kept calling her name— the last name he'd ever known. And I kept begging, please, Dear Friend, just go.

When he finally did, there was no light, no hallelujah. Just the silence of his fingers falling from the ceiling, the weight of his name left behind in the sheets.

I stayed a little longer, wondering if Mary had come, or if it was just the sound of her name that carried him through.

16
Girl on Twelve

There's a girl in apartment 12B, who's carved out a space so sad and silent, it echoes like the hollow of a tired moon. I don't know how I know this, but I do.

She never looks at me, never square in the face. Her eyes skim past like I'm a miserable dog, or a mouse darting under the fridge. When she does look, it's brief— a quick blink, a flicker of light snapping off. Her lashes seem to erase me, like old smoke lingering too long in a cheap bar.

Sometimes we pass on the stairs. She's always rushing down from her kingdom on twelve, while I crawl up from the depths of three. Three's my lucky number, which feels like a joke, because luck left me behind long ago, the day the city swallowed me whole.

On Sundays, I see her in clean, neat armor— a white Bible tucked in her arms like a newborn she doesn't trust the world to hold. She moves as if Sunday mornings belong to her, and maybe they do. I wonder which church takes her in, where she sits on a wooden pew, whispering her prayers, while I rot on the other side of town with a beer and no god to listen.

Sometimes I think about following her. Finding her church. Sitting in the back. Letting her God see me, just once, just long enough to call me lucky.

I think she wears a small cross on her neck, slender and pale, like something painted in winter. But I've never been close enough to know if the cross is gold, silver, or just imagined.

I pray sometimes— not for me, but for her. I pray she'll look at me, just once, with a kindness that doesn't slam the door in my face. I pray she'll slow down on the stairs, won't pull her coat tight like I'm the cold, won't blink so fast like I'm the nightmare.

I'll save enough someday, move up to twelve, get an apartment with a view of the same city that chewed us both up.

I'll meet her in the basement, in the laundry room, both of us waiting for the machine to stop spinning.

Then, in that damp quiet, I'll say hello, and she'll blink slow— not to erase me, but to let me stay. But maybe I'll stay here on three, watching her on the stairs, letting my prayers go unanswered. That's the kind of luck I'm used to.

17
Dreams

Sometimes my dreams were chocolate— rich, warm, melting on my tongue, a sweet nothingness that made everything feel possible. But other times, they hid behind a door, small and trembling, like a child afraid of his father's shadow.

They would dart ahead of me, Rudy barking at their heels, both of them chasing ghosts down side streets, or after cars with no destination. When they weren't chocolate, they just sat there— a lump, a meatloaf of a dream, stewing in its own juices. A bad baby with a full diaper and no one to change it.

How I miss those silly, innocent dreams— those harmless flights of nonsense, unspoiled by the rancid smells of this world's heavy breath. Now my dreams whine. They drag their feet through dark clouds, spill into nights that stretch too long. They bring gray-bearded strangers with hollow eyes, their faces collapsing like crumbling walls. These dreams are tired, just like me.

I know, I know— I have to live with them now. The nightmares, the terrors, the jagged edges of midnight journeys. Each one feels like a step closer to heaven— or so they say.

And those angels— God, those angels with their empty eyes and too-bright smiles. They promise knowledge but hand me nothing but the cold weight of hope, wrapped in silence.

Yes, I miss the dreams I used to have. The chocolate ones. The ones that ran, that laughed. I miss Rudy chasing them into the sun.

18

Song for Broken Souls

I have seen them— wandering like leaves in autumn winds, carried, turned, and sometimes caught in the sharp branches of the world. They are not sick. They are not dying. They are moving. Forever moving, blown off course by strange winds that whisper promises of safe harbors, but lead them instead to wild, untamed seas.

They twist, these souls, like a compass at the North Pole, their needles spinning endlessly, searching for a truth they already hold but cannot see. They trust too much, too easily. And in their trust, they crack— fine lines spreading like a spider's web kissed by frost. But oh, what light enters there! What radiant beams break through those fissures, and what tender glows escape!

Broken souls are artists. They are makers of worlds. They paint with infinite colors, with textures that no other hands could shape. Their lives are not masterpieces of completion, but of becoming— a process that sings louder and truer than any finished work. And yet, beneath their beauty, there is pain. A deep ache that pulses like a second heartbeat, a constant reminder of their need— not for fixing, not for mending, but for healing.

When you come upon a broken soul, do not ask what shattered them. Do not try to stitch their fragments into something whole. Simply love them. Pour your heart into their hands as though pouring water into parched earth. Let them drink from your kindness. Let them feel the warmth of your gaze. Let them remember that love exists, even in the wilderness they have come to know so well.

Because this—this is the nature of true healing: not to seal the cracks, but to honor them. To show them that light still streams through, that their brokenness is their glory.

And as you love them, watch. Watch as their pain softens, as their spinning needle steadies, as their winds become a gentle breeze. For in the love you give, you will see the beginning of their becoming— a broken soul, a wandering soul, finding its way to the horizon of itself.

19
Creative Spirit

Art is spiritual— not in the vague, washed-out way of things forgotten, but in the crackling immediacy of lightning tearing through the fabric of a silent sky.

It is the breath God takes when He stirs the ocean's depths, when He kneads the stars into shape, again and again— an eternal hand in an eternal act.

Art is not a fleeting refreshment, like rain on stone that dries too soon. No—art stays. It seeps deep, soaking the roots of what we are. It adds to the permanent fullness of the soul, a quiet wealth that cannot be spent.

Its joy is sharp and clear— like a bell struck in the stillness. Its echoes discipline the heart, not as a master with a whip, but as a lover, holding you close to the edge of what you can become.

And in this dance— this steady ache of beauty— you are transformed. You are drawn beyond yourself, to where the horizon widens, and values bloom in the soil of the infinite.

20
Street Gospel

They walk slow, a shuffle of feet on broken sidewalks, tapping out rhythms older than the concrete beneath them. The scratch of shoe leather against the ground hums like a needle on a worn-out record, each step a story, each story a song. And they sing—low and deep, voices full of the blues, that soul-aching sound that doesn't ask permission, that doesn't beg for an audience.

Their voices are cracked and beautiful, like shards of broken glass catching the last rays of sunlight. They sing about love gone wrong, about husbands buried under cold ground and children grown into strangers.

They sing about aches that settle into bones and refuse to leave, and about the joy that, somehow, still lingers like a stubborn ember. The city grinds on around them. Cars roar, taxis honk, a man in a sharp suit sidesteps with a frown, but they don't care. They don't sing for the world.

They sing because they have to, because the rhythm is as much a part of them as their breath. Their laughter bubbles between verses, rolling out into the evening air like cigarette smoke curling toward a tired sky.

These old women, faces etched with years, with whiskey and tears, carry a fire that refuses to go out. Their steps are gospel, their voices a hymn for the lost and the found. They've turned these streets into their cathedral, their sanctuary.

And they don't need a thing— no crowd, no applause, no reason. They need only each other and the next line to sing, the next step to take, their rhythm stitching the night together, one verse at a time.

21
Breaking Seed

I hear glass breaking, or maybe it's just my heart. A billion leaves fall from the trees, a quiet storm of resignation, and I realize that autumn is less about the colors or the crackling of leaves and more about the human condition.

We are so weary, dragging ourselves through days that taste like rust, with dreams hanging by threads, fading like the last light on a November afternoon. Utterly exhausted, we carry the weight of our own surrender.

But deep inside, there's a seed, a stubborn, defiant thing, begging to die so it can split open. It aches for rebirth, to push its way through the cold earth, cracking the ground above it, reaching for a beam of sun like a whispered promise.

I am that seed— a fragile, trembling defiance. But the way up is a battle, each inch a war. The soil presses in like doubt, heavy and relentless. Rocks block the path— ancient, unyielding, indifferent to my struggle. The clouds hover, gray and unsympathetic, hoarding their rain.

There's that sound again— glass breaking, sharp and sudden— and I know now it's my heart. My heart is a seed too, cradled in a fragile shell, yearning to shatter. To burst from its own prison and find something, anything, worth rising for.

I push, and it hurts. The dirt is cold, and the sun is only a rumor above the blackness. But I keep going because that's what seeds do. They fight, they rise, even when the rocks mock their effort, even when the struggle feels senseless.

The sound of breaking glass echoes in the marrow of my being, reminding me that growth is a kind of violence, a kind of breaking. And sometimes, breaking is the only way to make it to the light.

I am the seed. My heart, the glass. My roots twist through doubt, tangled and trembling, but the green is still in me— waiting, straining for that one beam of sun, that one breath of rain.

I push past the rocks, past the cold, through the breaking. And I hope— someday— to become more than a seed lost in the dark.

22
Out of Chaos

It is during entropy— when the temperature spikes, when the pressure makes the whole system groan, when solidity and chaos blur like an exhausted lover's midnight gaze—that things break. They shatter, spilling into something unrecognizable, something terrifyingly new.

The particles lose their manners, forget their places, and spin into a ballet of rebellion. They dance like mad prophets, chanting the gospel of dissolution. Solids melt, dignity slips, and the world becomes a river of liquid sin, rushing in confusion, with no banks to guide it.

When even liquids can't hold their shame, they vaporize into ghosts— memories of what once was, what could never be again. Steam rises into the night, a chorus of what-could-have-beens, whispering secrets to the stars. But the stars blink back with apathy, cold and unfeeling.

This is how it goes, isn't it? The breaking, the boiling, the vapor trails of things trying to find themselves, losing everything in the process. Believing that disarray is death when, in truth, it's only a prelude. Entropy is the creative force of the universe, the hand that slams the table and sends the pieces flying. The pieces land in ways no sober mind would ever dream.

It is the collision of the mundane and the electric edge of the impossible, where form becomes fluid, and fluid forgets its name.

The world itself was born from such moments, from these discomposing transitions where all sense is lost, and the heart races with the panic of not knowing if chaos will ever still. Entropy laughs, its crown of decay tilted, drunk on disorder, smug in the belief it has the final word.

But entropy is a fool. From the froth and madness, the particles find a rhythm. The chaos remembers its purpose. A new order settles like dust, a structure more beautiful, more stable for having been broken and rebuilt.

In these moments, when everything seems to fall apart, when the floor cracks and the walls sweat, when the world howls its indifference, a secret is being told— in the language of shattered things. It whispers that to become whole, one must first break. One must surrender to the molten, the raw, the ruinous.

As the night cools, the pressure eases. The last gasp of steam sighs into silence, and a form emerges made pliant by chaos, baptized in uncertainty. It is ready for the next cycle, the next time the temperature rises, the pressure builds, and the dance begins again.

23
Darkness

If only there was light in this jungle, a lantern swung down from heaven into the muck, enough for each of us to see our own hands— the dirt ground into our palms, the lines worn deep, the truth etched in flesh.

But it's dark here. The only light is electric, buzzing neon like a fly circling a corpse, a sick joke of brightness flashing over the ruins, mocking the shadows it fails to erase.

If only there was a bowl of rice for every starving man, a bite for every child with ribs like cages. If only those with power cared enough to lift a spoon. But they sit on their thrones, heavy and clean, cloaked in silk and illusion.

They toss crumbs from a septic tank so rotten it leaks poison, throwing us dry bones stripped bare, leftovers from beasts that vanished long ago.

This is what they call civilization— an empire of rotting meat and plastic smiles, a dead garden planted in concrete. A song that doesn't sing but hisses, steam escaping from under blistered skin. It's broken, like glass beads scattered across subway tracks, and when you step on them, they crunch like brittle bones underfoot.

We hear whistles, distant and dead. The smell of burning fills the air— the charred remains of hope crushed under the wheels of progress. And no one cares. Not even a flicker of concern in their eyes. Just another day on the highway to nowhere, the sky thick with smoke and clouds, smothering whatever god might still be lingering.

The devils are ready, hands wide open, fingers long and greedy. They're in every mirror, every screen. We watch them— orange politicians with waxy grins, dark poodles with bald heads nodding along. Yes, yes, they say. More of the same. More.

And here I am— no control, no shield— standing in the face of the flood, watching the tide roll in, black and oily. The waves lap at the shore of decency, pulling the ground from under my feet. I know there's nothing I can do but wait.

Wait for the next mouthful of filth, the next scrap of meat they toss, the next bitter swallow of this poisoned feast. The light's out. The rice is gone. And we're all here in the dark jungle, waiting—empty-handed, with broken eyes.

24
Simple Humanity

Human beings, my children, my beloved, must walk into the pain of others. They must cradle the anguish, the tears, the raw, sacred truth of life. Hold the suffering close— not with pity, not from a safe distance, but with the intimacy of a lover's touch, tender and unflinching.

This is not a sermon of power, not a doctrine crafted by men, not a political dance or a game of thrones and crowns. It is a plea— a cry from the heart, an expression of hope, of love. It is a simple humanity, for humanity's sake.

Feel it, my dear ones: the wounds of another's soul, the silent scream in their eyes, the unspoken agony hidden in their hearts. Not for glory, not for gain, not for some celestial reward, but because in this broken world, we are all the light we have.

Think of the baby's cry in Gaza, the homeless beggar's outstretched hand, the mother's silent grief, the father's unending toil. Each one is a mirror, reflecting our shared human frailty, our shared Divine spark.

So here it is— my heart, my hope, my everything: a simple humanity for the sake of love. A whisper, a prayer, offered in this beautiful, suffering world, where each tear is a sacrament, each touch a blessing, each act of kindness a miracle.

Together, these are testaments to our shared grace. Do not turn away. Do not close your hearts. Embrace the pain, the joy, the full spectrum of this existence. For in the act of loving, in the act of caring, we find our truest selves.

Our salvation is not in grandeur or power, but in the quiet miracle of a simple humanity— for humanity's sake.

25
Edge of Flight

I look in the mirror and see confusion. Not even my face stares back, only fragments— the back of my head, my shivering hands, pieces that don't fit. Ghosts haunt the shattered glass, their edges sharp with questions I cannot answer.

I live in a world where the ground cracks and sighs beneath me, where I am perched on a precipice, off balance, teetering between the jump and the wild, trembling hope of flight.

In a breath caught in my chest, I realize I have wings. But what kind? Are they the mighty wings of an eagle, wide and weathered, knowing the wind? Or are they the fragile fluttering of a butterfly, just born, wings damp and trembling, uncertain whether the sky is friend or foe?

Caught between two ages, I stand— confused and conflicted, suffocating under the weight of choice, suffering in the stasis of not knowing which way to go. But then, there it is: a truth as small as a haiku, as loud as a train on broken tracks. We have an instrument for understanding ourselves, a blade to cut through the fog.

It is the knowledge of the universe, etched into every star, every sigh, every grain of doubt. And there is faith— true as clear water— in a God, whose love runs through veins, whose hands shaped both the eagle's wide span and the butterfly's first uncertain flinch.

The Spirit of God, creative and loving, transcendent, immanent, incarnate— dwells in the marrow. It turns confusion into a chrysalis. It turns suffocation into the labor of new wings.

I stand at the edge, looking into the mirror. I do not see my face, but the fragments of something rising. Something waiting for the shift, the leap, the wind beneath wings that are only now learning to believe they were meant to fly.

26
The Song of Being

Creation hums beneath all things, a melody woven in the fibers of existence. It whispers of dependence, of every atom leaning softly into the will of the Divine, of a universe spinning not by chance, but by the hand of love. The trees lift their arms in silent praise, the rivers run in rhythms of trust, the stars burn with the light of a thousand hallelujahs. And here, at the center of it all, we are, fragile and finite, but cradled in the infinite.

This dependence is no burden, no shameful tether to some distant throne. It is the secret strength of the cosmos: that all things lean on the One who does not lean, that all beauty springs from the fountainhead of goodness. We are not self-made. We are not self-sustained. Creation sings, not of subjugation, but of communion. It tells us that we are not alone— we are never alone.

And what of this goodness, this essential glow that runs like veins of gold through every rock, every leaf, every living thing? It is not a distant ideal, not a theory of philosophers in their towers. It is the hum of the earth turning, the warmth of the sun falling on bare skin, the laughter of a child echoing in an empty room. It is the presence of God breathing life into all that is, calling it good, calling it beloved.

But Creation's hymn is not complete without its crescendo: the Word, ancient and eternal, stepping down from glory into the dust of the earth. The Divine wrapped in skin, walking the roads of Galilee, sweating under the sun, weeping at the tomb of a friend, bleeding under the weight of a cross. Jesus, the Christ, in whom all things find their fulfillment. Not a distant deity, but a brother, a friend, a savior. He lived so that we might see what it means to truly live.

This is Creation fulfilled: that the One who formed the mountains walked among them. That the hands that carved the heavens were pierced for our sake. That the Word who spoke the stars into being became flesh to speak our names in love. This is not abstraction; this is intimacy. This is not theology; this is life.

Creation teaches us to see: to see the sacred in the ordinary, to see the eternal in the fleeting, to see the Christ in every face, in every blade of grass, in every breath of wind. It teaches us that creation is not a past event but an ongoing symphony, a song that sings us into being moment by moment.

27
Christ Within

What if I told you, waiting on Jesus in this cold, dark room, waiting on some grand return, is the biggest con job— the slickest deception— to distract you from finding the raw, authentic Christ dwelling within your own battered soul?

What if I told you, with the weight of every lost night and every broken dream, that the one you're waiting for— the savior in the sky— is tired of waiting? That He's waiting for you, waiting for you to open your eyes, to see the light burning not in some far-off heaven, but deep in your own heart?

Feel it. Feel the Christ within you. Feel the raw, untamed love, the fierce compassion, the burning desire to heal. To mend the broken, to comfort the lost. Not in some holy book, not in some church or temple, not in some distant promise, but here. Now. In the sweat and blood of living.

What if I told you, in the gruff, growling voice of truth, that every time you look to the sky, every time you pray for a savior, you're missing the point? Losing the plot? The plot that says: *you are the hands, you are the feet, you are the voice of the Christ within.*

What if I told you salvation isn't a waiting game, isn't some grand finale, but the quiet moments— the gentle touch, the simple acts of kindness, the grit and grind of everyday life? That's where the real Christ lives. That's where the real healing happens.

What if I told you the kingdom of heaven isn't a far-off place, but here, in this very moment? In the love you give. In the pain you share. In humanity you embrace, raw and unfiltered.

So, stop waiting, stop looking at the sky, stop dreaming of a return. Start living, start loving. Start being the Christ this world so desperately needs.

What if I told you that the one you're waiting for has been waiting for you all along? Waiting for you to wake up. To rise up. To be the light in the darkness, the hope in the despair. To be the Christ in this broken, beautiful world.

28
Arms of Love

In this gritty, smoke-filled room, where life's harsh edges cut deep, I think of God.

I think of the call to focus, to lift our minds above the grind, above the muck, and dwell on all things lovely, all things pure, all things praiseworthy.

It takes effort, doesn't it? To think those thoughts, to rise above the weight of this world, to imagine ourselves untethered, free. Free to float in a sea of peace, under a sky vast with love.

We know God is love. And maybe it's that simple. No dogma, no doctrine. Just love, pure and unfiltered— like a cold drink on a scorching day, like the touch of a lover in the dead of night.

Trust Him with your whole life. With all your mess, your broken pieces, your insecurities. Trust Him with those dark corners you hide from everyone.

Give it all to Him. Lay it bare. Feel the weight lift. Feel the peace descend, gentle and soft, like rain on parched earth. Imagine it, your mind unburdened, your heart unclenched.

Imagine walking through this wild, unpredictable world, filled with His love, surrounded by His peace. Not fleeting, not a spark that fades, but a constant truth, a quiet whisper in the storm. It isn't easy. No, life is tough— gritty, raw, unkind. But, if we trust, if we let go, if we surrender the fears and doubts that chain us, we can find that peace. That love. That praiseworthy, lovely truth.

Here's to trying, to lifting our thoughts, to embracing the simple, the pure, the beautiful. To trusting in love— a love so vast, so deep, it swallows the darkness, calms the storm.

And in that trust, in that love, we find our freedom. We find our peace. In this moment, in this breath, we are free. We are loved, we are at peace. And maybe that's all we ever needed. All we ever sought.

29
Blurred Reflection

We are born with a blurred image of God, stumbling through the alleys of existence— eyes half-open, half-shut— trying to reflect love, compassion, goodness. But we spill it, like cheap wine on a first date, clumsy and uncertain.

God's there, they say— in the trees, in the stars, in the silence— but our vision is smeared, like a filthy windshield on a winter's day, the light distorted by sin, by flaws, by the dirt under our fingernails. We reach for divinity, stretch out trembling hands, and grasp only air.

We're supposed to be mirrors of the Divine, shining back holy light. But what do we know of light? We're muddled beings, spinach between our teeth, debts we can't pay, hearts half-empty from the start.

The streets are alive with noise. Bars hum with laughter and sorrow, the air thick with voices and emptiness. Somewhere in the chaos, we think we hear it— that faint whisper of the Divine— but it's blurred by the roar of our own lives.

We paint over it with our egos, our ambitions, our mistakes piling up like beer cans in the trash. And God waits somewhere, quiet, patient, as we fumble with the lens, always smudged, our hands shaking.

The churches tell us we are made in God's image. But when we look in the mirror, we see lines, scars, flaws carved deep and wonder how that can be true. Because love doesn't always look like this, doesn't always feel like this— like a worn-out shoe with a broken lace.

We walk through the fog, pretending to know something, anything. But we're guessing. Guessing at who we are, who God is, trying to untangle the mess of our own making.

And maybe that's the point. Maybe the blur is part of it. Maybe Jesus is that blurred image— the human part, with the flaws, the imperfections.

Maybe God's reflection isn't meant to be clear. Maybe it's in the dirt on our sneakers, in the cigarette smoke curling in the air, in the empty bottles, in the falling down and the getting back up.

We are blurred creatures, worn out around the edges, but still reflecting something. Still catching glimpses of that light, faint but persistent, shining through the cracks of our messy lives.

30
Anchor in the Storm

Clinging to it— my anchor in life's rough seas— where the waves crash and howl, where the night swallows the stars whole. Patience walks beside me, an old friend. We've shared these streets, rain-soaked and grimy, weaving through back alleys and broken dreams. We pass cigarettes and stories back and forth, laughing at the absurdity, knowing the world doesn't owe us a thing.

In the tempest of trouble's storm, when the world spins wild and out of control, I cast off fear like an empty bottle. God guides my heart, a compass in the chaos, steady and sure, pointing me toward something I can't yet name.

I find my way, stumbling often, but always forward. Always reaching for that sliver of light, that fragile promise of dawn in a city that never seems to wake. Hope hides in the cracks here, faith dances in the shadows.

The streets are a labyrinth, tangled with lost souls and forgotten dreams, but I walk them with purpose. Head held high, eyes fixed on the horizon, heart beating to the rhythm of something bigger, something unseen yet undeniable.

In the quiet moments, when the chaos fades and the world holds its breath, I feel it—that Divine grace. It lifts me gently, nudging me forward, whispering that I am not alone.

31
Poets of the Air

Poets of the air, fluttering horns on wings— chaos births a rhythm, a melody unseen but deeply felt. A heartbeat in the wind, the rustle of pages, the whisper of leaves, a dance of shadows and light unfolding in their wake.

They swoop and dive, these aerial bards, etching verses in the open sky. Scribbling sonnets in the clouds, their ink the azure blue, their canvas infinite and untouchable. They are unbound by the ground's harsh grasp, unfettered by the chains that hold us to earth.

Amid the cacophony of the city, in the clamor of horns, the screech of brakes, the chatter of hurried feet, they find a symphony. A harmony hidden in the din— the pulse of life, the breath of existence. They weave it into song, a rhythm only they can hear.

The poets of the air see what we do not, hear what we cannot. Their eyes are sharp, their ears tuned to the fleeting, the ephemeral. They transform the mundane into the sublime, the prosaic into the poetic. They find beauty in chaos, order in disarray, and leave it hanging in the wind for us to wonder at.

They are messengers, carriers of dreams, heralds of hope. Their wings testify to freedom, their flight a rebellion against gravity's pull, a defiance of the ordinary, a salute to the extraordinary. We watch them and envy them— their grace, their vision, their unbroken bond with the sky. Longing to soar as they do, to see the world anew, to discover the rhythm in chaos and the poetry in noise.

And for a moment, as we watch, we too become poets. Fluttering horns on wings, birthing chaos into rhythm, dreaming of flight, of freedom, of an endless sky where the poets of the air reside. Forever singing. Forever free.

32
The Soft End

We visit. We talk. We soothe with trembling hands and heavy hearts, offering bread, wine, words, and silence thick with unspeakable prayers. We pray, and we pray, and we pray more. But still, they die.

Some suffer— clinging to the threads of life with a fierce, raw ache. Some simply vanish— a breath stolen too quickly to catch. And some fade, slowly, tenderly, like the sun slipping behind the hills, leaving a shadowed peace.

Christ always knows. He stands in the doorway, silent as our tears, present in our fumbling kindness. He walks beside us in this compassionate work, through the bitter end, the soft end, the only end we can give.

And yet— we feel it, faint and sure, a trembling beyond the veil of this sorrow. There is something more. Something alive, alive in a way we cannot name, but know. And that's all I can say.

33
Mourning as One

Whispers haunt my sleep— a woman's anguish, her voice a melody both haunting and strange, a requiem in the darkness, absurd and profound, mooing like a cow. It echoes through the restless corridors of my mind, surreal yet deeply human, a serenade to sorrow.

Loved ones gather near, their faces carved by grief, their eyes pools of lost dreams. They stand in solemn silence, a circle of mourning, their tears unspoken but loud, a testament to love and loss.

Memories hang in the air, fragile lifelines cast into the sea of despair, their weight heavy and unyielding. Tears and memories abound. Each drop tells a story, each glance reveals a chapter unwritten but felt.

Pain and love intertwine, threads woven into a tapestry by the hands of time. In their shadows, silent hearts beat in rhythm— grieving, aching, longing.

This is a symphony of sorrow— mourning as one, a choir of the broken, each note a sigh, each chord a lament. Their collective pain becomes a beacon, a lighthouse piercing the storm of loss, casting its dim but steady glow over the wreckage of their lives.

I watch from the outside, a spectator in my own dream. Their despair pulls at me, their love burns deep, their loss stings sharp. Their anguish seeps into my soul, their whispers becoming my own.

It is a shared burden, a communal grief that binds us, holds us, refuses to let go. In the darkness, I reach out, my hand grasping nothing but air. The emptiness presses in— a cruel reminder of what is lost. Yet in their silent sorrow, I find an unlikely comfort. Pain becomes connection, grief becomes bond, a fragile solace forged in the fires of loss.

Their faces blur, their voices fade, but their whispers remain. A woman's anguish. A loved one's cry. A surreal symphony lingering in the night, a reminder of our shared humanity.

Grief binds us, and even in despair, love endures—endless and unyielding. The surreal returns— a woman's anguish, her mooing like a cow. Absurd, beautiful, aching.

A symphony of sorrow. Loved ones gathered, tears and memories flowing, silent hearts grieving together, mourning as one.

34
Checkmate Warriors

Old men, battered by the grind, hunch over chess boards, the scent of hot city asphalt wrapping around their souls— a suffocating embrace of the urban sprawl. Each move on the board becomes a testament to endurance, each breath a quiet rebellion against the relentless tide of a metropolis that neither sees nor spares them.

Their worn-out fingers slide queens, pawns, and knights with the precision of men who've played life's last game too many times. This is the chess of survival, played in the shadows of skyscrapers where dreams crumble like weathered brick and hope whispers faintly, barely audible above the city's cacophony.

Heaven, for them, comes in a green concoction poured from glass to gut. Each sip a fleeting reprieve, a liquid escape from the concrete furnace that roasts them alive. Ice clinks against sweat-soaked glasses, a fragile toast to oblivion.

The sun, merciless as ever, drives them deeper into their folding chairs, their shadows dissolving into the pavement. Dogs, those streetwise prophets, dart through alleys chasing rats, barking at the absurdity of existence. Their howls echo like a protest— a canine chorus raging against the game humanity has forced them into.

Pink girls in red hats sashay by, their laughter a flash of melody in this discordant symphony of streets. It's a sweet tune, ephemeral and weightless, gone as quickly as it comes, lost amidst honks, curses, and the grind of another day.

Beneath their feet, the subway rumbles— a hum of steel veins pumping through the city's core. It connects the boroughs like arteries, binding the fragments of this fractured land. The screech of an arriving train pierces the evening air, a howl of despair and fury, the roar of a beast disgorging its weary souls at every stop.

And yet, here in this concrete carnival, under the unforgiving New York sky, the old men laugh. They laugh at the moon, a drunken, defiant snarl in the face of the cosmic joke. Their laughter is rough, ragged— a symphony of resistance, a rebel song played against the inevitable.

Checkmate warriors, they are, in a city of shadows, playing their moves under the fading light of another blistering day. Their eyes are glazed with the weariness of a thousand battles, their spirits bruised but unbroken. As the city hums its relentless tune, as the streets throb with the lifeblood of the damned, they remain—stubborn sentinels, guardians of their own small kingdoms. Their laughter echoes into the night— a defiant cry against the darkness, a whispered prayer to the indifferent stars.

35
Nora's Testament

Nora sits in her worn recliner, weathered hands cradling Elmer, the ancient cat with one ear and clouded eyes— a living relic of days long past. The room, dimly lit and thick with time, is filled with memories. Photos of children, grandchildren, and great-grandchildren line the walls, their smiling faces a testament to a life steeped in love and purpose. The lines on Nora's face tell a story, a road map of a long, winding journey. Pain sits there, quietly etched into her features, but she waves it off with a dismissive gesture.

Don't mind me, she says, her voice rasping like wind through dry leaves. *I'm not feeling a thing.* Her eyes, though— windows to a soul weathered by storms— betray her words. They speak of silent suffering, of battles fought and scars earned. They hold pride when she talks about her family, every word like a polished gem. She recounts their accomplishments, their adventures, her voice soft but vibrant, a twinkle defying the shadow of grief.

But her voice falters when she speaks of the grandson lost to drugs just a year ago. It grows heavy, a muted dirge echoing in the corners of her heart. Grief lingers in the air, weaving itself into her stories, a dark thread in the tapestry of her life. Her body, frail and fading, seems like a candle flickering in the wind. She hasn't eaten in days, her strength waning hour by hour. And yet, despite the decline, a quiet peace radiates from her, a strength forged in the fires of countless hardships. *I'm ready to go,* she says, her voice steady, firm— a declaration, not a plea. *I'm ready to join Tom and my grandson up there.* She gestures to the ceiling with a faint smile, a gesture heavy with faith and longing. *Jesus can take me anytime now. I'm really looking forward to it. Real soon.*

I am awed by her resilience. Her life is a beacon, her spirit a reminder that even in darkness, light persists. That light shines in her words, in her gaze, in the way her hands—frail though they are— still carry the tenderness of a thousand caresses.

Nora closes her eyes for a moment, and I wonder if she dreams of those she loves— of the life she built with her own two hands. A life brimming with laughter and tears, with triumphs and losses, a life lived fully and deeply. In that room, where time seems to pause, I see the true measure of her humanity. Not in her strength or accomplishments, but in her boundless capacity for love. Her resilience in the face of inevitability, her grace as she prepares to let go. Nora is ready. As I take my leave, I carry the indelible mark of her spirit— a lesson in the beauty of release, of meeting the end with the same dignity and grace with which one embraces life.

In Nora, I see the essence of what it means to be human: the enduring power of love, the quiet courage to face the unknown, and the luminous peace of a life well-lived. She leaves behind a legacy of light, a testament to the unbreakable bonds that tie us together, even in the shadow of death.

36
Garden Without Fear

In the shadow of the pulpit, fear blooms— a flower of ash, its roots deep in trembling hearts. They speak of fire, of an endless fall into darkness, and call it salvation.

They whisper of a God with clenched fists, an angry father who withholds love until you earn it, until you crawl, until you break. This is not holiness; it is a wound that will not heal.

But there is another garden— a place where fear has no soil, where love waters the roots, and grace grows wild and free. Here, the voice of God is a whisper, soft as the morning, saying, "You are mine. You are always mine."

No disapproval, no rejection, no abandonment— only the open arms of a Creator whose holiness is not a weapon but a light that heals, a hand that guides.

Toxic religion wilts in this garden, its false doctrines crumble like brittle leaves. Here is no fear of hell, but the hope of heaven alive in every moment, every breath, every beating heart.

37
The Living Thread

We meet as strangers, eyes brushing past like wind on stone. Your name, a sound I barely hold; mine, a word already fading. We nod, we pass, two islands adrift, separated by the waters we cannot see.

But beneath the surface, where the roots of being entwine, I hear your mother's laughter, your father's sigh.

The echo of ancestors hums in your blood— their stories written in the dark rivers of your veins. And mine hum with the same rhythm.

What lives in you is not yours alone. The old songs of earth, the murmur of forgotten prayers, the collective pulse of life— they rise and fall in us, woven into the fabric we did not weave but wear all the same.

Here, the silence speaks. We are not alone. The distance dissolves, and the sacred thread of living substance binds us. Your breath touches mine, and I know— we belong to a wholeness too vast to name.

In the meeting of depths, God moves unseen, pulling us toward one another and into Himself. What seemed ordinary becomes holy ground, a communion of lives woven into eternity.

38
The "Word" Chord

A single note trembles in the air, then another, bold and unyielding, a harmony that breaks the silence— the "Word" chord. It is no ordinary sound. It carries the weight of eternity, the echo of a voice that spoke galaxies into being. "Word of the Father," the hymn declares, and the chord sings what words cannot say.

This is not music; it is revelation. The Logos steps into flesh, not as a shout, but as a newborn cry. The stars lean closer, the heavens part their veil, and the chord presses against our hearts—sharp, yearning, filled with joy and ache.

For this is the sound of love bending low, of glory wrapped in the rags of the world. It shakes the walls of our certainties, reminds us of what we cannot grasp: that the infinite chose to become finite, the eternal dared to walk among the fleeting. And so, the chord lingers, resolves, whispers into stillness.

39
False Fire

They built a throne from trembling hands, a kingdom ruled by fear. Not the fear of wonder, not the awe that quiets the soul, but the fear that closes the heart, that builds walls instead of altars.

They speak of flames, eternal, unyielding, and call it mercy. They say, "Believe or burn," as though love is a blade pressed to the throat. But the Word never came with threats; He came with open arms.

They warn of disapproval, of a God who turns His face away. But who can look at the Christ, bleeding on the tree, and say He abandons? Who can see His hands, scarred and reaching, and believe in rejection?

Toxic religion writes its gospel in fear, but the true Word is written in love, spoken in kindness, and carved into the hearts of the forgiven. Hell is not the fire they sell; it is the absence of love they create.

40
Glorious Unknown

Embracing the unknown is clutching a ripe banana, squeezing it until the future oozes out— a slimy, whitish blob, unappealing and raw, falling onto your shoe and smearing your carefully planned steps.

And then there's that damned dog, a wretched creature with rotten teeth and matted fur, lapping it up as if it's the last meal on earth. You stand there, half in disgust, half in awe, wondering how life became this absurd play— no rehearsals, no script. Just raw, unfiltered scenes where you're both actor and audience, laughing at the tragicomedy unfolding at your feet.

You think of the plans you made, the dreams you sketched— all those neat lines and tidy boxes— now just a mess. A chaotic swirl, like that banana goo on your shoe, reminding you that control is an illusion, a joke told by the universe with a punchline you never saw coming.

The dog looks up, eyes glazed with a mix of gratitude and confusion. Its life is a constant scramble for scraps, a fight for survival in the alleyways of existence. And in those dull eyes, you see a reflection of yourself— both of you navigating the unknown, one step, one breath at a time.

You think of all the times you tried to grasp the future, to mold it, to shape it into something recognizable, something you could call your own. But it always slipped through your fingers, like that banana mush— elusive and unpredictable.

The world spins on, indifferent to your plans. And you realize that embracing the unknown means letting go of the need to understand, to predict, to control. It means letting it be— a chaotic, beautiful mess.

You take a step, the banana squishing underfoot— a sticky, absurd reminder of it all. And the dog follows, a faithful companion in this dance of uncertainty, both of you moving forward— one step, one stumble at a time.

In the end, there's a strange kind of peace in the embrace of the unknown. A recognition that life is a series of moments, each one unexpected, each one a gift, wrapped in the slimy, messy, glorious essence of being alive.

So, you walk on, shoes sticky with the future, dog at your side, hearts open to whatever comes next. Knowing that the journey is all there is— and that, somehow, is more than enough.

41
The Eternal Now

Christ makes God known. It is as simple as that. No need for towers or temples, no need for scrolls of argument, or words that confound and distort. She is the eternal flame, He the living archetype of all that is— transcendent, immanent, incarnate. The Word that speaks without ceasing.

Every second, the Word is born. In the cry of an infant, male and female, in the breath of the wind, in the spark of a heart awakening. The Word is born in this very instant, not in some distant past or some far-off future, but here, in the eternal Now.

Every moment, the Word is crucified, male and female. In the suffering we see, in all we experience, in the wounds we bear, in the love that bleeds for others. The nails pierce again and again, but not in despair— this is the crucifixion of renewal, the letting go of what was, so that what is, might become.

Every heartbeat, the Word is resurrected, male and female. Not in marble tombs or gilded halls, but in the quiet transformation of life. The risen Word walks among us still, see him in the mirror, see her as she looks through a window not bound by time, but alive—Now. It is not memory. It is not prophecy. It is presence, full and radiant.

42
Echoes of the Past

In a sad-eyed old woman's kitchen, her gray hair gathers like a storm, the lines on her face a wrinkled map of wars long fought and lost. A torn housecoat clings to her frail frame, its fabric as tired as the walls around her.

A cigarette, half-burnt and dangling from cracked lips, sends smoke curling toward the ceiling, a tired wish dissolving in the air. The room, dim-lit and heavy, holds grime like regret, counters coated in years of neglect. Dishes piled high, a monument to forgotten yesterdays.

Her trembling, veined hands cradle a cat as worn as she is—fur matted, eyes half-closed. The creature sits with a cigarette stuck in its mouth too, a cruel, mocking reflection of its mistress's despair.

The open window is a porthole into a very dark place, framing a city slum sprawling like a wound. Buildings lean like drunkards, graffiti scrawled across their faces— cries of desperation. Trash swirls in the wind, a twisted ballet of abandonment.

Her tired eyes look beyond the broken streets, seeing the ghosts of what once was. The laughter of children echoes faintly in her memory, colors once vibrant now faded to gray. Every drag of her cigarette is a slow suicide, a quiet rebellion, a fleeting escape from the world crumbling around her.

The cat, her silent witness, sits in shared resignation. Together, they are grotesque reflections of survival in a wasteland, clinging to the last frayed threads of a life that has slipped through their grasp. She remembers when this kitchen was alive— when the air was filled with the smell of food, the sound of voices, the warmth of a family now lost to time.

Outside, the city slum sighs in restless sleep, its heartbeat measured in distant sirens, shouts of despair, and the whispers of dreams abandoned. The noise seeps through the window, a cruel reminder of the life beyond— vivid and alive but forever out of reach.

She drags again, letting the smoke fill her lungs, her mind. A fleeting comfort, a numbing balm for the chaos. The cat purrs softly, almost a whisper, acknowledging their shared silence, their shared burdens, their shared tears that refuse to fall.

In this kitchen, time stands still. Each minute stretches into eternity, each breath is a fight— a testament to an unbroken spirit that refuses to shatter, even as everything else around it falls apart.

43
Path to the Stars

What's the best thing you can do when your shoes are too tight, your arms too short, and there's never enough time to clean the windows? Get on that crazy path to the stars, the one that starts in the basement and winds its way up to the roof.

Leave the dust and grime behind. Step over the broken dreams, climb those creaky stairs. Pass the old boxes of forgotten hopes, the echoes of yesterday's regrets, until you reach the top, where the air thins, and the sky stretches wide.

Celebrate with the pigeons up there— gray, gritty angels of the city. Let them eat from your hand, those crumbs of doubt, the seeds of your fear. Sing with them a chorus of the forgotten, a symphony for the lost. Let them know you're one of them— a fellow traveler, winging it through the mess and the madness of this crazy planet.

Stand on the parapet wall and stretch your wings. Feel the wind—the breath of the world— pushing you, pulling you, whispering secrets of the sky. And if you have the guts, stare over the edge.

Look down into the abyss of your anxieties, the swirling vortex of what-ifs and why-nots, and then—take off—Fly! Soar beyond the rooftops, above the grind and the grime. Watch the city shrink below you, a patchwork of chaos and creation, a mosaic of madness.

Feel the freedom in your bones, the lightness in your soul, the thrill of breaking free. Free from the shackles of shoulds and shouldn'ts, the chains of can'ts and won'ts.

Glide through currents of possibility. Dive headfirst into the unknown. Embrace the uncertainty— the exhilarating, terrifying, beautiful uncertainty of a life lived fully, without restraint.

Remember those tight shoes, those short arms, those dirty windows. They're just distractions, reminders of the ground. But you—you were made for the sky. For the vast, endless expanse of potential.

So, when the world tries to squeeze you, to box you in, to weigh you down, remember the path to the stars. The one that starts in the basement and takes you to the roof.

Celebrate with the pigeons. Sing with them. Fly with them. And let them remind you, every time you look down, that you were born to rise above. That you were born to stretch your wings— and fly.

44
Voice Without Chains

They said the road was narrow, lined with thorns and fire. They spoke of gates that slam shut, of books where sins are written, of hands raised in judgment. But the Voice that called the stars to sing was not their voice.

They built a faith from stones, stacked them high and cold. "Fear," they said, "Fear is the beginning of wisdom." But love was always the first word, the seed that broke the soil, the light that kissed the dark.

They made God small— a judge, a jailer, a shadow waiting to condemn. But the Christ who walked among us, who washed the feet of doubters, who wept at the tomb, was nothing like the God they made.

The Voice does not call from towers of fear. It whispers in the wind, sings in the trees, and shouts in the breaking of chains. The Voice says, "Come as you are. You are mine. You have always been mine."

45
The Shadow's Work

A healthy faith does not build walls, does not fear the shadows. It walks into the dim places of the soul and lights a lamp, saying, "This, too, is part of you. Own it. Heal it. Transform it." But who teaches this?

They train their august men of faith to defend, not to liberate. Apologists for systems, not healers of souls. They protect the walls of their ancient traditions, while the people inside crumble, their shadows unowned, their pain unchecked.

If you wish to be just, if you wish to love without condition, you must do the work no sermon will do for you. You must name the cruelty within, see the injustice in your own hand. You must lay down the armor of every story that excuses you, even the ones wrapped in sacred words.

Religion should not imprison, should not be a lock on the heart. It should break the chains, teach us to dance in the light and the dark, to hold the world as it is, and to make it better with our hands. A healthy faith whispers—no, shouts! "You are more than your shadows. You are called to love."

46
Journey to the Moon

When was the last time you walked to the moon or stepped on a star? Was it when your eyes met the fiery beauty of a sunset, the sky ablaze with hues plucked from dreams? A fleeting moment of perfection, the heavens painted with wonder, whispering secrets of the universe into your ear.

Or was it when you gazed into the face of a loved one, their eyes reflecting galaxies, their smile a constellation of hope? Their warmth wrapped around your soul like a celestial embrace, making you believe, for a moment, you'd found your place among the stars.

Perhaps it was in the rain— the kind that cools the earth and quenches more than thirst. Each drop a kiss from the clouds, promising renewal. The parched soil of your heart drank deeply, grew lush, as the storm passed, leaving behind a world cleansed and alive once more.

Maybe it happened in the stillness, in those stolen moments when the chaos of the world fell away. You felt the rhythm of the cosmos align with your own, a reminder that you are part of something vast and infinite. Beautiful. Terrifying. Endless.

Or perhaps it was in the laughter of children, their eyes alight with wonder, their steps brimming with adventure. The moon wasn't far then— it was a friend to visit in dreams, a companion in the endless exploration of shadowed corners and secret skies.

Was it in a melody, a song that lifted you on wings of sound? A symphony of emotion that resonated deep within, carrying you to forgotten heights, each chord a vivid reminder of what it means to be alive— truly, madly, deeply alive.

Or was it in the silence of night, when the world slept and the stars sang their ancient song? Alone with your thoughts, you felt the thread of time weaving you to the past, present, and future— a fragile yet unbreakable connection to all that is and will ever be.

Maybe it was in the touch of a hand, a fleeting gesture that spoke of love, trust, and bonds unbreakable. A touch that conveyed what words never could, one that made you believe in the impossible, if only for a moment.

Or was it in the quiet strength you found within when life's storms raged? When you stood tall, unwavering— a star shining bright in the darkness, a beacon for others as you walked your own path to the moon.

Perhaps it was when you dared to dream, reaching beyond the mundane, grasping at the extraordinary. When you believed you could fly, soar above the clouds, and touch the very face of the heavens.

Or maybe— it is now. In this moment of reflection, as these words stir something within you. A spark. A whisper.

47
The Price of Peace

The world mutters about peace, sells it like a shiny trinket. They line up for the knockoff version— the kind that costs nothing and leaves them empty. True peace, it's a rough road. You've got to bleed ego for it, strip yourself bare, until there's nothing left but the soft pulse of humility.

I saw a man— he lived it. Quiet hands, steady eyes, not a trace of the noise in him. He carried his peace like a candle, shielding the flame from the wind that howled around him. You could see it, feel it— it burned, but it didn't consume.

You want that peace? Start by breaking— your pride, your demands, all the things you think you deserve. Let go, let it fall, and what's left will surprise you. It's not loud or bright, but it's real. And it stays.

48
Dance of Breath and Being

In the stillness, we find an unexpected compassion— a tenderness for our own fragility. For the brittle bones, the cracked veneer, and for the world's relentless beauty. A beauty that heals and hurts, cradles and crushes, a paradox both brutal and breathtaking.

We sit with the wind, letting it wrap around us. It is a lover's embrace, a parent's touch—soft and fierce, gentle, and wild. An element unbound, roaming the earth and sky, filling our sails and lungs, our hearts, and souls.

In the quiet, we hear its whispers, the stories it carries— of lives lived and lost, of dreams chased and shattered, of love found and forgotten. Each breath is a testament. Each gust, a eulogy.

We let it all wash over us— the sorrow, the joy, the mundane. Every moment becomes a grain of sand, every breath a fleeting eternity. And in this, we find a strange peace: resignation, a resolve to keep breathing, to keep living, to embrace both the chaos and the calm.

We see the scars on our souls, the wounds that never healed. And we begin to understand— the beauty in the broken, the poetry in the pain, the strength in surrender. The wind roams free, unchained, a reminder of the wild within us. That untamed spirit that refuses to bow, that fights, loves, and dreams, even when the world presses hard against us, even when it tries to break us.

And so, we breathe deeply. We let the wind fill our lungs, let it whisper its secrets, its truths and lies. In its currents, we find a reflection— a mirror of our own existence: beautiful and brutal, wild, and wondrous.

We sit with the wind and learn that life is not about the battles won or lost. It is about the moments felt, the breaths taken, the hearts touched.

In the stillness, we find compassion. A tenderness for our frailty and for the relentless beauty of the world. For its capacity to heal and hurt, to cradle and crush— a paradox as old as the wind itself.

And in this, we find our place. Not as conquerors or victims, but as participants in the dance— the endless, timeless dance of life and wind, of breath and being.

49
Operating Theater

In the operating theater, suctioned, sealed, but still, we bleed. This sterile battlefield of white walls. and cold steel holds no promises. Hope hangs by a thread, and every breath is borrowed time, ticking against the chaos within.

Here, endings are marked in silence— the steady beep of machines, the whispers of nurses, the sharp antiseptic sting that bites into the air. These quiet moments stand in stark contrast to the storm raging beneath the skin, where life fights to hold its ground.

In this harsh, unforgiving room, hearts falter, cease, and are coaxed back to life. The surgeon's hands move with steady precision, a scalpel slicing through flesh and fear, navigating the labyrinth of pain and dysfunction that brought us here.

Stripped bare, we are laid vulnerable under the blinding lights, no armor to shield us, no shadows to hide in. Each incision, a reminder of fragility, each suture a whispered plea to survival. The sterile white above exposes every flaw, every imperfection, casting us into the relentless march of time where each second edges closer to the unknown.

We lie motionless, lives placed in another's hands, trusting in their skill, in science, hoping for a miracle, fearing the inevitable. Outside, the world spins on, oblivious to the silent wars waged within these walls— moments of despair tangled with fragile threads of hope.

In this theater, we are more than flesh and bone, more than the sum of our parts. We are the dreams we chased, the loves we held, the memories etched into the marrow of who we are. Each beat of the heart, each flutter of breath, a testament to our will to endure, to remain. A reminder of our mortal threads, our fragile design, our shared fate.

When the heartbeat fades into the void, when the final breath is drawn, the silence swells. A life extinguished, a soul released, leaving behind echoes— a ghost in the machine, faint traces of what once was.

Even in this room of cold steel and clinical precision, there is more than biology at work. The spirit lingers, refusing to vanish. It testifies to our will to live, to fight, to love, to dream, even in the face of inevitability. We are more than our bodies, more than the blood that pulses through our veins.

We are the light that shines in the darkness, the hope that rises in despair, the quiet rebellion against the roar of silence.

50
The Dark Smell of a Man without a Heart

The dark smell of a man without a heart lingers, thick and acrid, like cheap whiskey on a drunk's breath. Stale, bitter, it clings to the air like the smoke of a thousand unfiltered cigarettes burned down to the filter in a dim room where time has stopped.

The scent is in everything he touches— the stolen cash tossed carelessly on a counter, the hollow laughter ricocheting down empty streets, the way his eyes skim over faces but never connect. Always looking past, through, beyond, searching for something that was never there, something he lost before he knew it was his to hold.

He is a volume of forgotten dreams, each page etched with regret. A barren heart where nothing blooms but weeds, a deserted wasteland where joy dared not linger. The smell is rusted iron on forgotten playgrounds, the creak of swings abandoned mid-motion, the graffiti on walls crying out in bleeding colors.

Anger and desperation scrawled like wounds, shouting at a world that turned its back. He drifts, shadow to shadow, a phantom in a city that never stops moving. His loneliness cloaks him like a shroud, his silence speaks louder than screams. He is the absence in a crowded room, the void in a lover's bed, the empty chair at a table where laughter has died.

The dark smell of a man without a heart reeks of regret— chances not taken; nights spent staring at ceilings that offered no answers. It smells of isolation, of burned bridges and untrodden paths, of wounds hidden under layers of bravado and booze.

To those who see him, he is a warning— A reminder of what apathy costs, of how indifference claims its victims. A man who once felt too much, now numb, his heart a casualty of a world too sharp, too cold.

He is despair made flesh, emptiness given form. A man who once dreamed in vibrant colors now lives in shades of gray, his heart a broken compass spinning aimlessly in a sea of numbness. The dark smell of a man without a heart is a second skin, a story told in absence and ache.

It speaks of love misplaced, pain endured, and the abyss of living without feeling. It warns us— of how close we all are, one heartbreak, one failure, one betrayal away, from becoming him.

We see him, fear him, pity him. And in the secret corners of our souls, we understand him. His reflection whispers our own capacity for emptiness, the fragility of our hope, the vulnerability of our hearts.

The dark smell of a man without a heart reminds us to hold on. To cherish the light, embrace the pain, and fight the numbness that stalks us all. To live. To love. To feel. To resist becoming shadows drifting in the dark.

51
Grief Doesn't Knock

Grief doesn't knock— it kicks the door in, makes itself at home. You sit across from it, trying not to meet its eyes. But it's got patience, and eventually, you look. That's when you see what it's holding— the thing you lost, still glowing, even as it fades.

The weight of it presses down, not just on your chest but on the whole world. And yet, there's a strange light in the cracks it leaves behind. You breathe out, pushing the fog aside, and there it is: a pinpoint of brilliance, sharp enough to cut. You let it.

Grief is no thief. It's a cruel teacher, sure, but it shows you what matters, what remains. And when the fog clears just long enough— you see it, the thing you lost, woven into the fabric of the infinite. It's not gone, just transformed.

52
Divine Sufficiency

She is the essence of simplicity— lovely and plain, a beauty that resists words, that unfolds only under the moon's gentle gaze, where shadows play tender games on her unadorned skin. She moves through the cluttered world, calm amidst chaos. She rejects the superfluous, the gaudy trappings of ornamentation, stripping life down to its bare bones, to its purest form. There, truth lies naked and unashamed, awaiting her quiet embrace.

In her eyes, the suffering of the cosmos lingers, a silent secret shared with grace. In her quiet rebellion, she discovers solace in simplicity. She carries the unembellished truth of existence as both burden and blessing. She is a whisper in a world that screams, a single perfect note rising above a cacophony of noise. She reminds us that beauty dwells not in excess but in essence, in the raw core of being that breathes life into the mundane.

Beneath the moon, its silver light brushes her face like a soft benediction. In that stillness, she knows less is not just more—it is sufficient. It mirrors the transcendent nature of God, a Divine simplicity that reveals deeper truths and higher planes.

In her simplicity, she glimpses the Divine, the eternal shining through the ephemeral folds of her life. Every moment becomes a prayer, every breath a meditation, every step a journey toward the sacred. Her beauty rests in the quiet lines of her face, the grace of her hands, the unspoken wisdom in her silence. It does not demand attention but gently commands it, filling the space around her with a subtle, profound light.

She moves like a poem written in the language of the stars— each word chosen with care, each line a testament to the power of restraint. Hers is the elegance of simplicity, the grace of a life lived attuned to the whisper of the wind, the hum of the earth, the song of the cosmos.

By rejecting excess, she embraces essence. She finds strength in what remains, a foundation built on the bedrock of truth— unshaken by the whims of the world, unmoved by the tides of time.

She speaks of the Divine in the mundane, the eternal in the everyday. A living testament to the power of less, she is a breathing prayer to the sufficiency of simplicity, the sacredness of the unadorned, the grace of the essential.

She understands, in the quiet, in the stillness, in the simple act of being, she touches the face of God.

53
Journey of Trust and Meaning

What does a man know at the end of the road, but death's cold breath stirring old fears, the void calling him home? Forgive me if I don't know if I don't care. This whole thing feels like a joke— a grand parade of fools marching in circles, chasing ghosts, clinging to dreams that slip through their fingers like sand. Each grain, a lost moment.

Take my hand, walk me to the edge, to where the path meets the unknown, where the story fades to black. Stand with me as the sun sinks low on fleeting passions and persistent sorrows, those twin weights we've carried too long.

Trust—just a word carved from broken hearts, a promise made of glass, fragile and easily shattered under the weight of fear and betrayal.

In the end, what does a man know? The vastness of death, the endless night that swallows us whole. But also, those tiny flashes of light— laughter shared, love given and lost, the small joys that carried us forward, even as they slipped from our grasp.

Forgive me if I seem lost if I seem a bit mad. Life is a cruel, beautiful joke— a puzzle with missing pieces, a story with no clear start or end, just this messy middle. Here, where we fight and love and fall, where we rise again, imperfect but persistent.

Take my hand, lead me to the place where the path fades into dark, where the last breath whispers out. Let me face the void with open eyes, unflinching, unafraid, for I have seen the absurdity— the dance of shadows and light, the endless cycle of birth and death. In the end, what do I know? Only this: I'm here with you, right now, in this fleeting breath. And that is enough—that is everything.

Forgive me if I can't offer answers if I can't make sense of it all. Trust, that fragile bond, is all we have— the thread that holds us together even as we drift apart.

Take my hand. Let's walk into the night, into the vast unknown. Face it with courage, with grace, knowing we are travelers, searching for meaning, for connection, for some small truth.

Whether we find it or not doesn't matter. The journey itself is the answer— the path we walk, the steps we take, the moments we share. And that, my friend, is everything. That's enough.

54
Between the Shadow and the Light

God, grant us strength to stand steady when the winds of doubt rise, when fear curls around our feet like a fog that hides the way ahead.

Teach us to seek your bright face even when the sky feels like stone. Let our hearts learn the language of hope—one breath, one step at a time.

Give us boldness to walk forward with trembling feet if we must, but with faith as our compass.

And when the time comes, may we have the humility to bow, not in defeat, but in surrender— to the grace that holds us upright when we can no longer hold ourselves.

55
Where Hope Digs Deep

On scarred, hardened ground, where the earth bears its wounds without shame, your hands search for seeds to plant—fingers pressing into the brittle dust, as though belief alone could make it soft again.

Hope, a stubborn weed, with roots that defy reason, climbs through the cracks like a whispered rebellion—uninvited, but unwilling to die.

The sun bears down, ruthless, but faith does not wilt— it blooms against the drought, fragile yet unbreakable.

Not every field yields a harvest, but still, you kneel and plant—because something in you knows: the ground remembers rain.

56
Frail Man in the Sea of Stars

Try as I might, I can't escape the sight of an evening drenched in stars, a cascade of cosmic dust lifting into a sea of chaos. Whispers of infinity drift through the sky, pulling at the edges of my soul. Unless the maidens of delight descend, I am lost in the turmoil, drowning in the vastness, their laughter a fading echo just out of reach. Eyes stare without faces— latent, haunting. Taste the current that flows between the earth and the unknown.

It's a dream, a fleeting layer of inference over reality. Finished is a word I speak in vain, for it doesn't hold here. Not like the warmth of summer's end. Come to me in the brightness of spring. Take my flowers, fragile offerings, and give them to God. There is a frail man here, with a broken heart and heavy steps, shrouded in sorrow. Each breath is rebellion, each step a testament to pain endured, to quiet hope against indifference.

In the stillness of night, he looks to the stars, those distant beacons of light, and wonders if there is more— more than suffering, more than the cold rain of tears. The maidens of delight are gone, their touch a forgotten dream. He walks alone, a solitary figure in the vast expanse. Yet, in his eyes, a spark remains— a quiet defiance.

He drinks from the cup of uncertainty, finding solace in life's unpredictable flow. There is no permanence here. Change is constant, and he embraces it, carrying the flowers of his soul to offer to the Divine. In the giving, he finds peace, a release from his burdens. Come to me in the brightness of spring, he pleads. Take my flowers and give them to God. In this act, there is hope— a surrender to something greater, a recognition of shared fragility.

We are all frail men, walking the same path, seeking the same light.
As stars lift into the sea of entropy, he stands at the abyss, gazing deep, finding peace—not in answers, but in the act of being. In the silent embrace of the universe, he accepts his place among the stars, where chaos and beauty collide, where life breathes, and dreams linger.

57
Sofia's Song

A child carries her doll to God, seeking a blessing, a baptism by the Spirit. Who is this child, and why should we care? She is the wisdom of the universe— Sofia, draped in purple, crowned with the jewels of knowledge and reverence. Her doll becomes my memory, an echo of innocence and loss. I carry it to the river, where we both receive a sacrament. There, we partake in the flesh of the Son, drinking deeply of the love of the Father— a love that fills the cracks we cannot mend.

Forgive me if my mouth opens but no sound emerges if my words are swallowed by the void. Forgive me if my eyes fail to see the wonder of a perpetual universe, its beauty blurred into streaks of forgotten dreams. Forgive me if my ears are deaf to the cracking of eggs beneath the mother, to the first breath of dawn, to the symphony of creation that hums beneath our chaos.

I stand beneath the falls of glory, letting the waters of salvation pour over me. Each drop is a prayer, each sip a redemption, cleansing the dust of doubt that clings to my weary soul.

Sofia, child of light, holds her doll close, a relic of purity and faith. She whispers secrets to the wind, her voice a melody that dances on the edge of time— a lullaby for the lost and broken. She knows truths we've forgotten, sacred songs buried beneath the noise. She hears the hymns of stars, the psalms of the earth, the silence that speaks louder than any word ever spoken. In her eyes, the universe unfolds— a tapestry woven of light and shadow, love, and sorrow. Each thread tells a story, each knot holds a mystery waiting to be unraveled.

We walk to the river together, Sofia and I, hand in hand. Her doll clutched to her chest, a fragile symbol of faith, of hope, of belief's delicate beauty.
The water bites cold, sharp against the skin. It cleanses, renews, washing away the grime of doubt, the stains of fear, leaving only the raw, naked truth of our existence.

We consume the flesh of the Son, an ancient ritual of connection. Each bite reminds us of sacrifice, of love, of the bond tying us to the Divine. We receive the Father's love— a timeless embrace, a warmth that seeps into hollow spaces, casting light into the darkest corners. Forgive me if I stumble if my steps falter along this path. The weight of memory's doll— this sacred duty to carry light through a shadowed world— is heavy in trembling hands.

Forgive me if my voice shakes, if my prayers break, if my songs stray off-key. For I, too, am a childlike Sofia, seeking blessings from a universe both vast and wondrous, both terrifying and holy. I will stand beneath the falls of glory, letting the waters wash over me. In that sacred stream, I will find my voice, my sight, my hearing. And I will join creation's chorus— a symphony of the redeemed, singing the eternal hymn of grace, carrying the doll of memory to the Divine.

58
Weight of Shadows

Your trauma makes you sick, seeping beyond dreams, beyond the specks of dust collecting in the crevices of your soul. It lingers like grease in a pan, stubborn, refusing to be scrubbed away. It seeps into your veins, turns your laughter bitter, your smiles hollow, a shadow always whispering, reminding you of what was taken, of what was lost.

Your nights fracture with broken sleep, wounds echoing in your mind. A symphony of pain plays on repeat, each note a scar carved deep, shaping your every step. In the quiet, when the world falls silent, your trauma speaks. Its cruel lullaby lulls you to calm only to tear you apart again.

Dust clings stubbornly, remnants of stolen moments, of memories that refuse to die. A second skin, a weight you carry with every breath, a fight against gravity. You try to scrub it clean, but the grease remains— a mark of permanence, a reminder that some stains never fade.

It sours everything: your joy, your colors, your world. Each step feels heavier, every smile a lie to yourself, a bitter surrender. Yet beyond the dust, beyond the dreams, a flicker remains. A stubborn light clinging to hope, to healing, to redemption. But trauma is a beast— it thrives on doubt, nourishes itself in shadows. You fight it nightly, armed with courage born of desperation, determined to reclaim what was stolen.

Your sickness bears witness to your fire. A flame refusing to be snuffed out, even as storms rage. The grease may never disappear, but you live with it. You find beauty in brokenness, light in the corners of shadow. You learn to carry what once threatened to break you.

You are more than pain, more than scars. You are a survivor, a warrior, rising step by step, breath by breath. Beyond the dreams, beyond the dust, you forge a path— not unmarked but strengthened.

The weight still lingers, but you rise. Not because it is gone, but because you've learned to bear it with grace, to transform it into power. You rise. A testament to the indomitable spirit— yours.

59
Grace of Imperfection

She is grace, a silent beauty, incomplete yet whole, etched by time's careful hands. Her flaws are her charm, a masterpiece of imperfection, where life's truths reside.

Humble and modest, she moves like a quiet force through a noisy world, graceful in her simplicity. She treads lightly, cherishing each leaf, each whisper of the wind, each fleeting moment.

She walks between air and surface, a specter of subtlety, indifferent to taste's rules. Her shoes, her ribbons, her flowing robes, and hats— a kaleidoscope of textures and colors, each piece a story of where she's been.

On the subway, she is unseen, small, compact, slipping between the seats. Lost among wide shoulders and heavy boxes, her presence still lingers, gentle and profound, a whisper in a crowded world.

She conspires with feral creatures, soft spirits, quiet souls. Her comfort lies in simple pleasures— kittens, glasses of Cabernet, anchors in chaos and cacophony.

Vague and blurry, she exists at the edges of nothingness, a living poem in pastel hues. Her outline fades into dreams, her colors a quiet celebration of nature's miracles.

She pares life to its essence, leaving poetry intact. In the spaces between certainty and doubt, she reminds you: beauty lies in unanswered questions, in what cannot be fully grasped.

Grace dwells in the corners of your vision, a fleeting glimpse of the extraordinary. A moment you cannot hold, a feeling vanishing just as you reach for it. She is art in its purest form— a canvas painted by time, a sculpture carved by experience, a melody of sighs and whispers, a dance swaying to her heart's rhythm.

Through her, the world reveals itself— not as it should be, but as it is. A mosaic of broken pieces, infinitely more beautiful than perfection could ever dream.

She is a testament to imperfection's power, to incompleteness' grace, to the quiet poetry of being. She reminds you to look closer, to find beauty in the cracks, to embrace the tender truth— life, in all its flaws, is enough.

60
True Gospel

The ultimate truth lies beyond words— doctrines are shadows, echoes of something greater. The True Gospel speaks in silence, vast and still as the void between galaxies, delicate as the gap between breaths, fleeting as dreams dissolving at dawn.

Words are illusions, phantoms of the restless mind. No different from visions of the night— palaces, carriages, silver ponds— beautiful, ephemeral. They fade with the first light, leaving only a whisper, a trace.

Remember this when you stand at the edge of the unknown, when death approaches with its quiet certainty, when the final curtain falls, and the last breath escapes. Do not cling to appearances, to shifting sands of perception. Let them go, and you will break every barrier, like a bird shattering its cage, rising into boundless sky.

Wherever delight resides, bondage lingers close. Pleasure and pain—two faces of one coin— bind you to the wheel of craving and suffering. But awaken, pierce the veil, see your original self, the truth beyond shadows, and you are free. No longer tethered by desires or fears, you shed fleeting joys and sorrows. You step into the quiet freedom of what simply is.

The True Gospel is wordless, a silent song humming in your bones, a light softly shining through cracks, a whisper cutting through the world's clamor, guiding you back to the essence untouched by illusion— the place always waiting.

In stillness, you find yourself again: a drop of water returning to the ocean, a flame merging with the sun, whole and complete, untouched by chains that once held you. When the road grows hard, when your steps falter, when the weight of the world presses your chest, remember the silence.

Remember the silent spaces between words, the truth dwelling in the void. Do not clutch at fleeting shadows dancing on your mind's walls. Let them come, let them go. In their passing, discover the vast freedom of emptiness.

The True Gospel is not a doctrine, but a path—winding and wordless. It leads through wilderness, through dark nights of the soul, through valleys of despair, peaks of ecstasy, always bringing you back to the truth never lost—only forgotten in the noise.

Awaken. Chains fall away. Walls crumble into dust. You stand in the light—naked, whole, free. The illusions fade. The world, once confining, opens wide, revealing its vast, quiet beauty.

The True Gospel always points to the Incarnate God, the Christ— a silent song singing in your heart, a light guiding you gently through the darkness, a whisper telling you: *You are free.*

61
Fairness of the Universe

Tell me about the fairness of the universe. Place it in a thimble with a drop of water, then wait—forty days, forty nights. Release the floodgates. Let the demons out, casting them one by one into the sea. If the sea turns red, remember this: the sun will rise, transforming crimson tides into golden sands.

Walk the shore. Let the waves wash over you. Repeat, and repeat again, until fairness appears— a fleeting shadow before your eyes. Close them for seventy years. Open them to truth: life is not fair, nor cruel— it simply is.

Fairness is a mirage, a myth spun to make sense of the tides. The demons we cast out return— not as enemies, but as fragments of ourselves. Changed, yes. Familiar, too. They carry lessons still unlearned.

The sea once stained red with what we cast away, dries into a desert of shifting sands. Each grain holds a memory, a hope, a fear— fragments of a puzzle never meant to be complete.

We walk the beach, gathering fragments, seeking patterns in waves, meaning in the whispers of wind, truth in the glow of a setting sun. Yet truth, like sand, slips through our fingers— soft, fleeting, eternal.

Close your eyes again. Let silence fill the spaces where fairness cannot tread. The fairness of the universe is no promise, only rhythm: a dance of light and shadow, chaos and calm, pain, and joy— threads woven into existence.

Open your eyes and see. Fairness is not found in answers, but in the experience of the living God. It is the taste of tears, the sound of laughter, the warmth of a sunrise, the beauty of imperfection.

Tell me about fairness, and I'll tell you about the chains we bear, the demons we face, the grains of sand we collect— seeking meaning in chaos, truth in shadow, fairness in silence.

62
Sunday Afternoon

It's a nice Sunday afternoon somewhere. Eggplant and cabbage, bean curd dusted with salt, carrots bright as small suns, a bowl of steaming rice. Little Neck clams pirouette on a plate, a baby's foot bounces on a grandmother's knee.

The scent of fish drifts lazily, mingling with the mew of a newborn kitten. Walls hum with children's fingerprints, their echoes painted in laughter.

A dog ambles by, tail wagging, a metronome of contentment. Through an open window, sunflowers sway, and mushrooms tumble in a playful waltz with peas that somehow rolled in from Brooklyn.

They all pause for a family photo— even the peas—frozen in a frame of joy. Then, the image dissolves. They run to the field, a ball tossed into the wind, its shadow long on the grass. The air fills with laughter's symphony, the melody of a life unhurried.

The baby giggles, the grandmother beams, the dog chases the ball, his paws catching the rhythm of joy. On the windowsill, the kitten watches, eyes wide with wonder, cradled by sunlight. Somewhere, a concerto of small pleasures plays, its notes drifting across the earth.

As the sun dips low, the sky blushes in pink and gold, painting the world with the quiet magic of endings. Shadows stretch, the day softens, but the warmth lingers— threaded through the hearts of those who shared its glow.

Eggplant and cabbage, bean curd and salt— simple fare for a simple day. Yet in that simplicity lies richness, a feast for the soul that no banquet could rival.

The family gathers again as the horizon embraces night. Together they weave a tapestry of love, shared breaths, gentle joys— a testament to the beauty of the ordinary.

Stars blink awake, soft reminders of the infinite. The world quiets, the day slips away, but its memory lingers— a glow that warms, a whisper that soothes.

It's a nice Sunday afternoon Somewhere— a fragment of peace stitched into the chaotic quilt of existence. A reminder of what matters: the laughter, the fleeting magic of sunlight and soft hands, lives entwined in the rhythm of love.

63
Being and Non-being

Beauty and ugliness define one another, a dance of shadows and light. Night rises to frame the day; joy blooms brighter against sorrow's shade.

Being and non-being create each other, an endless cycle of presence and absence, a rhythm of existence pulsing like the beating of time's heart.

A girl moves without seeming to move, her grace as fluid as wind tracing branches, as effortless as a river meandering toward its destiny. Her actions are unforced, natural— the world bends to her rhythm.

She teaches without appearing to teach, her lessons quiet as whispers, indelible as ink soaked into bone. Her wisdom lives in silences, in glances, in moments felt but never explained.

She speaks without words. Her silence resonates louder than a shout, a language of the heart, where meaning transcends sound and becomes something we know before we understand.

Creation flows endlessly. The universe swirls in constant motion, a ballet of beginnings and endings. The girl moves with it, letting things come, welcoming the inevitable as though greeting an old friend.

When things fade, she releases them, graceful in her letting go, aware of impermanence— the transient beauty in all things. She knows moments are meant to pass, lives and loves are fleeting, their essence only borrowed.

When her work is done, she lets it slip away— unattached, unburdened. Her touch as light as air, yet her impact as deep as the roots of mountains.

Ripples spread from her actions, echoes resonate in the canyons of existence, each one a quiet testament to her being.

Her work, though released, lasts forever. Its essence weaves into the fabric of the cosmos, a thread binding presence to eternity. Her actions carry purity of intention, the wisdom of letting go, the power of simply being.

Hers is the art of acting without acting, teaching without teaching, speaking without sound— a legacy etched not in monuments, but in the quiet rhythm of the universe, in the spaces where contrasts meet and create the infinite.

64
Unstoppable Light

Jesus walks back from the wilderness, dust clinging to his feet, an unspoken testimony. Forty days behind him, forty nights of hunger, wrestling shadows that offered kingdoms and called it glory. The wilderness is silent now, but its whispers linger— sand in his sandals, wind in his ears, truth in his chest.

He steps into the synagogue on the Sabbath, air thick with centuries of ritual. Elders nod, children squirm, scrolls wait in sacred stillness. He takes his place, hands steady as they unroll Isaiah, each movement deliberate, as though cradling fire.

The words spill into the room— not soft, not gentle— they strike like thunder. *The Spirit of the Lord is on me,* he says, his voice slicing the air. *I bring Good News to the poor.* The poor lean forward, hope trembling like a leaf. *Freedom for the captives.* Chains rattle somewhere unseen. *Sight for the blind.* Eyes blink, searching for clarity, even as hearts veil themselves. *Release for the oppressed.* The oppressed dare to breathe. The words hang in the air— alive, electric, dangerous.

Today, he says, his voice firm, his gaze sweeping the room, *this scripture is fulfilled in your hearing.* The pause is heavy, a moment that could shatter the world. But they don't see it. They don't see the light breaking in, don't hear chains snapping in unseen realms. Their hearts are locked, their eyes clouded, their hands clutching the familiar, even as freedom knocks at the door.

Awe curdles into anger. Who is he, this nobody, this carpenter, to speak like a prophet, to wield Isaiah like a sword? Doubt hardens into rejection. They shove him out— not just from the synagogue, but from their town, their minds, their souls.

The dust of Nazareth rises, his footprints pressed into the earth of a place that will not claim him. He walks away, truth heavy in his chest, a burden carried in silence. Their blindness is sharper than the desert sun, their chains tighter than anything Rome could forge. He carries it all— their rejection, their fear, their refusal to see the dawn rising in their midst.

The wilderness was harsh, but this is harsher: to bring light and meet shadow, to offer freedom and hear only the clink of chains.

Still, he walks. His path is not theirs to choose. The Spirit burns within him. The Good News will not be silenced. The oppressed will breathe. The captives will be free. Even as they push him out, even as they bind themselves tighter, the truth moves forward, unstoppable as the rising sun.

65
Bucket of Sorrow

The one who grieves picks up a bucket, heavy with unshed tears, and carries it to the beach— a solitary figure against the horizon's endless stretch.

Each step is a burden, each breath a sigh. The sand beneath his feet whispers silently, witness to the pain that courses through his veins—a reminder of loss, of love, of life now left behind.

At the edge where land meets sea, he pours his sorrow, trembling, into the vast, indifferent ocean. The waves take it, swallow it whole— a drop in an infinite expanse. The ocean doesn't care; it never has. It takes and takes, unyielding, a mirror to the emptiness inside, a reflection of grief that refuses to fade.

The bucket is empty, but his heart remains full— a vessel brimming with memories, with moments now shadows, with love turned ghost, lingering in the corners of his mind.

He stares at the horizon, where sky meets sea, wondering if the pain will ever ebb, if tides of sorrow will recede, leaving him whole once more.

The waves whisper their eternal song— a lullaby of loss and longing. For a moment, he feels a strange comfort in their rhythm, in the knowledge that he is not alone in grief. Others have walked this path, carried their buckets, poured their sorrow into the sea, finding fleeting solace in the embrace of the endless ocean.

But for now, he stands, the bucket empty, his heart still heavy. The wind carries his whispered prayers to the uncaring waves, as he hopes for the day the tides will turn and he will find the strength to carry on.

66
God on the Hot Black Pavement

A man writhes on the hot black pavement, his face a mask of agony, his body contorted in pain. I rush to him, my arms open, the asphalt's heat searing through my shoes. Is there anything I can do, I ask, to end his suffering, to take him from his agony?

Kill me, kill me, he cries, his voice raw, a desperate plea. His arms rise to heaven, his finger trembling toward deities who have turned their backs— idols entombed in stone monasteries, bloated on scrolls of dogma, lost in the labyrinths of their own making.

His wild eyes search the sky, seeking a sign, a miracle, a reprieve— but find only the indifferent sun, blazing without mercy, a relentless witness to his torment.

I kneel beside him, my heart leaden with helplessness, bearing the weight of his suffering. The burden of his unspoken fears seeps from his broken body, finding cracks in my own soul.

Kill me, kill me, he whispers again, his voice a broken echo of prayers unanswered, cries lost in the void. I want to tell him: It's not your fault. We are all victims of this cruel, indifferent universe— gods deaf and blind, lost in rituals, unaware of the suffering staining the world.

But words are useless, hollow— a poor balm for wounds that run so deep. So, I sit with him, hold his trembling hand, share his silence, his despair, a witness to his pain. The pavement burns beneath us, the sun scorches above. Time stretches, an endless moment of shared agony— a testament to the fragility of existence.

Kill me, kill me, his voice fades to a whisper, carried away by the hot wind. And I feel the weight of his plea, the unbearable truth of it, the depth of his suffering.

I want to save him, to take his pain away— but I am just a man, bound by my own frailties, unable to touch the Divine, unable to change the course of fate.

So, I sit with him, offering what little I can— a hand to hold, a heart that understands. A man writhes on the hot black pavement, and I am with him, a witness to his pain, a companion in his suffering.

But then I offer a silent prayer to my God— not a god of stone, not one deaf to the cries of the world. And in that moment, I see my God writhing on the hot black pavement.

67
Man in the Mirror

The man in the mirror grapples with ghosts, their whispers haunting the corridors of his mind. Memories, long buried beneath the weight of time, rise like specters from the shadows, their bitter sting cutting deep.

He thinks of the woman in the red dress, her laughter a melody that once warmed the cold corners of his life. Her touch was fire, branding his soul. She left on a rainy Sunday, her footsteps dissolving into the downpour, her voice a faint whisper— *Goodbye. It's over.*

He lights his pipe, the smoke curling around him like a ghostly embrace. Years have passed, but the pain remains— a constant companion, unyielding, sharp. He tried drowning it in bottles and fleeting arms, but it always returned, stronger, crueler.

His father's face rises unbidden— a hard man with calloused hands, speaking with fists and silence. In his father's world, love left bruises, not warmth. The scars he carries—inside and out— etched like hieroglyphs, a childhood spent in fear and anger. At the corner bar, the bartender watches, a silent witness to his sorrow. Another shot burns down his throat, a brief escape from the memories clawing at his soul. Years of running end tonight, as his past corners him. There is nowhere left to hide.

He remembers cheap motels, the stale smoke, regret hanging heavy in the air. The women who came and went, brief reprieves from loneliness that devoured him whole. Mornings alone, sheets cold, silence deafening. Was this all there was? Could this be all there would ever be?

He's buried friends, lost to streets and demons. He's stood at gravesides, survivor's guilt pressing down. *Why them and not me?* The question lingers, unanswered, unanswerable.

He stares into the mirror. The lines on his face tell the story— a life both lived and endured. He's not young anymore. The years have carved their toll, but he's still standing.

He raises his glass— a silent toast to the battles fought, the scars earned, the ghosts that linger. The jukebox hums a melancholy tune, its melody weaving through the smoky air. But hidden in the sadness, a glimmer of hope: a promise of something more.

He takes a breath, the exhale carrying smoke, and the weight of his pain. For the first time in years, resolve flickers. The ghosts will haunt, the memories will sting, but he will stand his ground.

He is still alive. And that, he realizes, is worth raising a glass to. The man in the mirror has a story yet to write, a chance yet to change. As the night stretches toward dawn, it carries the promise of a new day.

68

Afterlife

Together, we explored the afterlife— a horizon shrouded in mystery, fraught with doubt, tinged with fragile longing. We walked through fields of mist, shadows whispering secrets, the air heavy with forgotten dreams. Above us stretched endless twilight, neither day nor night, a canvas painted with our questions, our fears, our hopes. I told her, honestly, I knew nothing for certain. Nobody does.

Still, she asked for scripture, for the words of Jesus, for something solid to anchor her soul. In the distance, a city of light emerged, its spires piercing twilight with an unearthly glow. Cautiously, we approached, our footsteps echoing in the silence, our hearts pounding. The gates stood open, inviting, but the path was lined with apparitions, their eyes reflecting our uncertainties.

Hand in hand, we entered the city, a labyrinth of ethereal streets where time flowed like a twisting river, carrying us on its mysterious currents. We met souls who had forgotten their earthly names, their faces blurred by eternity, their voices a haunting chorus of yearning.

In a hidden corner, we found an ancient library, its shelves lined with books shimmering with inner light. We searched for the words of Jesus, hoping for guidance, for answers, for a glimpse of truth amid the unknown. The pages we turned were filled with parables and promises, their meanings elusive, dancing just out of reach like smoke. The words were beautiful, haunting— not certainties, but echoes of faith, whispers of grace.

As we read, the library dissolved into a garden of eternal spring. Flowers bloomed in impossible colors, the air alive with angelic song, a melody born from creation's heart. We wandered through the garden, our doubts mingling with the scent of jasmine, our fears dissolving in golden light. She asked if this was heaven, if this was the afterlife we had sought. I told her I did not know— perhaps it was a dream within a dream, a fleeting vision of what might be.

Beneath a tree with silver leaves, its branches shimmering in eternal light, we lay together. I held her close, the warmth of her soul pressing against mine. In that moment, the questions no longer mattered. Uncertainties faded. All that remained was the love we carried— through shadows, through mist, through eternity's echoes.

We closed our eyes, letting the garden's music wash over us. For a moment, we were at peace, lost in the embrace of the unknown, the infinite, the boundless. Perhaps this was the afterlife— not a place of answers or absolutes, but a realm where love endures, where the soul finds rest in the arms of mystery. Perhaps the journey itself was the destination, and the questions, as sacred as the answers we sought.

69
The Garden

We closed our eyes, letting the music of the garden wash over us. For a moment, we were at peace— lost in the embrace of the unknown, the boundless, the infinite.

The garden was quiet, but alive with sound: the rustle of leaves, the whisper of a breeze, a hymn sung softly by creation itself. Her hand in mine— warm, steady— a tangible reminder of what was real, what mattered. We had wandered far— through sun-scorched towns, across moonlit fields, chasing something we couldn't name.

Always, it lingered ahead, just beyond reach— a fragment of peace eluding our grasp. But here, in the garden, peace found us. Flowers stood in quiet bloom, vivid against the green, their fragrance a balm to restless spirits. She spoke softly— of dreams and fears, of fragile hopes and lingering shadows.

Her voice carried strength; a resilience forged in struggle. I listened, not with answers, but with presence. Listening became solace, a way to share the fullness of the moment. The past clung to us still, its memories haunting the edges of our minds. We had seen too much, lost too much, but here, the weight seemed to lift— as if the earth itself had taken on our burdens.

I thought of the sea— its vastness, its power, its duality to calm and terrify. Life was like that: waves both gentle and fierce, etching meaning into the contours of our souls. The garden became a refuge, a place where time slowed, where breath came easier. The rhythm of the world softened, freed from life's relentless push and pull.

We spoke of the future— not in grand declarations, but in quiet whispers, in the language of real life. A home, a hearth, shared meals, the comfort of routines built with love. There was beauty in the mundane, poetry in the everyday. Even this, we realized, was part of the infinite.

As the light dimmed, the sky turned to dusk, and we lay back on the grass, watching stars pierce the twilight— tiny beacons, whispering of eternity. The music of the garden lingered, a lullaby neither beginning nor ending, but simply being.

I held her close, her heartbeat steady against my own, a rhythm that silenced doubt. In that moment, the worries fell away— regrets, unanswered questions. We were here, together, in the garden. And that was enough. The world outside would spin on, its trials unfolding as they always had.

But we had found a fragment of the infinite, a touch of peace, and it would stay with us— a quiet strength, a source of hope. We closed our eyes, letting the music of the garden wash over us. For that brief, eternal moment, we were at peace— held in the embrace of the unknown, the boundless, the infinite.

70
Christ Does Not Wait to be Found

He is not on a throne. He is not on a cloud. He rides the subway, shoulder to shoulder with the weary hands gripping the cold metal pole as the train lurches forward.

The Christ wears tired eyes and a jacket missing buttons. He is the man staring out the window. He is the woman with too many grocery bags to carry, the kid with a song in his headphones and a tear he won't let fall.

He lives in the shuffle of footsteps down your apartment hallway, in the cough of the old woman next door who waters her plants but forgets to water herself.

You will see Him when you stop looking so far away, when the mirror catches your eye and you dare to hold its gaze. The Christ is there, in the lines on your face, the questions in your heart, the love you forgot you could carry.

Here He is. Here She is. in the scrape of your day, in the stranger who smiles without reason, in the silence that listens when you finally let it.

Christ does not wait, to be found in the pages of a holy book. He is here. She is here. In the now. In the all. In You.

71

By the River

The day unfolded, free of conflict. Even the animals, with their wagging tails, could not lift the veil of despondency clinging to me like a shroud. Morning arrived swaddled in mist, a dull gray blanket settling low. I wandered aimlessly through the streets, a shadow among shadows. Cobblestones, slick with rain, reflected the somber sky above. Echoes of laughter, distant and hollow, bounced off alley walls— remnants of lives lived with more vigor than mine.

In the marketplace, vendors called out, their voices a dissonant symphony clashing with the stillness within me. The scent of fresh bread, the sharp tang of spices, a dance of vibrancy, yet I remained unmoved. Children played, their shouts piercing the heavy air. Their innocence was a cruel contrast to the weight that bore down on my shoulders. Even a dog, tail wagging, eyes bright with silent questions, could not breach the fortress of my gloom. I knelt, hand outstretched, feeling the warmth of its breath, the softness of its fur. But my heart stayed sealed, locked by invisible hands.

Time stretched like elastic, snapping back to monotony. The sun hid behind clouds, offering no warmth, no light— only its indifferent presence. By the river, I found myself. The waters sluggish and opaque, a mirror to my stagnant soul. Ripples stirred, disturbed by an unseen force— a fish or the ghost of a forgotten hope stirring briefly before sinking.

The bench was hard beneath me, its wood splintered, worn— a testament to others who sought solace and found none. Bare, skeletal trees stood sentinel, their clawing branches a mute plea for mercy.

Evening crept in, shadows lengthening. Streetlights flickered alive, their pale orbs casting weary light on damp pavement. I returned home to the creak of the door, the familiar sights and smells, a reminder of isolation. The chair by the window beckoned, and I sank into its embrace. The hum of the refrigerator, the distant murmur of traffic, the faint tick of the clock— all became a lullaby of despair.

I dreamt of brighter days, of laughter that rang true, of touch that sparked life. But dreams are fickle things—slippery, fleeting. I woke to the same shroud, the same monotone existence, unchanged. The animals circled back, their loyalty a bittersweet balm. I stroked their fur, whispered empty promises, let the hours blur into the haze of routine.

The day unfolded without incident, devoid of crises or conflict— a monotone in the symphony of existence, a single, unremarkable note in the endless composition of life.

72
The Leap of Faith

Faith is not handed down like an old coat, worn thin by too many shoulders. It cannot be carved into stone or locked behind the heavy doors of institution. It is not printed in ink on fine paper. Faith is born where the ground gives way, and you find yourself standing on the edge.

This is where God waits, not in the comfort of answers, but in the tremor of the unknown. You cannot see Him, but you will feel Her pull, a whisper cutting through the silence. A new birth that says, "Come."

It is not reason that moves you— reason stays safe, staring at the chasm. It is the fire in your chest, the impossible hunger to step into the mystery and find yourself caught.

This is the paradox: the Fall is not the end. It is the beginning, the place where the sky turns to arms, and you land not on certainty, but on love.

73
The Spark That Remains

It was the ceaseless drone of bad news, the relentless barrage of negativity pouring from screens and speakers, poisoning the air, turning every breath into a struggle. Or it was the weight of the world— that invisible, crushing weight— pressing down on my spirit, leaving me adrift in a sea of uncertainty and doubt.

The morning broke pale and listless, the sun hesitant, peering through the haze. Birdsong, once a comfort, now felt distant— a mocking reminder of simpler times, when joy was effortless, when laughter unfurled like a banner in the breeze. The radio murmured its grim litany, a background hum of despair. Voices droned on, a chorus of calamity. Each note was another crack in my armor, each headline a fresh wound, bleeding hope into the ether.

I walked the street, a ghost among the living. Each step echoed heavy; the pavement unyielding beneath my feet. Faces passed by, blank and weary, eyes glazed, mouths set in grim lines— each person a mirror to my own desolation. The cafés and shops stood as silent witnesses, their windows reflecting a gray sky, a muted tableau of normalcy fractured. Even the trees seemed bowed, their branches drooping in silent lament, their once-vibrant leaves dull against the gloom.

In the park, children played, their laughter piercing the heavy air— a brittle thread in the fabric of the day. Their joy shone like a fragile spark, a reminder of resilience, but one that felt distant, like a relic of a world I could no longer touch.

Or maybe it was the ghosts of missed opportunities, the shadows of choices unmade, paths untaken lingering at the edges of my vision, haunting my mind's quiet spaces. I sought solace in routine, but even the familiar rituals felt hollow, their meaning stripped away. The coffee, once a comfort, was now bitter, a reminder of mornings spent in easier times, when conversations flowed, and dreams were nurtured. The weight of the world bore down, its tendrils wrapping around my heart, squeezing until each breath came shallow. Inhale, struggle. Exhale, reluctant release.

Yet in the midst of the storm, a flicker. A faint glimmer. Hope. A reminder that even in the darkest night, the stars still shine, their light steady, a beacon for the lost. I clung to that fragile hope, a lifeline in the tempest. Step by step, I moved forward, each footfall an act of defiance against despair.

Perhaps it was the crushing weight of the world. But in the end, it was the spark of hope— that unquenchable flame of resilience— that carried me. Toward a brighter horizon. Toward a new day. The promise of renewal, etched in the sky, waiting to be claimed.

74
Resilience in the Void

As I sat in the quiet of my home, the emptiness stretched endlessly, a vast expanse of nothingness yawning before me. It felt as though God Himself had stepped out for a moment, leaving behind only the echo of His absence. The walls, bare and unadorned, seemed to close in, their blank faces mirroring my solitude. The ticking of the clock, a relentless metronome, marked time's passage with indifferent precision— each tick a reminder of the void.

Outside, the world continued, unaware of the chasm within. The sun, pale and tired, cast a cold, indifferent light, its rays slicing through the curtains, falling in desolate patterns on the floor. I wandered through the rooms, each a repository of memories: ghosts of laughter, fragments of conversations, echoes of lives once intertwined. The photographs on the mantel, silent sentinels of a happier past, stared back at me— smiles frozen, eyes devoid of life. The kitchen, its empty table, spoke of meals unshared, the clink of cutlery, the murmur of voices— all swallowed by cavernous silence.

The kettle, once warm with life, stood cold and lifeless, its spout pointing accusingly, as if to question the absence of conviviality. In the living room, the armchair, worn and familiar, beckoned me to sit, to ponder, to lose myself in the endless expanse of my thoughts. The bookshelf, a fortress of knowledge, offered no solace— its volumes merely silent witnesses to my despair. I thought of God, of the Divine presence that once seemed so near— now a distant, receding shadow. Had He truly stepped out, leaving me alone to navigate this desolation? Or had I turned away, blinded by my sorrow, by my doubt?

The garden outside, once a sanctuary of life, lay fallow— its blooms withered, its pathways choked with weeds. The birds, their songs a distant memory, had flown to warmer climes, leaving behind only the whisper of the wind through barren branches. I sat in the quiet, the stillness of the house a heavy cloak, and felt the weight of my insignificance— a single grain of sand in the vast desert of existence. The universe, vast and indifferent, seemed to mock my solitude, its stars winking coldly from their distant perches.

Yet amid this profound emptiness, a flicker stirred— a faint glimmer of hope, a whisper of resilience. Perhaps even in absence, there was presence, a silent watchfulness, a promise of return. I closed my eyes, let the quiet wash over me, and in that moment of surrender, I felt a faint warmth— a gentle whisper in the void. The emptiness, though vast, was not unendurable. The silence was not eternal. For in the quiet of my home, amid the emptiness and echoes, a spark remained— a faint, persistent light. It was a testament to the human spirit, its capacity to endure, to hope, to find meaning even in absence. The emptiness stretched on, but it was no longer a void, no longer a mere absence. It had become a space— a canvas upon which life could be painted anew, and to wait with patient hope for the return of the light.

75

Communion

Amid the darkness, a flicker remained— a glimmer of light on the horizon, beckoning. Perhaps all I needed was to shake off the lethargy, to rise from my slumber and embrace the day anew. The stillness of night, deep and consuming, held me in its cocoon— shadows and whispered memories. Yet in the distance, faint but persistent, was a promise of dawn, a whisper of renewal.

With a heavy sigh and quiet resolve, I rose from my bed, the weight of sorrow lifting, as if drawn upward by unseen hands. My steps, lightened by morning's call, led me into a world bathed in the soft glow of first light. I walked through a small garden, touching flowers, each bloom a testament to resilience, each leaf a story of survival. The cherry blossoms, delicate and fleeting, spoke of beauty in transience, of grace in letting go.

The path before me, once shrouded in mist, unfolded gently in the light. Each step became a pilgrimage, each breath a prayer. The tall bamboo grove swayed with the wind, its song a hymn to impermanence, a reminder of the sacredness of change. In the east, the sun began its ascent— a golden orb of new beginnings. Its rays pierced the lingering night, painting the world in hues of gold and amber. The mountains, stoic, and eternal, stood as guardians of this sacred moment, their peaks glowing with the first light, offering stability amid change.

As I walked, the lethargy fell away, replaced by a quiet strength. The stream beside me flowed steadily, its waters clear and purposeful— embracing each bend and turn. In town, life stirred. Morning emerged as a symphony of renewal. Voices called greetings, chores clattered in rhythm, and children's laughter rose like a song. I joined them— a solitary figure finding solace in the rhythm of the day, in the dance of existence. For even in the darkest moments, there is always the promise of dawn— a chance to begin anew, to find hope in the simple act of moving forward.

Communion, at the clinic, became my meditation: each movement deliberate, each gesture imbued with grace. A ritual of mindfulness, a reminder of the sacred woven into the mundane. Bread, flesh. Wine, blood.

As the sun climbed higher, its warmth filled the day. I found peace in routine, joy in small acts of kindness and care. An open window, once a symbol of loss, now brought in life's light. The trees, once bare, whispered promises of spring— buds swelling with life's potential. Birds sang in celebration; their melodies filled the air with hope and renewal.

In the simple act of holy communion and embracing the day, I found a profound truth: life, fleeting and fragile, is a gift. Each moment, in its sorrows and joys, is to be cherished.

As the sun reached its zenith, I stood tall— spirit renewed, heart light. In the embrace of dawn, in the promise of a new day, I found strength to move forward— to live, to love, to hope.

76
Edges of Eternity

Life after death— a topic shrouded in mystery, steeped in centuries of contemplation. It is not spoken of lightly, especially in the somber rooms of hospice. But when Amara broached the subject, her eyes alight with curiosity, I was drawn into the depths of her inquiry. The room, hushed and still, bore witness to the quiet struggle of souls on the brink of a great journey. Walls, heavy with unspoken fears, absorbed the weight of antiseptic and hope. Amara's voice, soft but steady, carried the gravity of wonder— a yearning to understand the unseen, the unknown.

We sat together, the world outside reduced to a distant hum, time marked only by the rhythmic beep of machines and the rustle of sheets. Her question hung in the air, delicate as a spider's web, glistening with the dew of contemplation. I spoke of the ancients— their beliefs in the eternal cycle, the endless wheel of life, death, rebirth, and renewal. "In the East," I told her, "We speak of samsara, the soul's journey through lifetimes, each death a doorway, not an end."

Amara's eyes, pools of quiet resolve, reflected the flicker of candles, their fragile flames dancing against the shadows. She listened, her spirit reaching to touch the edges of the Divine. I told her of the Japanese— of samurai facing death with honor, of poets capturing fleeting beauty in the fall of a cherry blossom— a symbol of life's impermanence. We spoke of ancestors, their spirits lingering like incense, guiding the living with unseen hands.

Outside the window, the world moved on, oblivious to our sacred dialogue. The garden, blooming and withering in quiet harmony, stood as testament to nature's cycles. The birds, flitting among branches, sang songs of ephemeral beauty, a backdrop to our musings. Amara's hand, frail and delicate, rested in mine. Her pulse, faint but steady, echoed life's fragile rhythm. She asked of the afterlife, her voice a whisper, a prayer.

I spoke of the Pure Land, of Amida's vow— a realm of peace and light, where souls find rest, free from the turning wheel. Her eyes closed, a sigh escaping her lips, as though the words wrapped her in an embrace of solace.

Of course, we spoke of the blessings of God through Jesus, and that The Christ stands at the threshold, not as a sentinel, but as a guide. Life does not end; it bends, turns into light, and walks with Him into forever.

The shadows lengthened, the day yielded to twilight— a metaphor for our conversation, the passage from light to dark, from life to death. We sat in silence, the unspoken words between us a bridge across the great divide.

Amara, on the cusp of the great mystery, found comfort in ancient tales, in the promise of continuity, of an eternal journey. The hospice room, once stark and somber, became a sanctuary— a sacred space where life and death intertwined. As evening deepened, I rose to leave, my heart heavy with our shared conversation, yet lightened by its understanding.

77
Sand and Ashes

The sand in my shoes, the missing boards of the beach house floor, the twisted branches overhanging the roof— pieces of a story too familiar to notice. A mouse peeked out from beneath a slice of bread, as waves crashed, and the ocean boiled.

The car broke down again. I walked into town to grab a bite to eat. The sun bore down— hot, relentless— each step a reminder of the weight of the world. Dust rose with every footfall, clinging to my shoes, to my thoughts.

A child, small and stern, stood in my path. *Go home,* he said. *Your house is on fire.* His wide, innocent eyes held a truth I couldn't deny. I nodded, picked up my coffee, and briskly walked home. The streets were quiet, the town a whisper. Faces passed, familiar yet distant— each lost in their own story, their own struggle. The sea breeze tugged at my shirt, cool against the heat, a reminder of the ocean's pull— its relentless ebb and flow.

When I reached the beach house, smoke rose like a black plume against the blue sky. The fire crackled—hungry and unforgiving— devouring the old boards, the window frames, the memories they held. I stood, coffee in hand, feeling the heat on my face, the sand in my shoes. The waves crashed. The ocean boiled. The sounds mingled with the flames, a symphony of nature's duality—its power to give and to take.

The fire spread, flickers of orange and red dancing in destruction. The mouse scurried away, the bread abandoned, seeking refuge from the heat. I took a sip of coffee— bitter, strong— a grounding taste amid the chaos. Neighbors gathered, silent witnesses, faces etched with concern, with resignation. Someone called the fire department, their sirens a distant wail— a promise of water, of relief.

But I knew it was too late. The beach house was already gone, a sacrifice to the flames. The child stood nearby, watching with unscathed innocence. I walked to him, knelt by his side, and placed a hand on his shoulder.

We watched together— the fire's dance, its hunger, its finality. In the destruction, a shared understanding grew. The sirens grew louder, closer, but the house was lost. The waves crashed. The ocean boiled. I took another sip of coffee, breathed in the smoke, the salt air, wiped tears from my eyes, and found an unexpected peace. In the ashes, in the ruins, there was clarity. For in the destruction lay a beginning.

The sand in my shoes, the broken boards, the twisted branches— reminders of what was and what could be. I stood, trembling, crying, cup in hand, and walked back toward the town. The child followed beside me. The past smoldered behind us, the future stretched ahead— an unwritten story, a blank horizon.

78

Servant Song

Satan and his angels came one night to sit on your pillow. You'd talk about the tempter often as you lunged in pain in your hospital bed. And they watched you sleep, seeing your mouth open, your tongue sink back into your throat. They heard the wheeze from exhausted lungs, the pitiful plea to God for release, for deliverance. The streetlight flickered—a silent witness—the room heavy with their presence, their dark laughter barely audible, like the hum of the refrigerator in the kitchen down the hall.

You were lost in dreams, or maybe it was nightmares, trapped in a web of your own making— a life tangled in regrets and broken promises, an old lover's kiss turned sour, the bottle empty beside your bed. The clock on the wall ticked on, indifferent to your suffering, the seconds slipping away like sand through a sieve, like the love you once had but couldn't keep. Your fingers twitched, grasping at the sheets, your face contorted in pain, the sweat on your brow glistening in the dim light. They leaned in closer, their breath, cold against your skin, whispering promises of release, of eternal rest, if only you would let go.

But you clung on— to the memory of better days, to the hope that somewhere, somehow, there was still a chance, still a way out. You glared at the door at the end of your room. The night stretched on, an endless parade of shadows, and they stayed with you— watching, waiting, for you to make your peace, for you to give in. But you fought, with every ragged breath, every beat of your weary heart, refusing to surrender, refusing to let them win.

And when the first light of dawn crept through the window, they slunk away, back to whatever dark corner they had come from— leaving you alone, still breathing, still fighting, still alive. The world outside was waking up, another day beginning. And you knew you would rise, face it all again, because that's what you did, what you always did.

And you'd find a way to make it through— to outlast the darkness, to find some semblance of peace in this broken world. You turned your head to the side, saw your old Bible on the nightstand, its pages worn and stained. And you reached out, your hand trembling, and opened it to a random page, reading the words with tired eyes.

And in that moment, you felt a glimmer of something— hope, faith, maybe just a stubborn refusal to let the bastards win. So, you closed the book, laid it back down, and waited for sleep to come, knowing that the battle wasn't over, but that you were still in the fight—still breathing, still alive.

79
Echo of the Creator

The morning was quiet. The sun rose slowly over the hills, its light touching the earth like a hand— soft, steady, making no sound. You could feel it then— the weight of the world waking up. Not heavy, but real. The way the sea is real. The way the wind moves the leaves and never asks permission.

They said we were made in His image, but no one really understood. Not in the cities, not in the fields. Not in the wars or the marketplaces. Not where men stacked stones on stones and called them kingdoms.

But you could see it if you looked long enough. If you sat in the shade of an olive tree and watched a boy cast his nets into the water. If you listened to the woman singing while she swept her porch. If you stood still when the world demanded, you move.

It was there. It was always there. God's image wasn't in the perfect things, the smooth things, the things men polished and held up to the light. It was in the rough hands of the farmer, the cracked skin of the fisherman. It was in the laughter that broke through the silence when all seemed lost.

We were scared, they said. All of us. Not because we deserved it. Not because we earned it. But because it was placed there, inside us, like a fire that doesn't go out, even when the storms come.

But men forgot. They built their towers and their armies. They counted gold, combed their silken hair, spilled blood, and called it wisdom and the right thing to do. They looked at their brothers and sisters along the way and saw nothing but shadows.

Still, the image remained. In the old man who gave his bread to the hungry. In the soldier who knelt, weeping for the life he'd taken. In the child who reached out her hand to touch the face of a stranger.

The light was there, always. It burned quietly in the silence, in the stillness. It called us back, even when we didn't listen. And when the day came when the sun fell low, when the earth grew cold— we stood together, faces turned to the sky, and saw ourselves for what we were: not perfect, but whole. Not broken, but unfinished. Made in His image, like the sea is made of salt, like the earth is made of stone, like the stars are made of light. And it was enough.

80
Path of Becoming

The path winds through the forest, dark and shadowed, where roots twist like old memories, and the light flickers—uncertain, a fragile flame. Here, in the deep silence of trees, I search for meaning. I was told once, by a voice soft as dawn breaking over hills, that we are made in the image of God. Not in the steel of strength, nor the glitter of pride, but in the quiet dignity of being— fragile and Divine. A paradox, like the unseen wind that bends the bough but never breaks it.

And so, I walk. The trees whisper their secrets, and the stream hums a hymn older than time itself. They speak of Him— the one who came not with thunder or sword, but with open, empty hands, ready to heal, and a heart vast enough to hold the world.

Christ, they say, was more than a man. But He was also no less. In His breath was life's rhythm, love's cadence, compassion's pulse. He walked among us, not above us. He wept as we weep, laughed as we laugh, bore the weight of sorrow, and the fleeting joy of things too precious to last.

By the stream, I stop. Its waters, clear and cold, tremble with my reflection— imperfect, fractured by ripples. Is this not who we are? Images of the eternal, distorted by restless motion. And yet, the essence remains: to love, to forgive, to gather the broken pieces of the world, holding them tenderly, whispering, *This, too, is sacred.*

This is what He showed us. Not in grand sermons or in theological diatribes, but in touching the untouchable, carrying the weight of cruelty and betrayal, and still calling us His own. I rise and walk again. The forest opens into a meadow, the sun spilling like gold. I think of the world— its crowded cities and endless wars, its starving children, sickly elders, its lonely hearts. How often we forget. How often we see each other as dark shadows, not as bearers of light.

Yet even in forgetting, the flame remains. It burns quietly, steadfastly. It is there: in the stranger's smile, in the hand reaching out, in the moments when love is chosen over fear. Christ's path was not easy. It led to the cross, to pain, to the breaking of His body. And yet, it did not end there.

The path turned, like a changing wind, rising like the dawn, showing us that even in death, there is life. And so, I walk. Not alone, but with the echo of

His steps guiding mine. The wind carries His song, and the earth remembers His touch.

We are all on this journey, bearing His image, called to love with a love that does not demand, but simply is. In the end, it is not the destination that matters, but the walking— the becoming. To see the Divine in the fragile, the eternal in the fleeting. To hold the world as it is, and still believe it is sacred. This is what it means to be human.

81
Pain is the Poet's Shadow

I don't know why pain is the poet's shadow, always there, always whispering its secrets in my ear. They say it sharpens the words, makes them sing like a blade against stone. But I'd trade the whole damned song to be the fool dancing on tabletops, shouting at the moon, falling in love with the stars or the girl next door.

Instead, here I am, sitting on the edge of a tall building, my aching legs dangling like a question no one dares to answer. The sidewalk, a million miles below, smiles up at me, its teeth cracked and waiting. But I don't want to fall; I just want to fly.

I reach out, grasping at the wings of a butterfly— fragile, shimmering, like a hymn whispered in a cathedral. It flutters just beyond my fingers, leading me to some far-off flower I'll never know the name of. I wonder if this is faith, or just another kind of madness.

Leaps of faith, they call them, but nobody tells you how to land. Nobody says what happens when the flower you were flying toward isn't there anymore, or maybe it's just a Venus flytrap.

And so, I sit, flirting with the sidewalk, waiting for the butterfly to come back, or for God to finally answer me.

82
Dialogue with The Divine

Scripture is alive, but it won't chase you down the alley, won't knock the bottle from your hand or stop you from running headlong into a wall. It just stands there, waiting for you to stop yelling and start listening.

If you let it speak to you, you may not end up on the wrong side of town, or worse—on the backside of the Moon, watching your breath freeze in the void, wondering why the stars never told you the truth. Bring your dirty laundry to the Bible, the torn shirts, old socks and underwear, the unwashed jeans. Lay them out like confessions. It will hand you a clean wardrobe, or a one-way ticket to the edge of the Universe or the nearest cleaners, where silence hums like a hymn.

Sing with Genesis. Take a bite of that bright, shiny apple. Let the juice run down your chin— it's sweeter than you think. But don't stop there. Get burned at Moses's bush. Let the flames climb your soul, purge the sickness from your body, burn the mildew from your heart.

And when you sit with Jesus, don't let it just be a monologue. Speak. Whisper. Shout if you have to. You know, it's called prayer. He's not just a bookend for the good parts. He's the fire and the breath, the ears that hear you before the words form, the hands that already hold the answers you're too scared to ask for.

The Bible doesn't end. It doesn't close the door unless you slam it yourself. Dialogue with the Divine isn't a thing to finish; it's a life to walk, a path through fire, a song that never stops singing.

83
Hour of Flight

What time is it when you break out of your shell, climbing into the real dirt of the nest? Mouth wide open, begging for worms, screaming your lungs raw until momma throws you out— because you just can't control your urges.

To spout truth and lies, to howl and sing and demand— it's the hour when the sky's just gray enough to make you question the colors you dreamed. When your bones ache under the weight of unspoken words and half-formed desires.

You claw your way up, feathers sticky with the muck of yesterday's regrets. The world, a discord of desperate cries, each one a mirror of your own hunger. You scream. You bellow. You beg for sustenance— for that slimy, wriggling proof that life is more than just existing, that something can fill the emptiness gnawing at your insides.

And momma, oh momma, she can't stand the noise, the chaos you bring. So, she shoves you into the abyss, her eyes a storm of frustration and sorrow. You fall, flailing, flapping, failing, but never silent, never still. Truth and lies spill out of you like the relentless sound of rain on a tin roof. Each note a defiant declaration, a refusal to be muted, to be molded.

You are nothing but raw sound, a screaming, singing force of nature. And then—oh, then—the worm comes. You snatch it up, gulp it down, a lifeline in a sea of despair.

For a fleeting moment, you are invincible, a conqueror of your own small world. You spread your wings, unsteady but determined. You fly—fly away from the nest, from the safety of yesterday's lies.

Momma's voice fades, a distant echo, warning you of poisoned berries. But you don't care. Not now. Not ever. Because deep in your marrow, you know you're beyond her diet of worms.

The world is vast, terrible, and beautiful. And your song— your glorious, reckless song— is the only truth that matters. The world listens. Each note pierces, a needle stitching together the tattered remnants of dreams and realities. They love you for it. For the raw, untamed beauty of your voice. For the way you bare the world— the struggle, the pain, the fleeting moments of grace.

You sing because you must. Because silence is unbearable. Because the world needs your song as much as you need the air, the sky, the endless possibilities of a life lived on the edge— where truth and lies blur, and only the music remains. The story you tell with every ragged, glorious breath.

84
Dark Age

The coming dark age will be full of electric light, streams of color pouring from black screens, glowing in the twilight of our own making. We sit, eyes wide and empty, absorbing flickering pixels that promise escape but deliver nothing.

Cities hum with the low drone of a million machines, speaking a language of code and silence. The stars fade behind the haze of neon dreams, smog-choked ambitions rising like smoke from a dying fire. We've traded the warmth of the sun for the cold glow of artificial illumination, the crackling hearth for the hum of fluorescent bulbs.

In crowded streets, faces lit by phones, the lonely walk together but apart. Each heartbeat is a solitary echo, bouncing through concrete canyons. Where once there was conversation, now there is only the hum of data, the endless scroll of lives not lived.

The poets write in binary, the lovers touch through glass. And the children— oh, the children— grow up knowing only the synthetic dawn. Their lullabies are the soft hum of servers, their dreams filtered through algorithms, their innocence tangled in wires that pulse with fabricated meaning.

Libraries stand empty, their books gathering dust, pages yellowed and brittle, whispers of a time when words were enough— when stories were told by firelight and not by the cold, calculated voice of a digital assistant.

The coming dark age is bright with the glare of screens that show us everything and nothing. A parade of images, fast and fleeting, leaving us hungry, unsatisfied, always searching for more.

In the shadows, the old gods laugh. They see our chains, each link forged by a like, a follow, a click. We've built this cage of light, bright and shining, but a cage, nonetheless. We've forgotten the taste of rain, the feel of dirt beneath our feet, the sound of wind through trees. Lost in the din of notifications, we've traded the wildness of the earth for the hum of servers, the endless stream of updates, the false promise of connection.

The dark age is here, too bright to see the stars, too loud to hear the whispers of the earth beneath our feet, too fast to catch our breath. And yet, somewhere in the distance, there is a flicker, a spark— a reminder of what was, of what could be. A whisper calls us to unplug, to step out into the night, to feel the darkness, to find the light within. But for now, we sit, bathed in electric light, eyes wide and empty, waiting. For a sign. For a signal. For something— anything— to break the silence.

85
Manifestation of Spirit

I and the sunflower are one. No difference between us. Same atoms, same molecules, same quantum mechanics binding us to the soil and the stars. We stretch to the sky, searching for God, our faces turned toward the light.

We bend our heads in sorrow, then languish in the soil, waiting for the next manifestation of spirit. The sun rises, the sun sets, and in between, we exist— barely noticed, barely there, a whisper in the cosmic wind, a flicker of light in the vast darkness.

We reach, always reaching, hungry for warmth, for meaning, for something more than this— this endless cycle of growth and decay, this eternal dance of life and death.

The sunflower and I know the taste of the earth, the feel of dirt coursing through our veins. We know the pull of gravity holding us down, and the yearning—oh, the yearning—to break free, to soar, to be more than matter and energy.

To touch the Divine, to see the face of God. But the world spins on, indifferent to our dreams, to our silent prayers whispered into the void. The sunflower bows its head, heavy with the weight of its existence, and I bow mine too, knowing we are but specks of dust, blown by the winds of fate, lost in the grand fabric of the universe.

We wait, patiently, for the next manifestation of spirit, for life to breathe into our tired bones, to lift us from the soil, to set us free. But until then, we stretch, we bend, we break, we endure. The seasons change, the petals fall, the world moves on.

And we, we remain— a testament to the fragile beauty of being, of existing, of searching for something more. We are the same, the sunflower and I—made of the same star stuff, the same cosmic dust, the same dreams and fears and hopes. The same longing for the light. The same sorrow in the darkness.

And when the end comes, when the final petal falls, we will return to the soil, to the earth from which we came. In that final embrace, we will be one— truly one— with the universe, with the spirit, with the Divine.

Until then, we wait. We stretch. We bend. We search. We dream. We endure. We are but a moment, a fleeting breath, a single note in the symphony of existence—a sunflower and a man, reaching for the sky, searching for God.

86
Life is a Stone Mason

Life is a painful stone mason, chipping away at granite, each strike deliberate, revealing the rough edges and hidden veins of gold.

We walk through the dust, carrying the weight of every lost love, every broken promise— a silent procession of souls, marked by the scars of living.

In the dim light of a city street, truth is etched deep— lines on faces like a well-worn map, each crease a story, each scar a testament.

We drink to forget, but the memories linger— persistent shadows in the night, whispering their cruel truths. The bottle dulls the edge but never smooths it completely.

The streets are a gallery of our shattered dreams, each step a reminder of the pieces we've lost, scattered like fallen leaves on the pavement of time.

And yet, we move forward, guided by some unseen hand, hoping to find beauty in the cracks of our souls, in the fractures that let the light in.

Life carves us down, strike after strike, until we are raw and exposed. But in that vulnerability, we find something true, something unbreakable beneath the surface.

So, here's to the mason— to the pain, to the grind, to the endless shaping that makes us more than we were before.

For in the midst of the suffering, we are slowly refined. Not polished, not perfect, but real— etched with the lines of a life lived fully, and glinting, just barely, with the veins of gold within.

87
Goodbye

I said goodbye to Rob today, not just a patient, he was my friend. He was my teacher of the spirit, the one who pulled angels from his bag of tricks and made them dance on those tiny pinheads of doubt and hope.

Never without a story— his buddies in the Navy, always reminding me he was on the ships, but never in 'Nam. He was proud to be a carpenter, just like his Lord.

We argued, sort of, that Jesus was really a stonemason. *Probably hauled rocks,* I said. *His hands must've bled; his knuckles smashed.* But Rob laughed, said Jesus could still roll out the Torah scroll in the synagogue, talk to his Father in heaven with hands rough but holy.

Rob was always ready to go. *Never afraid of death,* he said, looking forward to meeting his Maker. He was tired of this world— a world of abdominal pain, dense cataracts, diarrhea, and loneliness.

No real family to speak of. No wife, no kids. A sister in New England, a good friend from church who brought him communion. *That was enough,* he said.

He showed me his old, worn Bible. *Can't read it anymore,* he admitted, foggy eyes making everything dark, gray, and fuzzy— just like this world, which he was ready to leave behind.

So, I said goodbye to Rob at the inpatient unit, gave him his last rites, touched his hands, kissed the top of his head. I had a feeling he was already with Jesus when I left his room.

This was a man who taught me, not just through his words but through his life— a life of faith and courage, of pain and yet of joy.

A man ready to leave, but never truly gone. For in the stories he told, in the spirit he shared, he remains.

88
Jam on Her Toast

Lillian is tired. Too tired to eat, too tired to care. *Chemo sucks,* she says, and I can see it in her eyes— the weariness, the fight that doesn't feel like fighting anymore.

She's waiting for relief, waiting for a knock at the door, a familiar face, a grandchild with stories of a world that feels farther away every day.

She can't watch TV. *It's all depressing,* she says, waving a hand toward the dark screen. *Too much ugly nonsense in the world. But I won't be here for it anyhow.*

Her words are heavy, not bitter, just matter of fact, like the toast cooling on the plate beside her— bare, dry, waiting for the sweetness it may never see.

The toast needs jam. It sits there, a small detail, but it speaks volumes. She turns away from the news, breaking but broken, the headlines too sharp, too much to carry.

It breaks my heart, she says, but she has more important things to do— like just living another day. Living without pain, without fear, without the weight of the world pressing down on her fragile frame.

I want to help her. I want to bring her something— a little more than words, a little more than sympathy. But what do you bring to someone so tired, so stripped down by the fight, who's already seen more than enough?

I look at the toast, its plainness, its need. Maybe that's it. Maybe I'll just put jam on her toast.

Maybe it's not about fixing the big things, not about solving the endless ache of the world. Maybe it's about this— a small kindness, a gesture of sweetness, a moment that doesn't demand anything of her but simply reminds her that she is seen, that she is cared for.

Lillian watches me, her gaze steady, and for a moment, the weight in the room shifts. The chemo, the headlines, the quiet waiting for relief— none of it goes away.

But here we are, two people, and a piece of toast that just needed a little jam.

89
Girls in the Window

The girls in the window look out over the city, silhouettes framed by the soft glow of streetlights and the distant hum of life. They don't see me.

They lean against the panes, fingers tracing invisible lines on the glass, lost in their dreams. The world turns below them— cars and crowds, laughter, and sirens— but they are above it all, untouched, their gaze fixed on something only they can see.

They take long walks on the boardwalk, bare feet brushing the wood, their laughter mingling with the waves. Each step is a whisper of freedom, each breath a taste of the open sky. They carry the salt air in their hair, the endless horizon in their eyes.

When the wind catches them, they fly away. Their hair streams behind them, faces turned toward distant horizons. Unbound, untethered, they leave me behind— to watch, to wonder, to fade into the night.

I see their freedom, their lightness, their joy. And yet, as they disappear into the vastness of the world, I feel the ache of their leaving, the pull of their untouchable beauty.

I am rooted here, earthbound, watching them ascend like birds breaking free from the weight of gravity. The city holds me, its streets a web of familiarity, its lights a poor imitation of stars.

I walk alone beneath their window, where shadows dance against the curtains. I wonder what it is they see, what calls them so powerfully that they cannot stay.

Perhaps it is not me they are leaving behind, but themselves— their fears, their doubts, the smallness of the world we all try to escape.

Perhaps they are chasing what we all chase: the promise of more, the hope of becoming.

And yet, I remain. I stay in the quiet, in the spaces they leave behind. Their laughter echoes in my memory, their steps fade into the distance.

The night wraps itself around me, and I wonder if they will ever return, if they will look back and see me waiting, still watching.

90
Prayer of Salvador

Salvador touches the children with his big hands, rough like sandpaper, hands shaped by labor, by the unrelenting grind of survival. He gives them melons, ripe and sweet, his twisted smile a crooked testament to too many punches, too many falls off the back of vegetable trucks.

His face is a map of pain, etched with lines of struggle, a testament to a life lived on the edge of despair and hope. Each wrinkle tells a story— of droughts, of floods, of laughter too fleeting and heartbreak too common.

He hauls honeydews in a small red wagon, rescued from an alley behind a dilapidated tenement. Its wheels creak, singing the song of survival as he trudges down cracked sidewalks, past faded murals, past forgotten dreams, and shuttered windows.

To Mrs. Koch, he gives apples, her wrinkled hands trembling as they grasp the red gift of life. To anyone with a heart, he offers bananas— yellow crescents of hope. His own heart, a bruised fruit, still beats, still holds on, still hopes.

He asks Jesus to bless his eggplants. Each one is a prayer, a plea for tomorrow, for rain, for sunlight, for enough. Salvador carries the weight of the world in a brown paper sack, flimsy yet strong enough to cradle his burdens, his dreams, his quiet sorrows.

He waters his peppers with the tears of a thousand years— the tears of ancestors, of lands left behind, of loves lost to time and promises left unfulfilled. He prays for the life of his son, a phantom in his thoughts. Somewhere south of the border, or lost in a ditch in Mexico, his son's voice is a whisper on the wind, his face a shadow Salvador cannot forget.

His prayers rise like smoke, like incense carrying the ache of his heart, the weight of his fears, to a heaven that sometimes feels distant. At night, he will return to his wife, her eyes mirrors of his own pain, her hands tired yet tender. They will sit together in their small kitchen, she will cook him dinner— simple, warm, a feast seasoned with love.

They will eat in silence, the silence of shared burdens, of words left unsaid. They will sleep entwined, seeking comfort in the night, finding solace in each other's arms. Their dreams will weave together— a jigsaw puzzle of memories, of laughter, of loss, of prayers whispered in the dark. They will hold onto each other, onto the promise of dawn, onto the hope that tomorrow will come with a little more light, a little less weight.

91
Sacred Justice

The church barks sermons in echoing halls, its words reverberating against stained glass. But out here, on the hot, cracked streets, where the air tastes of rust and despair, the sermon is written in blood and sweat.

They call it the church— a dance of ideals, a tapestry of dreams, a return to the glory that never truly was. Yet noisy reality clangs louder than the pulpit, and the paycheck does not hear prayers.

Imaginative institution-building, they say, but what about the roaches on the walls? The lead in the paint? The smog that steals breath from children, the heat that presses down on grandmothers, the work that breaks backs and spirits.

The politicians preach about flourishing, of gardens in Eden, their white leaders on white horses, while brown children choke on fumes, on broken promises, on unspoken truths.

What alternatives, they ask, can rise in the face of suffering and oppression? Alternatives, yes, we need them. We need them in every brick, in every breath, in paychecks that mean more than survival.

We need air that doesn't suffocate, skies that don't poison slowly, homes that hold more than shadows. The church, this church, it is failing—failing in the lessons of living, of breathing, of seeing the world as it is, and not as a verse suspended in the amber of an ancient book.

Let us build a new church, from the ground up. Let its walls be made of justice, its floors of dignity. Let its roof shelter all who enter, and let its doors— yes, let its doors always open wide, always remain unshut.

Let the sermon be written not in lofty words, but in the laughter of children whose lungs are clear, in the hands of workers who build without breaking, in the breaths of the elderly who rest beneath its shade.

Let this church rise, not as a monument to ideals and wealth, but as a sanctuary of action— a place where prayers take flesh, where hope is a foundation, where love is not a word but a hammer, a nail, a bridge.

For the sermon of the streets demands a response, a reckoning, a rebuilding. And in the dust of the old, let the new church rise— not bound by walls of stone, but by the unyielding truth that justice is sacred and dignity Divine.

92
Eternal Belonging

Born again before you were born, in a time before time, in a place beyond place, you were known, seen, understood— held in the quiet, timeless reality of your being.

Before the first cry echoed in the night, before the first light touched your eyes, before you felt the world's cold breath against your fragile skin, you were already part of the story.

Not a story you wrote, not a tale you told, but a grand, ancient narrative etched in the stars, whispered by the wind, breathed into the fabric of all that is.

Your identity— not crafted by a decision, not shaped by a whispered prayer, but formed in the heart of the Divine, in the mind of Christ— a deep, abiding certainty.

From the foundation of the world, you were known. From the first spark of creation, you were a part of the Divine dance, woven into the endless tapestry of existence.

The cosmos, vast and unending, birthed from a virgin's womb— the stars, the planets, the endless night— all part of the grand design, all part of the sacred story.

And from the tomb, silent and dark, came rebirth, renewal, transformation. The virgin tomb gave birth to hope, to life, to an eternal promise.

You—there, in the midst of it all— a thread in the tapestry, a note in the eternal song. Known. Loved. Understood. Before you knew yourself, before you took your first breath.

No decision could shape this. No prayer could change it. It was always there— a part of you, a part of Him, a part of eternity.

In the silent moments, in the stillness of the night, in the whisper of the wind, you can feel it— a connection, a thread tying you to the Divine, to the eternal, to the sacred.

The world may change. The seasons may shift. But this truth remains: this timeless reality, this Christ certainty.

You were born again before you were born. Known, seen, understood. A part of the grand design, a part of the Divine story, etched in the stars, whispered by the wind, forever and always.

93
Faith is the Fear Itself

Because all faith requires a surrender to something we cannot control, all faith begins with anguishing anxiety— a clenched fist hovering above an open hand, the breath caught between a cry and a prayer, the moment when silence becomes unbearable.

There is a boy kneeling in the dirt. His shadow falls like a cross over the broken earth. He cups the soil; lets it slip through his fingers— dust that refuses to answer him. Still, he waits for something to bloom, for the whisper of roots beneath the surface.

And the woman on the edge of the sea, salt burning her cheeks, cradling her grief like a child too precious to let go. She asks the waves if they have taken him if they will ever give him back. The sea only sings its unyielding hymn.

Faith is not the absence of fear— it is fear itself, held in trembling hands, offered up like a fragile gift. It is the leap we do not think we can make; the surrender we do not think we can survive.

94
Christ Eternal

There never was a time when there wasn't Christ. Before the dawn broke the sky, before the stars found their places, He was there— an immanent presence, incarnate in mystery, a whisper in the silence, a flicker in the void.

In the beginning, when the world was unformed, a formless void, He was the thought, the Word, the breath that stirred the waters, the light that broke the darkness, the life that filled the emptiness.

Not just in the cathedrals, where the stained glass tells His story, not just in the prayers whispered in the stillness of a Sunday morning, but in the fields where the farmers toil, in the marketplaces bustling with life, in the laughter of children playing in the streets.

There never was a time when there wasn't Christ— walking with the weary travelers, sharing bread with the hungry, giving hope to the hopeless, light to those in darkness.

He was there with the ancient prophets, speaking through their words, a promise, a vision, a hope— for a world made whole, for lives redeemed, for love that knows no bounds.

In the quiet moments of despair, when the night seems endless, He is the steady hand, the presence that never fades, the light that guides the lost back home, back to the heart of the eternal.

There never was a time when there wasn't Christ— not bound by time or place, a presence in the storm, a calm in the chaos, a thread woven through the fabric of existence.

From the manger to the cross, from the empty tomb to the hearts of those who seek Him, He is there— a constant, a certainty in a world of change, a light that never dims, a love that never fades.

He is in laughter and the tears, in the struggles and the triumphs, in the quiet moments of reflection and the busy rush of life.

There never was a time when there wasn't Christ— a presence in the beginning and in every moment since. A thread that ties it all together, a love that holds it all in place, a hope that never dies, a light that never fades.

95
Breath of Life

The breath of life, it stirs within us— a spark in the darkness, a whisper in the wind. In the Beginning, it was more than air, it was God's breath—Ruach— not just oxygen filling lungs, but inspiration igniting the soul.

It is the force that pushes us forward, that makes us reach for the stars, that shapes us into creators of worlds.

Ruach—the spirit, the wind— moves unseen, yet it is always felt. It drives the heart, fuels the mind, and lifts the soul beyond what the body can bear. The breath of God is not a mere exhale; it is the unseen hand shaping dreams, lighting fires of imagination, breathing purpose into dust. This breath— it is the artist's lungs, the writer's pen, the thinker's mind, the dreamer's heart.

It is not just a pulse of existence; it is the very essence of being, the Divine force that drives us to create, to build, to dream, to love, to rise above the mundane.

In every breath we take, there lies a spark of the Divine, a connection to something greater, a reminder that we are more than flesh. We are vessels of inspiration, carriers of endless possibility, lit by the sacred wind that moves us to live fully and deeply.

The breath of life is the breath of God, a sacred wind that fills us with purpose, passion, and drive. In every inhalation lies the promise of creation, of transformation, of stepping boldly toward the unknown.

And as that breath fills us, the stair to destiny rises— each step carved in quiet resolve, illuminated by shadows and fleeting light. It climbs through the unknown, where every rung is a choice and every landing is a promise. Upward lies the horizon, the place where dreams meet reality, where purpose finds its voice and lives are shaped by sacred intention.

Each step is a journey, a testament to the Divine spark within us. We climb, driven by the breath of life, toward the endless sky, toward the place where fate unfolds.

This is the stair to destiny, where paths converge, where lives are made, and where the breath of God meets the will of humanity, lifting us into what we were always meant to be.

96
Silence at the Center

The silence at the center of the soul is an unrestrained space, a holy void where the inner voice rises, speaking untethered by the ceaseless hum of the world's relentless noise.

In the quiet of dawn, before the world stirs, there it waits—patient, profound, a whispering echo of thoughts untamed, a wilderness within, vast and boundless, where the soul stretches like a tree reaching toward the unseen sky.

The heart of a soul untouched by the rush holds secrets deep, like the sea's darkest depths, where light rarely ventures but life teems in hidden abundance. Here, the currents of truth swirl, steady and unbroken, flowing in rhythm with eternity.

In this sacred silence, truth finds its voice— not loud, not demanding, but steady, a murmur that grows in strength. It speaks of dreams forgotten, fears buried, hopes hidden, and regrets unspoken. The essence of a soul laid bare, unafraid, unmasked.

Yet we chase the noise, the fleeting thrills, the clamor that fills each passing hour. We run toward the chaos, toward the bright, loud world, seeking answers while the truth whispers softly just beyond our reach.

The silence at the center is a refuge. It is the unshaken ground, the still water that reflects the sky. Here, we can be— free from masks, free from roles, free from the charades we play.

It is a return to the self, the raw, true self, unclothed by pretense, known only by the Divine.

And so, we must listen. In moments stolen from the rush, in the spaces between breaths, we must let the silence speak.

For in this stillness, the soul speaks clearly, guiding us gently toward who we are, and who we were always meant to be.

97

Separation

Separation is the great lie. They tell you there's a gap, a void, a chasm— a distance too vast to cross. But how can you be distant from the Immanent, the all-loving Creator whose embrace is as infinite as the cosmos, as close as your own breath?

They preach of walls and boundaries, of sins unwashed and debts unpaid, as if the Creator's reach is limited, as if the Divine is bound by the fragile constructs of human frailty.

Yet in every breath, in every heartbeat, the Divine Light, the Christ, is near— closer than our thoughts, present in the silence that hums beneath the noise of the world. Forgiveness is not earned. It is not withheld. It flows like a river— unending, pure, eternal.

An all-loving Eternal Mother does not tally wrongs, does not keep records of failures. She opens wide Her arms, Her voice soft and steady, calling us home, always home.

In the quiet of doubt, when guilt wraps itself tight around your chest, when shame whispers lies in your ear, remember the truth. The truth that is not shouted, but whispered, gently stirred in the depths of the heart.

Separation is a myth. It is a fear-born illusion, a shadow cast by the flicker of misunderstanding. How can you be apart from that which sustains your very soul?

Look within— not to your flaws, not to your failings, but to the presence that abides in the core of your being. Feel the nearness, the undying love that beats alongside your every pulse. You are not cast out. You are not forgotten.

You are held— always held, always forgiven, always known. The greatest lie dissolves when met with the light of truth: we are never apart, never alone, eternally embraced by the One who is, was, and always will be.

98
Path to Wholeness

Jung saw it clearly, in the depths of the mind, a journey not grand, but true. A process unfolding— simple in its essence, complex in its details— a return to what we were destined from the start to become.

In the quiet dawn, with the world still turning, we walk this path. Shadows fall behind, light stretches ahead, each step a whisper, each moment a story unfolding within us. Becoming whole, as we were always meant to be.

In every heart, there is a silent call, a pull to the center, a yearning for the self. It is not a selfish quest, but a sacred one—psychological and spiritual, a reconciliation of fragments, a becoming of something greater.

Universal salvation lies in this: the way we heal, the way we grow, the way we find peace. Each soul, a thread in the grand tapestry, woven together, whole, and free, a reflection of the Divine image imprinted in us all.

In the light of understanding, and even in the shadow of doubt, we find our way. Together and alone, we press on, toward the place we were always meant to reach— a home within ourselves, a unity with all creation.

It is not the finish we seek, but the journey itself— a biological unfolding, a spiritual ascent. In every step, in every breath, there is grace.

We walk a universal path, to the best of our best, to the wholeness that already whispers within us.

99
The Yellow Flower

What gives meaning to our fleeting lives? It's not the grand gestures, not the fame or the spotlight, but the little things, the quiet moments that slip by unnoticed— like a yellow flower in the crack of a sidewalk, defying the concrete, standing tall and bright.

It reminds us that beauty can bloom anywhere, even in the harshest of places. It's the purr of a round cat on your lap, a soft vibration, a warm presence, telling you in its own gentle way that comfort and contentment can be found in the simplest of times. A reminder that connection doesn't have to be loud or grand— it is everywhere, waiting to be felt.

It's a glass of cold milk on a hot day, refreshing, pure, uncomplicated. It cuts through the sweat and the heat, offering relief in a world that so often burns. It's these small pleasures that cool the soul, which make the tough days bearable, the kind of gifts that whisper instead of shout.

We chase meaning in chaos, in the loud, in the urgent. But meaning waits for us quietly— in the yellow flower, in the purring cat, in the cold milk. It is in these gentle moments, these small joys, that our fleeting lives find their worth.

Life is a series of fleeting scenes, some bright, some dark, but meaning weaves through them all— in the details, in the overlooked, in the mundane.

Each moment, no matter how small, gives us a reason to keep going, to find solace in the everyday, to uncover poetry in the ordinary.

Take a moment. Look around. Find the yellow flowers in your life. Listen to the purrs, savor the milk. Let the small things remind you that even in a fleeting life, there is beauty, there is comfort, there is meaning waiting to be found.

100
One More Time

One more time, I tell this body, there's still a song at the end of the street. A melody drifts through the dusk, a tune that plays on despite the quiet— in the twilight where the sun fades and shadows lengthen into memory.

There's still a light that comes on when the refrigerator door opens, casting its glow on the remnants of yesterday's meal.

A cold, white illumination spills into the kitchen, revealing the small ghosts of what's been lost, a solitary flame against the encroaching night.

The smell of sausage in a pan— sizzling, popping, releasing its warmth. It pulls me back to mornings when the day was a promise, when life felt full and the future limitless. Now the smell lingers bittersweet, a memory clinging to the air, a shadow of joy, now distant and faint.

The fly, still buzzing at 2 AM, circles my head in maddening persistence. Its tiny wings beat against the silence, a stubborn reminder that life insists— even in the deepest hours, there's movement, there's breath, the unyielding pulse of existence.

There's still time, I tell myself, if only in the hands of my watch, each second ticking softly, a fragile gift. But time feels like a thief, stealing moments, leaving echoes— of laughter, of love, a relentless march I cannot halt.

The sound of the old lady next door, her creaky front door greeting the day. Her voice, gravelly and worn, meets the morning birds with quiet defiance. It is a ritual of hope, of stubborn resilience— an act of faith against the weight of years. Even now, she finds joy in the song of sparrows.

One more time, I tell this body, there's sadness in the spaces left behind— in the song that fades at dusk, in the light's faint glow from the fridge, in the smell of a lonely breakfast, in the buzz of the fly, in the relentless ticking of time.

But there is also life, quiet and unyielding. It hums in the shadows, it flickers in the small, stubborn lights. And, for now, that is enough.

101
Feline Grace

Crippled by the world, this broken body aches, each bone a monument to pain. The shadows in my mind stretch long and dark, whiskey nights bleeding into cigarette days. Pain ticks like a relentless metronome, counting out the seconds of a life that feels too heavy to carry.

The pills. The doctors. Endless corridors of white coats and smiles thin as paper. Their reassurances are empty, their words as hollow as the sterile rooms. They don't know. They can't feel. This gnawing, relentless ache, this deep infirmity that burrows into the marrow of my existence.

But then, there's you. Silent, soft, slipping through the cracks like moonlight in a darkened room. Whiskers twitching, eyes like golden moons— cats, my unexpected feline saviors.

A purr cuts through the fog, vibrating against my skin. Furry warmth presses into me, tiny paws tread softly on my chest. There is weight here, but it's the kind that comforts, that grounds me, that makes the world feel a little less cruel.

You don't ask for answers. You don't offer false hopes. You give only your presence— simple, true, a kind of companionship that asks nothing in return.

You curl up beside me, your small body nestled into my despair. You are a warm, living antidote to the cold sterility of this pain.

We share this battered couch, these silent nights. You, my feline friends, know the secret of the wounded heart.

In your quiet eyes, I see resilience. In the soft vibration of your purr, I hear a whisper of grace.

It's unspoken but undeniable, a truth deeper than words. And for a moment, this deep infirmity fades. The ache retreats to the background, replaced by the simple joy of loving cats, of being loved in return— a grace as soft as fur and as steady as the pulse of a purr.

102
Passing Through the Rain

Where there is rain, the streets shine— black asphalt glistening, stretching skyward as if yearning to touch the clouds that weep upon them.

They transform these wet streets into slender skyscrapers, each window a blinking eye, watching the world below with silent, indifferent curiosity.

Women stand under umbrellas, their faces hidden, shadows framed in the city's restless canvas. They wait— for a bus, for a moment, for a whisper of purpose to pierce the monotony.

Raindrops tap a rhythm, a soft percussion on nylon canopies, their tempo steady, insistent, as they clutch their secrets close like sacred relics.

The city hums, alive and indifferent, its veins pulsing with anonymous lives, each one a flicker of light soon swallowed by the dark.

In the wet shimmer, reflections blur, dreams mix with the murk of reality, visions ripple, then dissolve.

All of us, walking, waiting, hoping, are just passing through. Like the rain. Like the women under umbrellas. Like the silent skyscrapers stretching toward a heaven that seems so close, yet so far.

We are fleeting, our steps erased as the rain pools, as the city hums, as the sky moves on.

Yet in the rhythm of the raindrops, in the quiet of waiting, in the blur of reflections, there is a grace— a reminder that even in this passing through, there is beauty, there is purpose, there is God.

103
Breakfast with Pain

Pain moved in sophomore year and never left. He commandeered the couch, lit cigarette after cigarette, and drank his bourbon straight out of the bottle. At 2 a.m., he'd wake me up with his ramblings— his parents kicked him out at fifteen, he found God just long enough to reject Him after his priest said he was cute. Then came the transcendental meditation, the macrobiotic diet, and the weekly Tuesday fasts. All of it was supposed to fix something, but Pain's still broken, very broken, and now so am I for listening.

Pain has opinions. He tells me voting is a joke, that communism will make a roaring comeback before the end of the century, that climate change has orange hair. He doesn't read the news; he doesn't read anything. Just sits there thumbing through Facebook and "X."

He spouts nonsense and kicks me like I'm a bad dog who just crapped on the carpet. He's ignorant, selfish, and thoughtless. He doesn't care about anyone's suffering but his own. He doesn't care about me or my own suffering. And yet, we're sharing a table this morning, like we always do, at 6 a.m. sharp.

Pain likes his eggs runny, so runny they might as well still be in the shell. He drinks Earl Grey tea, no sugar, because sugar would make it sweet, and pain can't stand sweetness. I watch him eat, watch the yolk drip down his chin, and wonder why I let him stay. Maybe it's because he knows my name—even my pen name. Maybe it's because he's the only one who shows up every damn day like clockwork with his duffle bag of sorrows.

I've prayed to God—in Jesus's name, for God's sake! —everyday for Pain to just leave; just pack your bags and get out. Move back to your little ugly Momma in Brooklyn. I've searched the bible for a cure, but God just tells me to read a few psalms, think about Paul, and call me in the morning.

But Pain isn't going anywhere. He'll leave his cigarette butts on the table, his bourbon rings on the counter. He'll drag his chair into the corner of every room, watching me with that smirk that says, "I'm here for the long haul, buddy." And I hate him for it. But I also pour his tea, cook his eggs, and sit across from him in silence, listening to his stories I've heard a thousand times.

104
Her Absence Fills the Room

Her absence fills the room like smoke from her last cigarette, curling in the corners, settling on the empty chair.

She used to sit there, quietly, watching TV, drinking a Coke. The silence was their language, unspoken but understood.

He misses her presence— not just her body, but the way she filled the space, like milk in a bowl. Her being, her essence, smoking her cigarette, eyes on the old screen, never saying much, just being.

She left him. Went to heaven, they say, or maybe to a place with lots of cats and dogs, especially cats. She loved those furry children— more than people sometimes.

Now he's stuck here, with all that litter, the boxes she used to scoop, her hands so gentle, so precise.

They never talked much— that was their thing. The silence was golden, a comfortable void. Her presence was enough; her quiet, his solace.

He cries a lot these days, tears like rain on a dry street, staring at an old black-and-white snapshot on the dresser, her smile frozen in time— a memory he can't touch.

He pours another drink, the bottle his only friend (some friend!) thinking about her— how she used to sit there, her eyes soft, her silence deep.

He drinks to remember. He drinks to forget. Her absence, a wound that never heals.

The cats meow. The litter box fills. He scoops it out, stuffs it in a bag. Each act a holy sacrament to her memory.

She left him with this small act of love, this ritual of the mundane, keeping her spirit alive in the silence she left behind.

So, he sits here, in the quiet she loved, watching the TV flicker, smoking a cigarette, drinking a Coke, some Scotch.

Her ghost beside him, silent as always, but here—always here— in the stillness, in the dark, in the whisper of the night.

105
Sacred Space

As you draw me ever deeper into your heart, I find myself in a room full of strangers— yet not strangers at all.

Women and men, faces lined with stories, eyes reflecting the same longing, the same search for connection, the same thirst for something more. We gather here, drawn by your silent call, your compassionate heart a beacon in the dark city nights.

In your love, there is no hierarchy— no one more worthy, no one less. Each of us a thread in the tapestry, woven together by your gentle hands.

I watch them, these companions, each one carrying their own burdens, their own scars, and dreams. Yet here under your gaze, those burdens seem lighter, those scars softened by the balm of being seen, being known.

There's a woman with eyes like deep wells, a man with hands rough from years of labor, a child with a smile that hasn't yet learned to hide.

And I, with my own bruised soul, find a place among them— not more special, not less. In this room, there is no exclusion, no door barred, no heart left cold.

Your love flows freely, like wine poured into every waiting glass, a banquet of acceptance, where the only price of admission is the willingness to be vulnerable, to be human.

As I sit among them, I realize this is not just your love, but a love that expands, that encompasses us all, binding us together in our shared humanity.

We are each a piece of a larger story, a story written in the language of compassion, of understanding, of grace.

And in your heart, I see reflected a world where love is not a finite resource, not a currency to be hoarded, but an endless river— flowing from one to another, filling the empty spaces, healing the broken places.

As you draw me ever deeper into your heart, I discover that in loving them, you teach me to love myself, to love others, to see beyond the surface, to the core of what it means to be alive.

In this place, this sacred space, we find not just love— but the courage to live, to open our hearts to the world, to each other, and to ourselves.

106
God in Plain Sight

God is right here before us, after us, over here, over there. God is in plain sight, penetrating every cell and subatomic particle in your body. God has no secrets, no mysteries, no subterranean caverns of despair filled with burning bodies in utter pain. God is the Creator, the Destroyer, all in the same sentence, in the same second in time. God has no time, but God is wound up in the fabric of space and time. This is the immanent God, the uttermost force.

On one end of this continuum is the entire universe, and on the other is the vibrating string that is every electron in every star, in every ounce of material, in the beating hearts of everyone you love. The cosmos sings with the resonance of this truth, and every particle vibrates with the echo of its Maker's voice. Do not think for one moment that the divine is far off, relegated to the cold pages of history or the restrictive confines of theologies past. God is now, God is here, and God is utterly alive within you and around you.

"For in him we live and move and have our being." Yet even this is only a sliver of the truth. Don't look to the Bible for the full story of God, for it cannot contain the boundless, infinite, overwhelming torrent of reality that proclaims both God's transcendence and immanence. The scriptures are a lamp, but the universe is a wildfire. Every supernova, every ocean wave, every newborn cry—these are the gospel writ large.

Look at science, at Creation, at the intricate dance of atoms, quarks, and galaxies. See God's fingerprints in the spirals of the DNA double helix and the swirling arms of the Milky Way. Marvel at the overwhelming force that binds quarks together and keeps the stars aflame. The Creator's breath fills the lungs of every creature, while the Destroyer's touch dismantles the old to make way for the new. Life is born, life is taken, and life is remade—all within the palm of God's hand. That is God.

And yet, in that tiny heart that beats and loves, you will find the Christ who whispers, "God is Love." The Christ who walked the dusty roads of Galilee, who touched the untouchable and healed the broken, who died and rose again, radiates from the very core of existence. She stands at the crossroads of eternity and flesh, shouting in silence, "Behold, I am with you always, to the end of the age."

So, look—not only with your eyes but with the whole of your being. Look at the stars and the flowers, at the tears and the laughter.

Look into the depths of another's eyes, and see there the immeasurable, unfathomable, intimate God. Your Mother and Your Father. God is the pulse in your veins, the thought in your mind, the ache in your soul for something greater. God is not hidden. God is here, in plain sight.

107
Commuters

I can feel the sadness as it coats my dreams, a thick, heavy fog sinking into my soul. In the quiet of the night, I hear the echoes— the whispers of those I've seen, their eyes locked in a silent plea, staring into the abyss of their suffering. My patients cannot move, their bodies are prisoners to pain and decay. Their eyes speak volumes, their lips move as if to ask, *close our eyes, blow us into heaven.*

Some say this intermediate state, this liminal space between life and death, is the doorway to heaven. There is nothing more to do, they say, than simply wait—like standing on a platform, looking down the track, waiting for the train to downtown.

We are all just commuters, waiting for that train, that final journey to a place unknown. Jesus is the conductor, walking down the aisle, checking tickets, nodding with a quiet smile. We all get on eventually and ride the rails to a better place.

In this waiting room of life, we are bound together— not by our joys, but by our sorrows, our shared sense of the inevitable. We pretend not to notice the thinning line between here and there, but in the stillness of the night, it's undeniable.

I see them—my fellow passengers, each carrying their own load, their own secrets, and fears. The young, the old, the weary, all waiting for the same train— some with hope, others with resignation, and some with a quiet acceptance, a peace that eludes me.

The train will come, they say, and take us to a place where Pain is no more, where the weight of the world is lifted from our shoulders.

But until then, we wait— each day a step closer to the platform's edge, each night a deeper descent into the shadows of our own thoughts.

I wonder, will we recognize the conductor? Will his face be familiar, or just another in the crowd? Will he offer a kind word, a gentle hand, or simply guide us silently to our seats?

As I sit here in this dimly lit room, with the hum of machines and the soft murmur of breaths taken and released, I think of them—my patients, and their eyes that speak of things I cannot understand.

Perhaps the train is just a metaphor for something greater, something beyond words. It is the final act of surrender— of letting go, of trusting that the journey has a destination worth reaching.

108
The Middle Way

The middle way, a quiet path, where shadows play, and light is soft. Not the drunken stumble nor the monk's thin line, but a place where footsteps fall— steady, even, true.

In the midst of life's harsh pull, there's a space, a breath, where peace can find a home. It's not the blaze of glory, nor the cold of silent void, but the warmth of evening sun on weathered skin.

I've known the edge, the sharp drop, the rush of blood, the fall. And I've known the empty stretch— the barren land where nothing grows. But here, in this in-between, there's a steadiness, a calm.

It's a road not paved with gold, nor strewn with broken dreams, but a simple path with stones worn smooth by many feet, where each step is enough.

In the middle way, there's a kind of strength— not the raging storm, nor the frozen still, but the quiet persistence of a river's flow, carving its course through rock and time.

Here the heart beats slow, the mind is clear, and the hands find work to do— honest, steady, plain. It's a life not marked by fame, or hidden in obscurity, but one lived well, in balance, in truth.

Walk the middle way with eyes open wide and find the simple beauty in the days that come and go. For in this place, there's peace to be found— a quiet joy, a steady love, a life lived fully in the middle way.

109
The Word

I take this holy book of scriptures, its gold-trimmed whispers of prophecy, its thunderous declarations of ancient law, and hurl it skyward, a rebel act, a leap of despair, or perhaps a leap of faith, a prayer unspoken.

Its leathered spine bursts, its bindings flee their moorings, and its pages scatter like frightened sparrows, like a startled heart shattered into a million grains of sand, dissolving into particles of dust that glint for one moment before the wind carries them into the farthest reaches of existence.

The book disappears into the arc of the creation, its words undone, its voice silenced in the vortex. I sit in the hollow stillness, bereft of its weight, empty of its form, and wonder if I have unmade the only thing that ever held me whole.

And then, a wind— no, not a wind, but the breath of a thousand years, a sigh from a thousand unseen mouths, sweeps toward me, carrying with it the dust of its journey, the fragments of what I cast away. It settles on my lap, not with judgment, but with the tenderness of a dog curling into its master's embrace. The book returns, but it is not the book I knew. Its cover is soft with new skin, its pages woven of the threads of new burning stars.

When I open it, it sings with the voice of all creation, a hymn that is both new and older than the oldest song. Its words glow like embers— but there are so few of them now. And there is a hand, a finger that moves along its lines like the rabbi's pointer, guiding, seeking, revealing.

The Rabbi speaks one Word, and his tears fall like ink upon the unwritten spaces, writing what could not be said. And the Word is Love. Not a command, not a demand, but a presence, a stillness, a voice in the void that reaches, touches, heals.

This is the book that returns to me, the holy text rewritten in another universe, the scripture recast in the fire of stars. And I hold it now, not as a shield, not as a sword, but as a tender knowing— a Word that was lost, and found, and is now forever.

110
The River

The river always carries itself to the sea— a mindless traveler, a wanderer. It doesn't care about the bends, the twists, the fallen trees, just keeps moving, relentless, heading for that wide-open blue.

That river— like a tired old man at closing time, leaving the bar, stumbling over rocks and roots, always finding its way, never stopping to ask why. It's a wanderer, like me— never quite settled, never quite still.

The nights I've spent by its side, listening to its secrets whispered in the dark— they're my secrets too.

We're both heading somewhere, but the destination's a mystery— the sea, the end, the quiet place where it all makes sense, or nothing does.

It doesn't question, doesn't wonder what's next— just keeps moving, taking what comes, leaving what it doesn't need.

I envy that sometimes— the simplicity, the acceptance. To be a river, to flow, to wander, to always find the way to where you're meant to be.

I sit by its side— a fellow traveler, a mindless wanderer, watching the water as it carries itself to the sea. And I think maybe I'll find my way too.

111
Shape of Loneliness

Loneliness is an empty bottle, half-buried in the sand, a stray cat with one eye, an expired credit card lost at the bottom of a drawer.

There is no time for loneliness on an empty street— only the sound of clinking spoons in a diner at the edge of the city, where the neon buzzes like a broken heart, and the waitress's smile is a tired thing. The coffee is bitter as regret, but it's hot and cheap, and it keeps the cold night at bay— if only for a little while.

Lonely girls walk down dark streets, their footsteps echoing in the quiet, heels tapping out a rhythm that no one hears. They find strange scents clinging to melons at the fruit stand— too sweet, too ripe, like promises made and broken in the same breath. They cower behind doors, afraid of their own shadows that linger in the corners. They leave their mail piled up at the front door, letters unopened, bills unpaid. When the day is done, they climb six flights up, their bodies weary, their minds numb, and they hide in the dark, waiting for the sun to rise. But it won't.

The night will stretch on, endless and quiet, until the next blue moon— until the loneliness becomes a part of them, like a second skin, a shadow that never leaves.

Loneliness is a bottle of whiskey, half-drunk and forgotten, a cigarette burned down to the filter, ash crumbling in the wind, a song playing on a jukebox in an empty room.

It's the sound of a train in the distance, its whistle a mournful cry that fades into the night. Loneliness is the feel of cold sheets on an empty bed, the space beside you a void that nothing can fill.

112
The Ugly Face of God

God shows up late again, scratched knuckles, cigarette breath, hands in His holy pockets, smirking like He knows a joke you won't understand. Children die. Mothers claw the ground. And He stands there, nodding, saying nothing.

Immanence—the way He's in everything. The fist and the bruised lip, the cancer eating a child's bones, the entropy gnawing at the edges of stars. Creation, they say, is a feast of rot and bloom. You can't have the cherry blossoms without the reek of the grave.

I stand by the bedside, watching another body give up the ghost. I ask Him the same question I've asked a thousand times— Why? He doesn't answer, but I see Him in the tear that runs down the cheek of the man holding his wife's hand for the last time.

God is unfair. God is cruel. God is love. Wrap your head around that if you can. He's the kiss on the forehead of the dying, the scream of the ones left behind, the silence after the long grief.

And yet, somehow, I find Him in the hospice halls, in the faces of the nurses, in the hands of strangers. He's there in the way a dying man smiles when his granddaughter walks in. It doesn't answer the question. But it's enough to keep me going another day.

113
True Worship

True worship isn't a pearl-draped choir crooning sweet nothings to the ceiling. It isn't a ruby ring you kiss or a hand you kneel to. It isn't the muttered prayers of the guilty, cramming their sins into a box too small to hold them.

It isn't the Rosary rattling in the dark, or the preacher pounding his pulpit like a desperate gambler. It isn't your ticket to heaven, stamped and tucked in your pocket while you smirk at the poor on your way to the feast. It isn't simply facing East or turning the lights out on Friday night and saying a prayer.

It's not the latest version of the Bible on your nightstand, its pages yellowed with abuse and manipulation, its words twisted to justify your politics, your greed, your hatred, your shiny new idols, be they human or gold. The book doesn't save you. It doesn't even know your name.

So, better throw it out! Throw it into the fire along with your toxic politics and excuses, your golden calves, and cheap lies. You want holy? Start with the broken bodies, the dead children in Gaza, the ashes in your mouth, and build something true. Build an authentic holy dream.

The Word isn't what you take. It's what you give. The Word is something you meet head on. And in that collision, something new is born. It's called The Christ or simply the Divine Spirit. Perhaps it has no name at all.

It's the calloused hand that reaches for the broken, the voice that stands up when it would be easier to stay silent. It's love, dammit, and it's painful and it costs everything.

114
Womb of Being

In the womb of being, we cradle the seed of divinity, nestled deep in the marrow of our fragile bones.

Each soul is a vessel, a sacred chamber, where the birthing of God takes place— not with fanfare, but in the quiet hours of the night, when the world is asleep and the stars hang low, whispering secrets we're too deaf to hear.

We walk these streets, shadows in the moonlight, carrying the weight of the universe in our chests. Our hearts beat out the rhythm of ancient prayers we've forgotten how to say.

In the mirror, we see only flesh, wrinkles carved by time, eyes dulled by the grind of daily life. But beneath it all, the seed stirs, waiting, aching for the moment when the walls we've built come crumbling down.

In the womb of being, we are all mothers— laboring in the dark, birthing Gods we've never met. Gods we've cursed in our moments of despair. Gods we've begged for mercy when the bottle runs dry and the night stretches on forever.

We cradle the seed, nurture it with our tears, our laughter, our fears. And when the time comes, we let it go.

We release it into the world to take its place among the stars, to shine its light on the broken, the lost, the forgotten— the ones who've yet to see that they too are vessels.

Each of us, a sacred chamber, a temple of the Divine. Each of us, a womb for the birthing of God.

115
The God Who Comes

God comes to me, not in a blaze of glory, not with a booming voice from the sky, but in the quiet shuffle of slippers down a hospice hallway, in the way a child's drawing is taped to the wall of a room where death lingers, waiting for permission to enter.

I ask Him, why do You let children suffer? Why do You allow their bright songs to fade into silence? And He answers me, but not with words. His answer is the nurse sitting by the bedside, holding a hand that no longer grips back. His answer is the cup of coffee offered at midnight to a grieving mother who cannot stop shaking.

It is not enough— how could it be? I want a God who will stand up and fight, who will rage against the dying of the light. But He is not that God. He is the one who sits in the ashes with us, who cries our tears, and whispers, "I know. I know."

And yet, even in my anger, I see Him in the smallest things: a laugh that breaks through the sobs, the way a sunbeam falls across a tired face, the moment when someone says, "I'm here," and means it.

This God is unfair! This God is fragile. This God is Love. And that's why He came to us not as a warrior, but as a child. Not as an answer, but as a question.

116
Drive

Take me somewhere, anywhere but here. Relieve me of this burden, this weight pressing down on my chest like a concrete slab.

Borrow a big car— something with power, something that roars when you touch the gas— and carry me away. Away from these empty streets, away from hollow eyes, away from clocks ticking louder with every passing second, a metronome of monotony.

Let's fly, not like birds gliding on wind's whim, but like a rocket punching through the night, breaking the chains of gravity. Leave behind the noise, the grind, the endless cycle of days that blur into sameness.

Open the sky. Tear it wide with your hands, rip it like paper, and let's pour honey on the moon— drip by golden drip, sweetening the night. Turn that cold, distant rock into something warm, something worth reaching for, something we can hold between our trembling fingers.

Take me somewhere, anywhere but here. Somewhere the stars don't just flicker but blaze with holy fire. Somewhere the wind doesn't just blow but sings hymns to weary hearts. Somewhere the world isn't just spinning but dancing— dancing in step with our wildest hopes.

Relieve me of this burden, this life that feels too small to contain the dreams that keep me awake. Let's borrow that big car, turn the key, and drive until the road runs out.

Drive until the sky is no longer above us but wraps us in its infinite embrace. Until the moon spills honey into our hands, sticky and sweet, its golden warmth seeping into the cracks of our broken hearts.

Drive until we are no longer just surviving but living. Until the stars are close enough to touch, until the wind carries the sound of our laughter, until the weight lifts, and the dreams that once felt impossible become real— more real than anything we've ever known.

117
Edge of the World

In the quiet hour before dawn, when shadows cling to walls like old regrets, I stand at the edge of the world— holding nothing, seeking everything.

The stars above, older than the bones of mountains, wink with a secret knowledge: that to grasp is to lose, to hold tight is to fall. I chase the fleeting, the dream of solid ground, but the earth beneath my feet is sand, shifting with the breath of life.

The tighter I clutch, the faster it slips through my hands. There is wisdom in the wind— in the way it dances through the trees, never staying, never owning, only passing. And in that passing, it finds its freedom.

To let go— not in defeat, but in grace— is to find the lightness of being, the soft melody of existence that sings not in certainty, but in the gentle sway of doubt, in the tender embrace of the unknown.

I have walked the path of sages, listened to the silence that speaks in the spaces between words. And in the end, it's not answers I seek, but the peace of the question— the open hand, the heart that beats in rhythm with the world's quiet pulse.

For in letting go, I find a paradox: what is lost returns. What is given freely comes back tenfold— not as possession, but as a whisper, a truth carried on the wind.

And so, I stand, no longer holding, but being held. No longer seeking but found.

118
Grace in the Cracks

God's grace comes when you're raw, stripped down, like a tree in winter—bare and cold, but still standing. It's not in the preacher's chant, not in the hymns, or the fine-printed pages. It's in the nights when the soul feels dry, empty, a hollowed-out vessel aching for meaning.

When the room spins slow, and you're just a man— no more, no less—staring at the ceiling, wondering what the hell it's all about.

Grace doesn't come because you've earned it. It doesn't come wrapped in gold ribbons or delivered by angels. It comes when you admit you don't know and maybe never did.

It slips in when you stop pretending you've got it all figured out, when you let madness be what it is, without wrestling it into neat, holy shapes.

Open your clenched fists. Let the damn thing go. Let the chaos in— the noise, the questions, the rawness of being alive. And, just maybe, you'll find a sliver of light in the dark, where you least expect it.

God's grace isn't in the knowing. It's in the not knowing, in the cracks where doubt seeps in, where the polished masks fall away, and you finally let yourself be human. Flawed. Frightened. Free.

And in that space, in the trembling silence of surrender, you might just feel it— not as a roar, but as a whisper. Not as certainty, but as presence.

The grace that holds you even when you let go.

119
The Price of Consciousness

We walk the tightrope, day in, day out, pretending the ground isn't there, pretending we don't hear it calling. We wait for the snap, for the drop, for the hit that splits us clean down the middle, spilling out everything we've tried to hold together.

It's the price of consciousness. You've seen it— in the eyes of the broken, in subway faces etched with quiet despair, in stories whispered after midnight.

Stories that sting like bad whiskey, burning all the way down but leaving you no warmer for it.

You know it's coming. Maybe not today, maybe not tomorrow, but it waits, just out of sight, that black dog with teeth sharp as regret. It will catch up, tear you open, make you bleed out all the flimsy hopes you stitched together in the dark, when you thought nobody could see.

This is the curse— the cost of knowing, of feeling every inch of this strained life. The weight of what-ifs, the knowledge that any moment could be the one that shatters you, leaves you crawling through the wreckage of dreams you didn't even know you had.

But this is also the game, isn't it? The price of awareness. The burden of the thinking man, the one who sees too much, feels too deep, and still wakes up, still gets up, still puts one foot in front of the other. Because what else is there?

You live with it— that shadow in the corner, that itch in the back of your mind, the knowledge that it can all fall apart with a phone call, a glance, a whisper. And yet, you keep going. Because the bite makes the beer taste better, the sound of her laughter sweeter, the nights longer, and the mornings crueler.

A prayer for the walking wounded, for those who know and keep on anyway. Living like it matters because it does— until it doesn't. And that's enough. Just enough to keep you upright, to keep you alive, to keep you hoping for one more day.

One more day where the sun still shines, and the world doesn't break you all the way through.

120
The Mirror and the Flame

They say God made us mirrors of a holy light— yet in the glass, I see cracks, lines tracing histories untold. Scars etched by time, each one a story of breaking and mending.

"How can this be Divine?" I ask the empty room. The silence holds its breath, and I am left with the weight of my reflection. It is not flawless—but neither is it false.

The ancients spoke of the fire within, a flicker of God's eternal flame. I feel it faint, fighting beneath the ash, its glow hidden by doubts that gather like clouds.

Yet still, it burns. Not in the brilliance of noon, but in the quiet persistence of a candle in the dark. A whisper of warmth that refuses to yield to the chill of despair.

The lines on my face— are they not maps? Paths through shadowed valleys, over windswept peaks, leading me closer to the heart of the One who placed them there. Each scar is a testimony, not of defeat, but of endurance.

For God does not craft perfection as the world sees it. He weaves strength into the broken places, grace into the gaps, turning jagged edges into the latticework of His design.

The mirror lies, or perhaps, it tells a truth too vast for me to hold. For in its depths, I see not just myself, but the flicker of the holy flame, a reflection of the infinite.

"Let the light shine," He says, "Not as the sun, but as you are— a fractured lamp through which My love pours freely." And in the cracks, His glory finds a way.

So, I stand before the mirror, the flame steady now, and I whisper, "Thank You for the scars, for they remind me that You are here, making beauty from all that is broken."

And the light shines on, not perfect, but perfect in His hands. The image remains, holy and whole, though I see it only in glimpses. It is enough.

121
Norwegian Sardines

She opens her heart, like a can of Norwegian sardines, rusted and cold. The jagged metal cuts deep, but she doesn't flinch. She's used to the blood, the sting of it, the way it flows in quiet red streams down her fingers, painting her hands with memories of every sharp edge she's ever known.

Inside, the little silver fishes lie packed tight, shimmering faintly in the dim light, their scales catching glimmers of something— hope, or just the reflection of her own trembling hands.

She pulls them out, one by one, steady, unhesitating, no second thoughts. Each one she swallows whole, bones and all, tasting the salt, feeling the cold scales slide down— a comfort as icy as the world she knows, settling heavy in the pit of her stomach.

This is how she loves. This is how she lives. Cutting herself on sharp edges, bleeding just enough to feel alive, to remind herself that in a world full of blunt truths and serrated lies, there is still something to taste, something to hold, even if it hurts.

The world is full of sharp things, and she's learned to handle them. Learned to dig deep, to pull out the pieces that shine in the dark— even if they cut her open, even if they leave scars that never fade.

She knows the taste of metal, the bitter tang of truth. She knows the weight of survival, the ache of love that doesn't heal clean.

Still, she opens herself up, repeatedly, swallowing the silver fishes, because that's what it takes— to feel, to endure, to love in a world where everything cuts, and nothing is ever soft.

She'll bleed, and she'll swallow, and she'll keep opening that rusted can, because in the end, it's all she knows. It's all she has, and that's enough.

122
Package of Wisdom

I bought a package of wisdom today, shiny as a new dime, wrapped in silver foil, promising to fix my sorry life. A stamp of approval from *Good Housekeeping*, blessed by the Pope, nodded at by the Dalai Lama— how could I resist?

It was all there, neatly packaged, ready to go down easily, like a pill you swallow without a second thought. The checkout girl smiled, her braces glinting under fluorescent light. It's on sale, she said. Everyone's buying it these days.

Who has time to figure it out on their own? She winked. No need for therapy when you've got this. I took it home, peeling the wrapper like a kid at Christmas, expecting the secrets of the universe to spill out like cereal from a too-full box. But all I found was the same old stuff: platitudes, promises, and fog. Pre-packaged wisdom that melts in your mouth but never sticks to your ribs.

The Pope can keep his blessing, and the Dalai Lama his nod. Let them sell it to someone else. I'd rather take my chances with a good bottle of Johnny Walker and a walk down a dark alley, where the bruises you don't see coming teach you truths you can't unlearn.

I tossed the wrapper in the trash, sat down with Johnny, and laughed—a bitter laugh, the kind that scratches your throat on its way out. Another sucker looking for shortcuts, when the real wisdom is out there, in the street, waiting to kick you in the teeth and leave you smarter than before.

123
A Cry in the Desert

I rush to his side, the heat rising through my worn shoes, the sand beneath me alive, shifting, burning as though the earth itself aches. My arms open, my heart laid bare— a raw, trembling offering to his unrelenting torment.

His eyes meet mine, red-rimmed, hollowed, a wilderness of despair stretches within them. Is there something, anything, I can do? My words tumble out, clumsy, like stones falling into an empty well. "Kill me," he cries, his voice breaking against the sky, a raw, desperate plea that scrapes my soul.

The heavens are silent, the air thick with a tension older than the stars. I falter, my hands trembling, my heart shattering under the weight of his unbearable suffering. What answer can I give? I cannot lift his pain or drain his sorrow. I cannot pull him from the chasm of himself.

Yet I stand there, refusing to move, refusing to abandon the fragile bridge between his despair and my hope. "Friend," I whisper, though the word feels brittle, like dry leaves crumbling in my hand.

"Friend, I am here." The desert presses in, its silence a hymn of emptiness. The wind carries the taste of salt— not from the sea, but from our tears. I reach for him, not with answers, but with presence, with the trembling, futile grace of one broken soul holding another.

His agony does not relent, but he does not turn away. His eyes stay fixed on the heavens, as though daring God to answer. The sky remains unchanged, vast, and distant, yet beneath it, two small figures hold onto each other as though the act itself might summon meaning.

"Kill me," he pleads again, and the words sting. But I do not let go. I do not step back. I hold him tighter, as if my grip might keep him tethered to this fragile, burning earth. The sun begins to fall, casting long shadows that seem to stretch infinitely across the sand.

The torment remains, but in the growing dusk, there is a faint whisper of peace. Not from the sky. Not from the earth. But from the simple, trembling truth that neither of us stands alone.

124
The Cycle of Meaning

I envy those who find meaning— ultimate, shining meaning— in the vaulted ceilings of churches, in the stained-glass mosaics of belief. To believe, to belong: what a gift, what a shelter. Their hands steady on the railing as they climb toward something sure.

And here I am, in that strange liminal space— not here, not there, stretching, straining, my fingers grasping at fragments like a child clutching at fireflies only to find their glow fading in my hands.

But sometimes, I feel the hand of Jesus on my shoulder—or maybe just the tap of a good friend—his grasp firm on the back of my neck, not cruel, not harsh, but certain, steady, turning my head to see the one thing I've been too lost to notice: a hurting person, a bleeding soul, the living, aching epitome of meaning itself.

And then the bricks of the church fall away. The scriptures curl into ash. The dogmas dissolve into the wind. And all that remains is this: a solitary soul, fragile and trembling, to cradle with my prayers. In that moment, meaning doesn't whisper; it roars— a locomotive on slick tracks, bearing down on me with speed and certainty, and I know, for that fleeting instant, what it is to live.

I can smile again. I can breathe again. But then the tracks disappear, the moment shifts, and I fall into the next pit of self-pity, the next empty stretch of road where the glow dims and the questions grow sharp again.

This is the cycle of meaning-making: to lose and to find, to stumble and rise, to cradle the fragile pieces of ourselves and others, only to drop them and start again.

Perhaps this is faith, after all— not certainty, but the act of reaching for the next hurting hand, the next bleeding soul, knowing that when the walls fall and the words burn, the act itself is the meaning.

And when the locomotive comes again, I will smile. And when the pit comes again, I will pray. And when I reach, I will find another piece of the whole, another fragment of that great mosaic of belief, of belonging.

125
Sharp Things

The streetlights hum like tired angels, casting halos on puddles of regret. There's a guy at the corner selling maps to nowhere— He says he's been to the edge and back, but his eyes tell a different story.

I don't ask questions; the answers would only bleed and leave me in pain.

There's a sharpness to the night— not the cheap edge of a broken bottle, but the kind that cuts clean through the lies we tell ourselves. Wonder is a blade, and it's got your name on it. You can dance with it, or let it carve you open. Either way, you're going to feel it.

I saw a woman in a red dress, smoking like she owned the world. Her laugh split the air and for a second, I swear, I saw the whole universe collapse into her smile. It was unbearable, beautiful— and gone before I could catch it.

The mundane is a warm bed, for sure, but it's the sharp things that wake you up. The edge is where the truth lives, Where the heart finally remembers how to beat. Step out, step in, let it break you wide open. There's nothing more real than the unbearable wonder of it all.

126
Praise the Bloom

In the dark soil of failure, beneath the boots of rage, where the worms carry secrets to places we'll never see, something waits.

It is not hope, not yet— only a silence that stirs when the world crushes in like an iron fist.

You curse the manure. It stinks; it stains your hands. And yet, you press it down, you press it deep.

What is this stubborn heart that refuses to wilt? What is this shadow of green against the ruin?

A flower, ragged and small, its petals shaped like apologies, its stem tough as bone.

Do not praise the ground— it is full of rot. Do not praise the sun— it burns too easily. Praise the bloom, which took what it was given and became.

This is what remains: the small miracle of becoming whole from what was broken.

127
Grief Spilled

The sky cracked open last night, and grief spilled out like ink, staining the edges of the stars. The air tasted of burnt words, prayers unanswered, and the weight of what could never return. I tried to hold it all in my hands, but it slipped through my fingers, a tide receding into silence.

You said loss was just a shadow, but shadows are born from light. Grief, though—grief is the tearing, the ripping of the veil, the moment you see eternity and know it doesn't belong to you. Breathe out, you said, and I did, pushing the fog back to glimpse a pinpoint of brilliance— a light too sharp to name.

The world tilted under the weight of the unseen. I walked streets I'd never leave, stepping on echoes, dodging the ghosts of what was. Each breath cut deeper; each blink burned brighter. The light waits, you whispered. The veil will fall again, but not yet.

And so, I sit, holding the fragments, the unbearable sharpness of this grief, this gift, this ache that proves I once touched the infinite.

128
Love is Two Turtles in a Shell

Love is two turtles in a shell, bound by an inner cave, a darkness where people hide, only to come out in the evening, when the demons are restless.

They curl into each other, like whispers folded tight in the silence of the night, where the world can't see them bleed or taste the salt of their wounds.

They know the sun's a liar, promising warmth but burning cold, so they wait for dusk, for the shadows to stretch long, for the city's hum to drown out the sound of their own breaking.

It's not the kind of love that dances in the daylight, but the kind that grips in the dark corners of a room, where hands meet in quiet desperation and eyes close to forget the ache that never leaves.

Love is two turtles in a shell, hidden away from the world, knowing the fight is only theirs, and the night is where they breathe, in the comfort of shared demons, restless but never alone.

129
Pocket God

I found my car keys, thank God. checked the couch cushions, the fridge, even under the cat. then— there they were, in my pocket, all along.

I laughed, a dumb, tired laugh, the kind that feels like spitting into the wind. "Good one, God," I said. "Nice trick."

Then I thought about other things, the bigger things, the ones you can't laugh about.

I asked God why he didn't stop the Holocaust. Why do kids starve in the shadow of golden temples? Why does love always feel like it's dying just when it starts to feel real?

No answer. Just the hum of the refrigerator, the cat yawning, keys jingling in my hand.

God is busy losing things in his own pockets, too. Better check under the rug.

130
What I Know about God

I don't argue about God. What's the point? He does what He does—or doesn't. Who am I to hand Him a to-do list? Or perhaps I should hand Her a to-do list.

I'm just a poet writing poems not to explain, but to bleed onto the page. it's easier that way— no sermons, no lectures, no dogma, no pseudo religious toxic Christianity, just a heart trying to make sense of its own rhythm.

Don't ask me about women. They're poems I'll never finish. Don't ask me about sex— that's just a fire with no blueprint. Football? Men in helmets chasing their egos. Quantum physics? Ask a drunk monk or a couple of Rabbis with Ph.D.'s.

All I know is the weight of a pen, the click of a computer keyboard, the burn of a question, the way a blank page feels like both a challenge and a prayer.

And that's enough— not answers, but scribbles. not certainty, but ink stains on my hands, blurred vision from a computer screen and proof that I was here, thinking about it all.

131
The Still Small Voice

Reality sings—not one note, but all of them, woven into a hymn so vast we only hear its echoes.

The stars hum in their stillness, the rivers chant in their motion. Every breath, every falling leaf, every whispered kindness joins the song.

At the heart of it, there is a rhythm, steady as a pulse, ancient as the first light that split the void.

We are the melody, you, and I— frail, trembling, sometimes off-key, but always essential.

And there, at the center, is the Sacred Force—call it God, Divine Spirit, The Christ, Allah, Adonai—not distant, not silent, but laboring in the deep, spinning beauty from chaos, pulling harmony from discord.

Creation itself is a poem, each line a sunrise, each word a human heart.

If we listen closely, we might hear it, that Sacred Force— not in thunder or flame, but in the still, small voice of the totality.

132
Not Whole

Light cuts the shadow, a jagged seam across the dark. It isn't clean—never is. Nothing mends without a scar.

Broken pieces tremble, edges glinting with quiet ache. They move—not gracefully, but they move.

Not whole, not steady—but who said wholeness was a requirement for rising?

Even Jesus wasn't whole on the cross.

Just enough. Enough for the dawn to see and believe—something here still holds, still hopes to heal.

133
If You are the Silence

Tell me, God, why hide? Is it fear or mercy that keeps you unseen? Is the weight of our sorrow too much, or is it something else—something I can't name?

Where is your face in my grief? The nights press in close, but your voice drifts far, like a ship lost in its own sea.

Why no touch of peace? No breath to calm the storm inside? No hand to wipe these warm tears before they fall into the hollow of my heart.

No arms like a mother's love— soft, sure, sheltering—just the empty space where comfort should be.

If you are the silence, then teach me to listen. If you are the absence, then teach me to hold what isn't there.

134
Broken Knife

What do you do with a broken knife, too sharp to handle, but useless as a tool for incision?

Useless for cheese or brain surgery, can't even scare a cat with a broken knife.

Too dangerous to put into a box of cereal, as a secret weapon when you have breakfast, and your annoying brother-in-law is staying the weekend with his dreadful wife.

Try shaving with it, and watch the blood roll down your face into a waiting roll of toilet paper.

Maybe it's good for picking your teeth, better than dental floss.

Best thing yet— test it on your neighbor's tires. He deserves a big blowout on I-95— just leave that metal sucker stuck in a groove and let it do its work slowly.

Now go wash your hands and butter your bread with a good knife.

135
The Flicker and the Dark

In the blackest night, where even shadows forget their shapes, a flicker fights the wind—tiny, trembling, defiant.

Is this the Divine Spirit? Small. Stubborn. The touch of Christ. More whisper than roar, more ember than blaze.

It doesn't save the world, doesn't split the heavens open wide. But it saves enough—enough to remind the night that light still remembers how to be born.

Every day, every moment!

It stays, not because it can't break, but because it refuses to leave.

136
Where the Roots Remember

On scarred earth, where the songs of rain are only rumors, your hands dig—not for gold, not for relics of a better time, but for something that knows how to rise.

In the dry marrow of the world, where sorrow sleeps like a tired beast, hope rises—a stubborn green thread unfolding in the cracks of ruin.

The sun sneers down, but still, the seed listens to the dark. Faith blooms, uninvited, a wild thing that doesn't ask for permission.

Not everything beautiful needs soft soil. Some things grow because they must—because the dirt remembers every root that dared to dream.

137
Bittersweet Romance

Just a bittersweet romance— a Mr. Good Bar gone bad in the afternoon sun, twice melted in the backseat of a '62 Ford Galaxy.

My love mobile, a chariot from hell—high school, complete with plastic seat covers, and hanging dice from the rearview mirror.

A mirror that always looks back fifty years, when a burger was a burger, and a girl was something you put in your pocket and ate later in the day.

Those were the days, right? Sticky fingers and chocolate stains, grease on your jeans, and that wild grin that said you didn't care, wouldn't care, couldn't care if the whole world melted like that candy bar in the backseat— like love on a hot day, like memories, fading into a rearview that never quite reflects what it should.

But we were stars in that Galaxy, even as it rusted beneath us, even as the roads cracked, and our dreams cracked with them, because it was all just a ride— a sweet, sticky ride through the sun-drenched afternoons of a time that never really was, but felt real enough to make us believe in something close to love.

138
Where the Silence Lives

It's not the man, not the girls, not the woman on the stairs—it's the in-between, the pause between footsteps, the glance that doesn't land, the space where meaning unravels before it reaches the heart.

The cracks swallow sound, as though they were hungry for everything unspoken. The alleys sigh where the city exhales, a slow release of breath, like it forgot it was alive and now pretends it never was.

It's the quiet corners where stories go to dissolve, where streetlights flicker but never ask why. The moments between door slams and greetings, between arrivals and departures—those are the empty spaces where time sits still, watching itself fade.

What isn't seen, what isn't heard— those are the ghosts that linger longest. Not in the rooms where voices gather, but in the places where sound once was and never returned.

I walk those spaces, feeling the absence press against my skin. It's not loss I fear— it's the echo that stays behind, the reminder of how easily the pulse of a place can forget its own rhythm.

139
Life Sitting in a Chair

Life, sitting in a chair, watching TV—the dull hum filling the room like a lover's sigh.

A cold beer in one hand, caressing the cat with the other, the purr vibrating through my fingers— a soft rhythm of existence.

Touching the underside of life with a warm sponge, squeezing out the days, watching them drip down the drain, slow and inevitable.

Breaking the sound barrier with a good fart— a symphony of solitude, while a pepperoni pizza burns the roof of my mouth, the perfect pain of indulgence.

Telegraphing my thoughts to my mother in heaven— a conversation without words, just the flicker of memories, a nod, a smile, an understanding that needs no reply.

An interesting evening, of home movies playing in my mind— the reel spinning, old friends and faded laughter, drinks that never empty, a night that stretches into the quiet dawn.

140
Godforsaken Day

Don't talk to me about golden illusions, keep your bright lies and glittering promises—

I'm not interested in the shine of something that'll fade by morning.

Give me a beautiful smile, one that's real, one that hasn't been polished by the world's bullshit, one that cuts through the noise like a knife.

I just want a day with undulating clouds, the kind that roll across the sky, like they've got nowhere to be, no rush, no schedule— just floating, drifting, like the way I'd like to live if I could just let go of all this crap.

Talk is cheap, yeah, but so is this whiskey, burning its way down, reminding me that the truth's in the sting, not in the sweet words that slip so easy off a liar's tongue.

I'll take the burn over the buzz any day, because at least I know it's real, and it doesn't pretend to be anything more than what it is— just like that smile I'm waiting for, just like those clouds, just like this Godforsaken day.

141
Journey of Tears

Is there life without pain? Or is it the pulse that keeps us whole, the fire that burns, the thorn that pricks the soul? Can we walk through fields of joy without the shadow of suffering casting long, eternal footprints on the land of our hearts?

Where do we wander when the weight of the world pushes down upon us, and there is no place left to go? When the mountains rise too steep, and the rivers run too deep— do we wander into the night, lost to ourselves and to the stars? Do we take our pain and wrap it tight around our chest, wear it like a cloak, until we forget the warmth of sunlight?

What is the purpose of tears— these silent rivers that never lie, that carve paths down our faces, marking where the sorrow has flowed? Are they simply the body's way of telling us we've loved too much, we've lived too deeply, that the soul has bled too freely for its own good?

Tears are the sacred language of those who carry the weight of truth, too heavy for the tongue to speak, too deep for the heart to keep. Each drop a message— a prayer sent out to the heavens, a scream to the abyss, a confession whispered to the wind. Tears are the quiet song of all that we cannot bear yet cannot bury. They wash the eyes so that we may see and cleanse the soul so that we may be free.

But where do they lead us, these tears we shed in the dark, when we have given all we have and still, the ache persists? Where do we turn when there is nothing left to hold but the rawness of our need and the silence of our fear?

It is in these moments, in the weight of our loneliness, that we must learn to speak, not to the world, but to those who love us. To them, we say, *I am here,* and though I am broken, though I am lost, I still carry the light of your love in the depths of my heart.

Tell it to those who love you— those whose hands are reaching out, even when the world feels too dark to see. Tell them that your pain is not an end, but a beginning, a way to touch something sacred, something real, beyond the boundaries of flesh and time. Tell them that in the brokenness, you are whole, and that in the suffering, you have found your strength.

For there is no place left to go except the quiet places within, where the pain becomes a memory and the tears a river of peace. There, we wander not to escape, but to find the truth that waits, waiting in silence, waiting in the love we have so long denied.

And in the end, can life be without pain? Perhaps not. But there is life, and that is enough. It is enough to wander, to cry, to stumble, to stand again, and to love in the brokenness.

142
Reaching Through the Void

In the stillness of the night, when all is quiet except the heart's faint beating, I reach through the void— a hand stretched out, not knowing what I seek, only that something waits on the other side of silence, something that calls me, whispers without words, beckoning through the dark.

It is a fragile thread that binds us, thin as a breath, a flicker of light in a sea of shadow. We grasp it, and it pulls us back— back from the edge, back from the precipice of nothingness, where dreams fade and crumble into dust, where even the stars lose their shimmer.

We are all caught in the web of this struggle, each of us pulling, each of us reaching, trying to make sense of the thread that ties us together, though we never quite understand how it holds. It is the shared weight of sorrow that keeps us tethered, or the shared weight of joy, too fragile to stand alone, needing to be felt through the cracks of others.

Through the void we wander, not as separate souls, but as travelers bound in the same current, drawn by the same moon, under the same indifferent sky. We ask questions that echo back at us, unanswered and unanswerable, and yet we ask them anyway, for the asking itself is the search, the search that keeps us moving even when the road falls away beneath us.

What is the thread, this thing that pulls us back from the abyss? What keeps us from losing ourselves to the dark, to the cold, to the silent depths where nothing moves, where even hope drowns? Perhaps it is the shared struggle— the understanding that we are all, in our deepest core, broken, searching, aching for meaning in a world that never offers it freely.

I pull at the thread— delicate as a whisper, strong as a promise, and for a moment, I feel the presence of another hand on the other end, holding fast, not pulling away, not letting go. And in that moment, I know we are not alone, that the struggle is not ours alone to bear, but shared, woven into the very fabric of existence.

In the quiet of the void, I hear the distant hum of other souls, reaching through the same darkness, their hands outstretched as mine are.

We are all reaching through the void, each of us fragile, each of us desperate, yet each of us connected by the thread that pulls us back into the struggle, into the search. It is a fragile thread, but it is enough. In the reaching, in the struggle, we find our purpose. And in the finding, we become whole. For what is life if not the delicate balance between the pull of the void and the thread that holds us?

143
Embers Beneath the Ash

Deep down, whiskey burns slow, like a quiet fire in the hollow of night. Smoke curls up, soft and lazy, its path unhurried, as if savoring the air it climbs. A hunger lingers—not for the drink, not for the fleeting brush of skin, but for something raw, something real.

I close my eyes and taste the burn, letting it stir what sleeps beneath. The ache isn't for escape—it's for arrival. For a place where the masks drop, where words bleed true, and silence holds more weight than sound.

There's a pull toward the untamed— the parts of life untouched by polish or pretense. Not the gloss of memory, but the marrow of the moment. Where pain doesn't ask permission and joy arrives without warning.

The slow burn whispers of truths I've buried, embers beneath ash, waiting for breath. It isn't destruction I crave, but the heat of something unbreakable— the core that remains after everything soft has melted away.

I sit with the fire, feeling its slow, steady hum. I don't need the blaze to consume me, only to remind me that I am still alive— hungry for what I cannot name but know when it finds me.

144
Devil's Road Trip

There's a pit in my stomach, a postcard from hell— a bad handshake with the devil, his sly grin saying, *"The party's just begun."*

Tell Satan I'm not home, but he can have the keys to my car. Let him take a joyride to New Jersey, where the highways coil like regrets, and diners serve coffee strong enough to keep you awake through your own nightmares.

Maybe he'll meet a not-so-nice girl, one who's worn out her welcome on every block she's circled. She'll teach him the ropes— how to light a cigarette with a glance, how to swallow disappointment without even tasting it.

She'll drag him to Atlantic City, show him the slots, let him feed the machines his quarters of despair. Each spin a flash of hope, each loss another step closer to redemption or ruin.

And when the neon grows tired, she'll point him to the beach. *"Count the grains of sand,"* she'll say, *"like they're sins waiting for grace, until even you believe in the love of God."*

Meanwhile, I'll take a train to New York— but stop off in Newark first, where the streets don't bother with your name, and the corners whisper stories nobody's brave enough to hear.

I'll let the city swallow me whole, disappear into its concrete maw, because sometimes, nowhere feels safer than staring into the pit of your own stomach.

145

Lying Mirror

Okay, so mirrors don't lie, but they sure know how to twist the truth— sending back distorted messages, like sadistic postcards from Planet Reality.

They wrack the brain; make you question everything you thought you knew about yourself. Especially when I'm shaving, staring at my own face, and those little whiskers turn into gray spikes, like the universe itself is laughing at my expense.

Each stroke of the razor peels back another layer, and I'm left wondering— what's underneath all this skin? Am I just a glorified sausage, wrapped in a porcine casing, starting to split at the seams?

The mirror doesn't lie, but it sure as hell doesn't tell the whole story. It shows the cracks, the flaws, the relentless march of time turning youth into memory, strength into myth.

But it doesn't show the fight that burns behind the eyes— the stubborn refusal to go quietly, to be reduced to a sack of gray hairs and regrets.

So, I keep shaving, keep facing that lying mirror, because even if it's just a reflection, there's something worth holding onto. Something that says, *I'm here, and I'm not done yet.*

146

The Bottle and The Sea

I decided to put my head in a glass bottle, toss it into the ocean like a message no one wants to read.

The South Pacific sounds nice, or Iceland, where the cold can freeze my thoughts before they turn to stone.

Not sure where the currents will take me, but that's half the fun— letting the sea decide if I'm worth saving.

I just hope some little kid finds me on a warm sandy beach, small hands pulling the bottle from the surf, wide eyes staring at my withered face.

But please, not in Atlantic City, where dreams go to die, and the seagulls know your name. I'd rather not be picked clean by those screeching bastards.

Let some beautiful mermaid crack me open at a slot machine, like a tender oyster, devour my brain while I laugh at the absurdity of it all.

Glad I'm in a whiskey bottle— still a little Jack down here to keep me company, to keep me warm, while I float on through the endless blue.

The ocean's a big place, full of secrets and lies, but, just maybe, there's a piece of me that'll make it somewhere worthwhile— somewhere I can finally rest and stop looking for a reason to come ashore.

147

To Let Go

The current calls me forward, relentless and wild. I resist, planting my feet in yesterday's fading shore. But the ground dissolves beneath me, as if to say, "Nothing stays, not even your sorrow."

I asked for permanence, but permanence wears the mask of impermanence. Everything shifts—faces, seasons, dreams— and I am a wanderer in the in-between.

I once thought stillness was the answer, but even the stars move across the night. The universe hums with motion, and who am I to deny the song of the turning tides?

So, I unlearn the clutching, the grasping, the fear. I let the river take me—not away, but deeper—into what I cannot yet understand. The current knows the way home, even when I do not.

To let go is not to surrender to emptiness. It is to trust that what slips away leaves a space for grace to enter. And when I open my hands, I find them already filled with something new.

148
The Broken Parts

God forgive me for my blasphemy, but . . .

The saloon keeper is the chaplain's brain surgeon, steady hands pouring whiskey, fixing the breaks in his skull with every shot.

His mother is his urologist, measuring out his life in piss and pills, telling him to drink more water. He just laughs and says, *water is for the dead.*

Next door, the neighbor pulls out his own teeth one by one with pliers and a steady grin, while the rabbi in the corner makes matzoh balls and plays ping pong, reciting the Mourner's Kaddish through tears that speak the truth.

A thousand Sunday mornings, they all shuffle into church, except the rabbi—too busy with his matzoh balls. They hold hands as Jesus feeds them his bleeding body, his broken heart, washed down with wine that had been water five minutes ago.

The butcher—with very bloody hands—offers cheap forgiveness and dispensations, for a price of course, in waxed paper bags, smelling of rotting meat and despair.

The priest is a magician, pulling twelve-legged spiders and red demons from the bellies of sad old men who pick their teeth with rusty nails, hoping to erase the past with every dig and scrape.

In the back pew, a beautiful young girl knits her way to heaven— each stitch a prayer, each breath a blessing. The old ladies line up like beggars, healed with just a whisper from her lips.

The saloon keeper schedules surgery for the priest— after all, everyone's got sins to confess, even the ones who hand out grace like candy to children who never say thank you.

And in the end, they all go to heaven together, because even the damned need a place to heal.

149
Let God Love You

Let God love you the way He wants. Don't force it, don't twist His arm, don't dress it up in Sunday best or carve it in stone.

Let God love you the way He wants— in the street, in the tenements, in the emergency room where cold lights burn, where the night's full of regrets. Let Him find you there, where you are, not where you pretend to be.

He doesn't care about fancy words or polished prayers, or the list of sins you keep in your pocket like some kind of scorecard. He's not counting.

He's in the cigarette smoke, the last drag before dawn, when the city's asleep and your thoughts run wild.

He's in the ache in your chest, the one you can't explain, and the songs on You Tube that make you feel something you can't put into words.

Let Him love you in the moments you hate yourself the most— when you've screwed up again and you're drowning in it, when you've pushed everyone away and you're alone with the mess you've made.

Let Him be there, in the silence, in the stillness, when you've got nothing left to give, nothing left to lose.

He's not asking for perfection, never did. He doesn't need your bright ideas or your broken promises, or the way you keep trying to make it all make sense.

Let Him love you in the chaos, in the uncertainty, in the not knowing, because that's where He is.

Let God love you in the way you can't love yourself, in the way no one else can, because He's been here all along, waiting for you to stop running, to stop pretending, to just be.

So let go of the control, the need to steer the ship, the idea that you know better— because you don't, and you never will.

Let Him love you in the mess, in the wreckage, in the broken-down moments when you're ready to quit.

Let Him pick you up, dust you off, and remind you that you're still here, still breathing, still worth it.

150
Let the Poet Slap You in the Face

Let the poet slap you in the face, hard enough to make your teeth rattle, and kick dog crap on your pretty red dress— watch it smear and stain like the truth you've been trying to avoid.

Receive those words like a summons to pain, a license to kill every soft lie you've been spoon-fed since birth. Because if it doesn't make you vomit, if it doesn't make you faint, then it's not good poetry— it's just another bedtime story meant to lull you back to sleep.

Real poetry should make you bleed, should carve out pieces you didn't even know were there, leave you gasping for air— like a punch to the gut, like love that turns to rot in the blink of an eye.

Let the lines hit you like a speeding car, wrecking everything you thought was safe, everything you thought was beautiful. Because the truth isn't pretty, it's not dressed in lace— it's raw and ugly, like the world we live in. And if it doesn't hurt, it's just another lie wrapped up in verse.

Let the poet excise your soul. And if you're not standing after that, then maybe you've found something worth reading.

151
Girl with the Eggplant

A large girl with green hair on the G train to Brooklyn, holding a big fat purple eggplant, looks at me like I'm Hitler with two heads.

She's probably a nice girl, heading to Bensonhurst or Sunset Park, or maybe just downtown to get her teeth fixed at the Williamsburg Savings Bank.

I'm thinking eggplant parmigiana would hit the spot right about now—with a few bottles of chianti, or even a merlot, if I were feeling fancy.

But I've only got a few bucks, enough for a gallon of cheap sweet red table wine, blended in Little Italy by a guy with dirty hands and ties to the Mafia.

I stare at her eggplant, and she shields it like it's something delicate, like it's her own tender bosom.

Her eyes are dark, and she looks at me like I'm just a filthy college student—long hair, bloodshot eyes, and terrible shoes. And she wouldn't be wrong.

I smile, get off at Hoyt-Schermerhorn, thinking about that eggplant, and the wine, and how sometimes it's better to keep moving before life tells you what you already know.

152
Trust the Breaking

There are seasons when the soul folds in on itself, crumpled like a paper crane under the weight of rain. Times when everything that held you steady—names, places, faces, even your own reflection—slips through your grasp like water through trembling fingers.

You try to fight it at first, scrambling to hold the pieces together. But the harder you clutch, the more they dissolve, until you're left with nothing but the ache of your own empty hands.

This is the chaos we all must pass through. A necessary undoing, like the earth cracking open to let the seed breathe, like nightfall pressing close to birth the dawn.

I have been there, too. Lost in that darkness where nothing feels real, where even your prayers seem to echo back in unfamiliar voices. It is not a place of comfort, but it is a place of truth—a wild, untamed truth that strips away what no longer serves, leaving only the raw essence of who you are.

And it is from that rawness that the new self is born. Slowly, quietly, like a sapling reaching toward light it cannot yet see. The chaos becomes the soil, the tears the rain, the breaking the space where growth begins.

So, if you find yourself there now, in that hollow of unknowing, let me tell you this: You are not lost. You are in transition. Caving in is not the end; it is the clearing of the way.

Hold on. Trust the breaking. There is a new shape waiting to emerge, one that is truer, stronger, and freer than you ever imagined.

And when you rise—and you will rise—remember this: growth is not a straight path, but a spiraling one. Each collapse, each moment of disorientation, is a step closer to the whole of who you are becoming.

153
Kill the Buddha

My favorite professor in seminary told me if I see the Buddha on the road, just kill him. I never had the nerve and failed his course.

But there was this guy, owned a Chinese restaurant in Brooklyn— looked like a real smiling Buddha— and I didn't have the heart to kill him, or even punch him in the face.

So, I just bought some kung pao chicken and a pint of wonton soup, sat at a little table in his shop, and gave him the evil eye.

He just kept smiling, brought me a fortune cookie, said I'd be dead before the night was through.

Well, so much for killing the Buddha. Sometimes, you just eat your chicken, slurp your soup, and wait for your destiny in a pastry shell.

154
Death at the Table

Death sits down next to you, a quiet guest at the table, and you realize it's not the monster you thought it was— just another part of the deal, the final page in the book you've been writing your whole life.

Dying strips you down, takes off the layers of bullshit you've been piling on for years— the rent, the job, the black screens, the endless chase for something shiny that never felt quite right. All of it falls away, like an old coat full of holes.

You start seeing things clearer, like a window finally cleaned. The things that mattered, the things you fought for, are now dust in your hands.

But the touch of a lover, the laugh of a friend, the warmth of a dog at your feet— those are the things that stay. Those are the things that mean something when the lights start to dim.

In those last breaths, you find something sacred, something you never knew was there— a flicker of light, a whisper of love— something that makes the whole damn mess worth it in the end.

Close your eyes, not in fear, but in a kind of peace you didn't know you had in you. And for once, everything just makes sense.

155
Live Real

Live real— without the hot sauce from the talking heads.

Finish your sentences with good periods.

Learn to laugh with both your ears. Let the sound fill you up, because life's too short to listen to fools and ass holes.

Stand on some beach, let the waves lick your feet like an old dog. Walk into the sea until the foam fills your nostrils, until you forget what it means to drown in other people's noise.

Dance like a fly on a donut or a piece of rotting meat, because life's full of decay, and you might as well move to the rhythm of it all.

Build a house of ice, invite the neighbors with their torches. Let them watch it melt and tell them nothing lasts forever—and that's the best part.

Look into the mirror, see a nice guy with pimples and a pepperoni pizza, because we're all just grease and dough, trying to get by.

Sit in the middle of the street, wait for the bus that never comes, because sometimes it's waiting that makes you feel alive.

Sit in the back with the peasants, the migrants, the lost souls, the throwaways, the ones who've seen too much, and drink your beer with a smile.

Sit back, let the world spin without you, because you're too busy being real, being here, being now.

156
Waiting for Jesus

She's 103. She says, *I'm waiting for Jesus. Please, Jesus, take me.*

But Jesus missed the bus too, He's on the wrong platform, headed to Manhattan, not Coney Island.

I hand her a road map of heaven, but the streets aren't paved in gold— just a few craggy footpaths filled with gravel and sand, crab grass growing wild on the edges.

Lots of cats lounging around, each with a guidebook, pointing to the famous mansions Jesus' Father promised, each one filled with fine spiritual food, endless television, and old Bogart movies with blondes who never age.

I look down the track, and here comes the A train, doors wide open. She gets right in and slides into eternity.

157
Love Becomes Whole

They say love is bright, a flame unyielding, a thread unbroken. Yet here it lies, a cloak patched and frayed, its edges unraveling with each tug of the world's weight.

Shoes cracked, soles worn thin, laces pulled too tight— this is the love we bear, not golden, but weathered, not perfect, but steadfast, a pilgrim's journey carved on the path of our hearts.

Was love ever meant to gleam? Or does its beauty rise from the pain of its forging, the scars of its endurance? For in the breaking, in the bending, love becomes whole.

The old shoes tell a story, of fields crossed, of rivers forded, of mountains climbed together. Every crack, a memory; every worn thread, a testament to its strength.

Love's pain is no enemy— it is the shaping of the stone, the softening of the soil. It digs its roots deep, holding fast through storms, its blossoms hidden until the season of grace.

So, take this love, cracked and worn. Tie its laces once more, and step into the journey ahead. For even in its weariness, it is holy, a gift given and received, blessed by the One who bore love's weight first.

158
The River Beyond the Shore

The water murmurs secrets to the reeds, but the reeds are still. We press our ears to the soft hum of the universe, hoping to catch the echo of our first breath—God's whisper shaping clay into song. Consciousness stirs before the earth knew our names. Before the stars blinked awake, we existed in the warmth of the Unseen Hand.

The body is a door, not a prison. It swings open at the appointed hour. On the other side, the fields bloom golden with a light that no shadow can touch. Death is only a pause, a gathering of feathers before the flight homeward.

The heart remembers what the mind forgets: that we are pilgrims of eternity. God, our maker, does not abandon His own. He cups our souls like fireflies, releasing them into the endless sky of His love.

In the great quiet after the storm of flesh, we will remember our truest name— the one He spoke when He made us, before the world spun its illusions. And the last word, as in the beginning, will be His. And that word will be *welcome.*

159
Slow March

Time drags its feet, no rush to be found. Its shadow sprawls across cracked linoleum floors like a drunkard forgetting how to walk straight, its breath heavy with the stale stench of regret.

Liquidate all care, let trouble drown in a puddle of beer inside a grimy, discarded glass. Worries swirl with cigarette ash and shattered dreams, while ice cubes clink like whispers of lost chances.

Forget who you are—the name, the face, those labels that pin you down like moths on a board. Build a tower of water in this desolate place, a monument of mirages rising from cracked pavement, each drop a ghost of yesterday's thirst.

Seek only the sparks that set your blood on fire— those fierce, fleeting flashes in the dark corners of the bar, where desire dances like a mirage on the edge of a glass and the only truth is the heat that burns your fingertips.

Tomorrow's a coin—it flips, a liar in disguise, a crooked fortune-teller spinning in circles, promising new beginnings with each toss but landing on the same old faces, the same old pain.

Fix the wells that run dry, the echoes, the moans, those dusty relics of dreams gone stale. Patch the cracks in the walls of your solitude, but know the best repairs leak again, like tears from a soul too worn to weep anew.

Then stagger home to the soft, empty tones— the quiet that wraps around you like a shroud. The silence hums with ghosts of what could have been, while the only company is the steady tick of a clock that's stopped, mocking your wandering steps with its endless, indifferent march.

160
The Thread That Binds

A single cry, half a world away, tightens the thread in our hands. We cannot pretend we do not feel it pulling. A stranger's grief knots with our own, for we are woven into a tapestry larger than our small ambitions. We stand together beneath the same wide sky, though we call it by different names. The prophets knew this—they sang it from the mountains and cried in the streets: no one is free until all are free.

The ancient laws were written not on stone alone but in the chambers of every human heart. "Love your neighbor," they said—not because it was easy, but because it was holy. Justice is not a distant throne but a daily bread shared with the hungry, a shelter for the exiled, a promise to the forgotten.

To tear one thread is to weaken the whole. We cannot blind ourselves to the suffering of another without unraveling the soul's own peace. Christianity and Judaism do not whisper justice—they roar it. We are commanded not only to pray but to rise, to mend the world with mercy, stitch by stitch.

And when we are called to account for our days, the question will not be who we claimed to love, but who we failed to see. Justice is not abstract. It wears a human face. It is the very breath of God moving through us—the great web pulling us homeward, hand in hand.

161

The Snake Oil Salesman

The snake oil salesman— slick as bourbon on a liar's lips. He slinks through the cracks in your mind, selling blessings, dispensations, and holy water like a cheap prophet in a back-alley chapel.

He's a serpent draped in fine silk, a grifter in a three-piece promise with a heavy golden cross around his neck and his right hand on the Bible. You're the mark, and he's got the deck stacked. Every word he spins is a noose of sugar, sweet and sickly.

In the corners of your skull, he sets up camp and builds his personal shrine, sacred whispers curling like cigarette smoke, making you doubt the reflection staring back.

The mirrors crooked. The clocks—melted. Time's all wrong, *but it's your fault, he says, kneel here, now!* He'll twist your spine until you believe the floor is the ceiling and the stars are just pinpricks in black velvet.

You'll dance 'till your feet bleed, drink a little poison from the mouth of the snake, and wait for your heart to sputter like a dying light bulb, flickering in a basement of bad dreams.

And when you finally see the tentacles tied to your every limb, he's already gone—but he's left his indelible mark on your soul, and he's got you for eternity.

162

Silence of the Void

The wind carries no message, only silence, and the trees bend to hear it without questioning why the sky remains empty.

The nothingness gnaws, like a silent wave lapping at the shore of your mind. But it's not hunger, just the tide's gentle reminder that all things are born from its retreat.

Sit still. The void says nothing because it has already spoken— in the sound of your breath, in the space between thoughts where truth hides like a shadow under a leaf.

You feel the weight of emptiness, but what is heavy? A cloud drifts through your chest, and suddenly, there is nothing left to carry.

Do not despair. The void is a mirror, reflecting the face you've never seen— the one beneath the layers of names and stories, the one untouched by dust or time.

In this emptiness, there is a door that leads nowhere, yet opens everywhere. Step through, and watch the world fall behind, like water from a blade of grass.

This is your soul calling, not from the depths, but from the center, where all is still and where death is a ripple in a pond that returns to silence.

The nothingness whispers: you are not bound to the shape of your skin, nor the thoughts that flutter like paper birds. You are the space between the wings, the wind that carries them.

In the emptiness, you are full. In nothing, you are infinite. And there you will find the peace of the Divine Spirit.

163

The Mensch

No mask, no pretense, just the weight of presence— like the stillness of a mountain, rooted deep in the soil of the heart.

A mensch— not a title, not a role, but a quiet fire that warms without burning, a light that does not seek to be seen yet illuminates everything around it.

In the curve of a hand, in the sound of a voice, there is something that moves— like wind through trees, unseen, but known by the way the leaves tremble.

This is the quality of being that shines through, not as an effort, but as water flows from a spring, clear and unforced.

It's not the absence of self, but the fullness of being— so deeply human, it forgets to try. It simply is.

When you see it, you feel it— the unspoken truth of someone whole. They are not perfect, but in their imperfection, you glimpse the infinite.

And so, in the midst of the world, a mensch walks, quietly shaping the air, being human in the most human way possible.

164
Shadowed Corner

No matter how good we strive to be, there is a corner deep within— a shadowed place we try to hide, where brokenness begins.

In the light, we walk, our hands full of deeds, but somewhere, in the quiet folds of our soul, a cry rises, for forgiveness unseen.

For though we stand and offer love, our hearts still tremble with the weight of sin— that corner where pride or Pain remains, and grace must enter in.

It's there, where words can't reach, that mercy knocks and gently calls, not to condemn but to embrace the wounds we thought too small.

For Christ alone can touch that place, the part of us we cannot heal. And in His hands, our broken' hearts are softened to His will.

So, no matter how good our lives may seem, there's always a place that bends— a need for grace to fill the gaps until the journey ends.

In every heart, a corner cries and only love Divine can trace the path of forgiveness to the soul and bathe it all in grace.

165
Wounds of the Earth

We bang the earth, her groans rise like morning mist, her tears seep through cracks we carved with greedy hands. Her veins bleed rivers of fire, and still, we take, never looking back.

We pull her guts, the sinews of mountains torn, the bones of deserts broken, feeding the flames of our unrelenting hunger. Each spark a prayer unspoken, a plea she cannot voice.

The soil, scratched raw, bleeds beneath our plows, her lifeblood mingling with seed. We eat from the wounds we've made, unthinking, unyielding, and wonder why the sky grows dim and the rain tastes of ash.

God of the soil and the green hills, of the deep roots and quiet streams, help us mend what we have broken. Teach us to sow not only for harvest, but for healing— to tread lightly where we once stormed, to give back what we have stolen.

For the earth is Yours, not ours to plunder, but a gift to steward, a sacred trust. Grant us the wisdom to see her Pain, to hear her cries, and to put her back in order before her voice falls silent.

166
Light and the Pain

I will love the light, for it reveals the path before me, each curve of the trail, each stone, each whispering blade of grass. The light is a teacher; it shows the way but never walks it for me.

Yet I will endure the darkness, for it unveils the stars, a tapestry of hope in the void. In its silence, pain becomes a quiet song, a low hum of the universe that reminds me I am alive.

Pain is the fire that shapes the blade, the sculptor's chisel on a stubborn stone. It carves my heart open, making room for joy, for wisdom, for the softness of compassion that grows in its wake.

I walk with pain, not as its captive but as its companion. I listen to its lessons, even as it screams, even as it whispers in the small hours when the world feels too heavy to bear.

For the light and the dark are lovers entwined; one cannot exist without the other. The brightest day finds its echo in the deepest shadow. And the stars— oh, the stars—sing only in the dark.

I will love the light, and I will endure the night. I will feel the pain, let it wash over me, until it leaves me cleansed, reborn in the quiet stillness of being.

For pain, like the stars, is not forever. And when the light returns, it finds me stronger, my heart larger, my spirit unbroken.

167
Unlock the Shadows

Throughout our lives, we pass by windows of ourselves, glimpsing faces we love and faces we refuse to name. The light is a gentle liar, hiding what we cannot bear to see.

The shadows move differently— they crouch, they linger, their hands are cold, but their truths burn like fire. They are the silent witnesses to the lives we've hidden.

We turn from them, bury them in the soil of denial, but they grow roots, their branches brushing the edges of our dreams, their leaves whispering truths we try to unhear.

To face them is not surrender, but a reclamation of the whole self. Each shadow holds a key, each rejection, a secret door to the vast room of who we are— not broken, but infinite.

Step into the dark. Feel the weight of it in your chest. Hold the shadows in your hands until their sharp edges soften.

For it is here, in this meeting, that the stars begin to sing, and the sky unfolds like a gift. Only by knowing the shadows can we see the fullness of the light.

168
The Son

The Son— image of the invisible, firstborn over all creation. In Him, all things came to be, heaven and earth, the seen and the unseen, thrones that crumble, powers that corrupt, rulers that bow only to their own reflection. All was made— through Him, for Him.

Before all, He is. And yet, we scurry to piece together unity in fragmented idols we make with trembling hands. In Him, all things find their center, held together in a quiet strength we mock as weakness.

He is the head, and yet we sever Him daily— the body, the church, unwilling to bear the weight of His crown. He is the beginning, firstborn from the dead, yet we cling to the dust, hoping our kingdoms will rise without His breath.

God's fullness dwells in Him, not in the towers we build or the wars we wage.

He is pleased to reconcile all things, but are we? Earth and heaven, torn apart by our defiant hands, can only be mended by a peace we fear— a deep and final peace, paid for in blood we refuse to acknowledge was ever shed.

169
Bitter Spark

A twist of families—like a lemon peel in a cheap martini. That tang sticks to your tongue, forces a breath, deep and slow, and you realize—anything that tastes good is just dumb luck, a fleeting accident of flavor.

But still, you hold on, searching for the bitters, though you hate the bite of it. You chase that spark anyway, knowing it'll sting, knowing it's fleeting, but craving the heat it leaves behind.

Mix those juices, the ones that burn and settle in your chest like only a bartender's touch can command. Add some spice, a sprinkle of laughter, a few soft kisses to dull the sharp edges. And suddenly, you've got a masterpiece— something you sip, something you can't quite explain.

Just be careful how you swallow. Too fast, and it'll scorch you all the way down, leaving you gasping for air. Too slow, and you'll miss the buzz altogether, watching the ice melt, wishing you'd taken the chance when the glass was still full.

170
The Silence and The Revelation

Beyond time's grasp, In the shadowless reaches where light fears to tread, God hides. No hands may hold this Holy emptiness, no eyes may see. No voice may name it. It does not exist, yet it is All. The silence of the silence, The void that births voids. We know nothing of this, yet the whisper of its absence is the hymn of eternity.

God within all things, saturating every breath. Binding every mote of dust to the sky. Here, the eternal Creator spins galaxies from whispers and dissolves them back into forgetting. In the Planck pulse, the quark's dance, the Divine writes equations we struggle to understand. Through devices of science, we glimpse the depths of Creation, a glory both veiled and unveiled. This God is knowable through atom and ache, through the crumbling of galaxies and the flowering of weeds. It is creation and destruction in every moment.

And then— God steps into the room. Breathes. Speaks. Becomes the Word in your mouth, the warmth in your hands, the fire in your questions. The God who meets you in the wound and answers your cry with another cry.

This is the God who bleeds, who touches your face and says, "I am here." The God who loves as mother and father, as child and stranger, whose eyes you find in the quiet reckoning of a friend. We are The Christ, in flesh and blood. Manifest in the now. Alive only in the holy instant of touch and truth, where prayer is dialogue and dialogue is Love.

Thus, God is the unknowable abyss. God is the all-encompassing field. God is the face before you, the whisper behind you, the love between you.

171
The Stranger

In the restless din of the outer world, where every voice demands allegiance and every face mirrors a borrowed dream, there is a silence that belongs to you alone. It does not compete; it does not scream. It waits, like a seed beneath snow, patient for the thaw of your attention. The hero in each of us stirs not when the world applauds, but when the stillness calls.

Turn away—not as a deserter, but as a seeker. The cacophony of the world's demands will not quiet itself; it will only grow louder, more insistent. You must choose to walk through its noise, past its bright banners and hollow promises. For beyond the outer clamoring lies a threshold, one marked not by gates but by the courage to say, *enough*. Step through, and you will find the wilderness of your own becoming.

There, in that wilderness, the old roads vanish, and the familiar names fall away. The journey of individuation is not a linear path; it is a spiral, descending inward before it rises again. Each turn unravels a lie you believed was yours. Each step reveals a truth you had forgotten. In this solitude, you will meet the one who waits—the *YOU* who has been shadowed by expectations, hidden beneath roles and titles. You will see them not as a stranger but as the face you were born to wear.

And when you dare to live by this voice—this quiet, persistent urging— you will find yourself transformed. The world may not recognize you. You may become a stranger to those who thought they knew you. There will be questions, even accusations: *Why have you changed? Why have you left the path we all agreed upon?* But in the solitude of your own heart, you will know the answer. You did not abandon the world; you reclaimed yourself.

To achieve personhood is to accept the price of authenticity. It is to trade the fleeting approval of the outer world for the lasting peace of inner alignment. This is not a bargain for the faint of heart. It requires the courage to stand alone, to walk through fire and shadow, and to emerge with the unshakable knowledge that you are no longer a stranger to yourself.

And so, the hero in each of us is called not to conquest, but to communion— not with the world, but with the truth that resides within. To heed this call is the sacred task of a lifetime. To ignore it is to wander forever as a ghost in borrowed skin. Listen. Turn. Answer. For the voice that calls is yours, and it will not be silenced.

172
Quiet Truth

In each breath, a quiet dignity resides—not earned, not bartered, but stitched into the threadbare fabric of simply being. And yet, we claw at titles, collecting medals that tarnish, as if worth can be hung around our necks.

No status, no achievement, no golden ladder can alter this: we are simply enough. Enough to shatter, enough to rise, enough to stand bare before the Divine and still be called beloved.

Made in the image of something eternal, we walk a tightrope between fragility and greatness—between the cracks and the stubborn light that seeps through them.

Our imperfections—sharp, jagged stones beneath the water—are worn smooth by the relentless current of grace. And in the stillness, when the river settles, we see our reflection and wonder how we ever doubted our potential for holiness.

We are both the fragile leaf, trembling in the wind, and the towering tree, unyielding against the storm. Both are held by the same unseen root, the same ancient truth.

In this balance—this dance of breaking and becoming—we find a fleeting peace. And, just for a moment, we stop chasing what we already are.

173
That Worry

So, what is it that I'm worried about? Can't find it—not in the sock drawer, not in the fridge—but it's somewhere, pounding like a headache that forgot to leave.

No meaning, no desire, just sitting there, like a fat bastard on the couch, won't move. Like a constipated anomaly with green horns and a twitching leg, it takes up space, refusing to leave.

But I'm still worried. It comes back like a rusty boomerang, a kid's frisbee on the cracked city street.

Don't turn around—it might smack you in the head, might pretend it knows me, sees me in the subway, like an old friend. But it's no friend.

I want to send it back, back to the Bronx or Jersey, one of those places where dreams go to die, where even the rats don't bother running.

Think I'll take the train east, just to find it, just to get rid of it, watch it slip away into the shadow of some abandoned lot.

And if I don't? Well, that's the worry. Or maybe it's nothing at all.

174
Truth in the Thorns

Suffering's the teacher, not pleasure. The serpent slithered knowledge to Adam, Eve took a bite—a taste too sweet. But the truth wasn't in the bite; it was in the aftermath: banishment, pain, the long crawl through the thorns.

Ulysses heard the sirens sing, songs wrapped in honeyed tones. But the wisdom lay in the ropes, in the resistance, in the ache of wanting but not having.

Pleasure has no answers, just distractions. It makes you think you've won while you're sinking deeper. Knowledge doesn't live there—it hides in the scars, the bruises, the long nights of wrestling with your own soul.

Pleasure's innocent when you don't expect much from it—a brief kiss in a dark alley, a cold drink after a long walk. But when you go digging for truth in the height of a smile or the warmth of a touch, you lose something. You fall.

Suffering's the real deal. It whispers the truths pleasure hides, because only in the breaking, in the bleeding, do we find the pieces that make us whole.

175
Edge of Joy

The more you taste joy, the sharper the edge when it cuts away.

You know what's out there—the sunlight, the laughter spilling over, the easy days where nothing aches, where everything hums like a tune you've always known.

But then the fall, the darkness creeping in, and the joy you've felt makes the drop even harder. You know what's been lost, and it's not the kind of ignorance you can unlearn.

The fuller you've been, the hollower the pit. And suddenly, you see the cracks in everyone else—in their eyes, in the way they shuffle through the day, carrying weight you can feel, because you've been there.

Compassion comes not from pity, but from knowing joy and suffering are lovers, dancing in the same breath. The higher you fly, the harder you hit the ground.

But you get up again, and you walk, knowing every face you pass is somewhere between the two, just like you.

176
The Stick, Not the World

We stumble through this place, hands outstretched, feeling for something solid, something real—like a blind man with his stick, tapping, tapping, trying to make sense of it all.

The body, this world—it's all just a tool, a way to find our way to something bigger, something unseen. But we treat it like the whole show, clinging to what we can touch, and taste, and hold, as if that will save us.

We forget it's all just the stick, not the destination.

The stick's not the world, just a way to feel it, to navigate through the dark until we hit light. The body's not the truth, just the vessel we use to fumble toward something we'll never quite grasp, but know is there, somewhere.

And maybe we're not meant to see it all, just enough to keep moving, to know there's more than this—this flesh, this dirt, this noise.

Tapping along, trusting the unseen road will lead us somewhere better than what we thought we were after.

177
Knocking on the Wall

Two men sit in concrete boxes, steel bars, cold walls—the kind that suck the air out of your lungs and make the silence scream.

They knock on the wall, tap tap tap, the rhythm of the lonely, the pulse of the forgotten. Each knock says, *I'm here, are you?* but all they hear is the echo, bouncing back at them like a ghost.

Funny thing, that wall—it keeps them apart, but it's the only way they talk. Their prison and their connection, a barrier, and a bridge, all in one breath of concrete.

And isn't that the way with us and God?

We knock on the walls of this world, knuckles bloodied, looking for some sign He's on the other side. We shout into the silence, and what do we get? Echoes. Like He's there but just out of reach, just behind the wall.

The thing that keeps us apart is the same thing that holds us together.

We knock, He knocks, and the wall stands between us—thick and heavy, but also the only way we know He's there.

Every separation's a thread, a thin line, like spider silk—fragile but stronger than we think.

We knock on walls, and somewhere in the echo, there's a link, you know the One just waiting to pull us through.

178
She Died of Love

She died of love, or something like it—a quiet ache that spread like smoke through her veins, turning her bones to dust while nobody noticed.

It wasn't the kind you write songs about—no roses, no letters sealed in wax—just the slow burn of days wasted, waiting for something that never quite came.

Her hands, always empty, still reached out, fingers grasping at the air like it held answers. But love isn't in the air; it's buried deep, under the weight of too many cigarettes and bad decisions.

And maybe she wanted it that way—to dissolve in the wanting, to let the hunger swallow her whole. Because what's left when you've found it? What's left when you've got it all, and it's still not enough?

They say she died of love, but I say love just watched her, like a vulture circling slow, waiting for the moment her heart finally gave up.

It wasn't tragic—no violins, no moonlit tears—just the quiet click of a door closing on a life lived too far in the shadows, too far from the fire.

And when they asked why, when they searched for reasons, all they could say was love. As if love was the cure and the disease all at once.

179
Looking for the Neanderthals

I'm looking for the Neanderthals—yeah, those big-brained bone busters, the ones who ate alligators raw and crafted jewelry from mammoth tusks.

They weren't dumb Fred Flintstone clowns. No, these guys had style, grit under their fingernails, brains in their skulls, survivors with swagger.

I checked under my bed, lifted the dust bunnies and last year's chocolate Easter eggs. Just a couple of insect wings and a broken pen. No Neanderthals here.

Poked around the backyard shed, found rusted tools, a bucket of screws, but no sign of my hairy geniuses.

Where the hell did they go? Did they pack up and leave, hitch a ride with aliens while we were too busy watching reruns and scrolling our lives away?

Maybe they're up in heaven, kicking back with the Nephilim, trading stories about the old days—how they punched grizzly bears and walked barefoot across glaciers like it was a Sunday stroll.

Bet they're laughing at us, thinking we've got it all figured out—while they sit on some cosmic throne, smart as hell, not a single caveman grunt between them.

180
A Mess of Brokenness

My pain splits me open, cracks in the soul—like an old, busted pot leaking out everything I thought I was. I stumble around, all jagged edges, but then it comes—God's love.

Not gentle, not soft, but a flood, rushing in, filling the cracks, patching the holes. I'm still shattered, still walking with pieces missing, but healed somehow. Like a scar you wear with pride, I'm connected to the One who holds me together.

He holds the doors of heaven open, lets me peek inside, soothes this burning body with holy water, cool and fierce. I keep walking—a mess of brokenness and Divine Grace—knowing He's there with each fragile, unfinished step.

181
Stubborn Hope

Pain's a punchline, always there, like your dumb cousin at the bar, spilling your drink while you're just trying to sit and breathe for a minute.

But there's hope too. It crawls in through the cracks, like sunlight leaking under the door—not flashy, not loud, just there, persistent, whispering, get up, keep going.

You don't ask for it, don't even believe it sometimes. But hope's a stubborn bastard, refusing to leave you alone.

And in that hope, there's love. Not the Hallmark kind, not roses and violins, but the kind that shows up with scraped knuckles and dirty boots, saying, I'm here. Let's make this work.

It doesn't solve anything, doesn't erase the pain. But it holds you up when everything else is falling apart.

182
Trembling Before It

Intimacy always carries the sense of something hidden, a breath held just beneath the surface, a seed split open in the dark. What we feel is not the touch—but the trembling before it.

The sky moves without hurry; a bird glides in silence. The water mirrors neither. It does not need to. There is wisdom in what remains unseen, the ripples too subtle to notice.

Sit by the tree long enough, and you will hear it hum. Place your hand on the stone; its patience will teach you stillness. We meet the world as strangers but leave it as kin.

The unseen beckons. What is hidden blooms. This moment, this breath, is enough.

183
Like a Shirt Drenched in Sweat

Like a shirt drenched in sweat, anguish sticks, clings to your skin, doesn't let go.

Every damn breath tastes like metal, like hot molten blood, and you're pulling air from somewhere deep—some pit of sadness you didn't even know you had.

But beneath it, beneath all that torn muscle and raw nerve, there's something. Small. Thin as a thread, delicate as a spider's web, catching the light, a whisper you can't quite hear but know is there.

You hold on because what else can you do?

Life's always waiting to kick your teeth in, but, just maybe, there's a way out—something in that thin thread that won't let you sink completely.

And all the while, you keep breathing in all that metal, because the thread isn't ready to break.

184
Sky Unfolds

The mountain bows—not in defeat, but in knowing its place, its power etched in stillness, its majesty found in surrender.

A leaf falls, and in its descent, there is grace. No resistance, only the quiet acceptance of gravity's call.

To carry another's burden is to carry your own. In the quiet pain, a door creaks open—not to answers, but to silence, a vast, unbroken stillness that holds it all.

In each face, the Divine breathes. In each tear, the self dissolves, melting into something greater than the sum of its fears.

Humility whispers, you are not separate. In suffering, in the breaking, the whole sky unfolds—a canvas of stars, a truth too vast for words to hold.

185
The Shadow's Whisper

There is a door in the forest of your mind—half-hidden beneath the overgrowth of years you pretend never happened. You stand before it, hesitating, because you know what's behind it. The shadow that bears your name but walks with a different stride. You've seen it in dreams—the stranger with your face who loves what you fear and fears what you long for. You shut your eyes, but the door pulses like a heartbeat.

Jung said: *Until you make the unconscious conscious, it will direct your life and you will call it fate.* But how do you speak to the wild animal inside yourself without trembling? How do you greet the chaos you've spent your life avoiding? The path inward is lit with flickering lanterns—some held by angels, others by ghosts. But both call your name with the same tenderness.

Your shadow isn't your enemy. It is the part of you exiled for being too strange, too broken, too real. Integration is not the triumph of light over darkness—it is the embrace between them. To own your shadow is to reclaim the parts of yourself you once buried out of shame. And when you finally step through that door, you won't find a monster. You'll find a quiet child, sitting alone, waiting for you to come home.

186
Rush Hour Apocalypse

Breath mints scattered on the subway floor, a big green cabbage rolling down the aisle. One kid bleeding from the nose, the other sucking his finger, like he's trying to taste the fight.

The old ladies scream, scrambling for the doors, while an old man shits himself, just sits there, eyes glazed over, waiting for the next disaster like it's already late.

Where's the cops? You'd think you'd see one, but no—here comes a flying eggplant, or maybe it's a turnip. Who the hell knows anymore?

Jay Street stop. Everyone bolts, fast as they can, like they're trying to outrun the stink that's settled in—burning rubber, hot tar, the screech of the wheels ripping through your skull.

On the platform, an old knish rots in the corner, next to a half-eaten hot dog draped in limp sauerkraut, like some sad culinary crime scene.

It's 3 p.m., school's out, and this is the ride home—a symphony of chaos, a masterpiece of the mundane.

187
Lament of Lazarus

Jesus, you've come to the tomb to crack it open, to peel away this body of death, but here I am, in front of my family, in rags, stinking, skin like old cloth, only days from the grave, and what now, Lord?

They stare at me— my sisters, my friends— with eyes that dart like birds. Even they look like I should've stayed beneath that rock, like I've dragged the dirt of death back with me, still smeared in grave dust, still heavy with the weight of life that crushed me and laid me down.

You've pulled me from the dark, Jesus, but where do I go? What do I do now? Will I be a footnote, a name whispered, a trophy for your victory, a Lazarus pulled up to prove a point, or will my story live beyond these crumbling walls?

I am Lazarus, the poor, the one who was left, forgotten, and now they look at me like death itself, like I've brought back ghosts to their table. I've climbed out, yes, but I'm marked, Lord, every bone remembers the cold, the silence, the weight of days in the dark.

What am I now? Point me somewhere, Jesus. Turn me toward light, to something that doesn't ache with every step.

Only you, Lord, can raise the dead and give breath to those who've crossed into shadows, only you can lift the eyes of a man four days gone, who's seen things he'll never unsee.

188
Tuna and Bad Luck

Two girls on a bench, tuna salad stinking up the air, cheap perfume mixing with the sweat of the city.

A big ugly guy, beard like a dirty mop, gives them the eye—the kind that sticks, clinging like gum to the sole of a shoe.

They don't flinch, just sit there, like he's nobody, like he's Farmer Gray from New Jersey, the kind of man you walk past and forget before he's even out of sight.

He lingers, scratches his belly, but they don't bite. They're too busy laughing, shoving chips into their mouths, tuna still dripping from the sandwich, like nothing else matters.

The guy spits on the sidewalk, wanders off. But the stink of him hangs in the air—like bad luck, like the day itself was just waiting for something worse to happen.

189
Scatter Kindness Like Seeds

With open hearts and willing spirits, we embrace a vision both ancient and new, rooted in the timeless Gospel of Compassion, yet ever evolving to meet the challenges of today.

The wildflowers do not wait for permission to bloom, nor does the rain ask the earth for a place to fall. We live within a song that was sung before we had names, and long after we are dust, its echoes thread through the bones of our becoming—mercy unfurls where our fears once stood guard.

Who tends the quiet fires of our restless yearning? Who whispers that peace can be a storm's afterthought? Not certainty, but faith—that tender, wavering flame—calls us to scatter kindness like seeds across the bitter soil of despair.

And so, with feet muddied by the path, with hearts broken open like rivers after the flood, we stumble, we rise, we become. This is how the story turns from shadow to light—one grace-fed breath at a time.

190
The Hollow Becomes the Flame

We walk alone sometimes—not because we are abandoned, but because the world cannot follow where the soul must go. Loneliness becomes a vessel, an empty sack we carry until it fills with something unexpected. The desert in our hearts whispers truths that cities drown out. In the silence, love sharpens its wings.

There is a darkness that belongs to God—a shadow thick with grace. We turn toward it, trembling, only to find it holy. The absence we feared is a presence we couldn't name. It presses against us like the wind before the dawn, unseen but undeniable.

The mind's desert is vast, yet somewhere within it, a spring begins to rise. Love has never abandoned its post—it waits in the quiet of our yearning. And when we search the dark with unflinching eyes, we often find the light we could not imagine, shining back like the first star on a moonless night.

Open the hollow places. Open them wide. What you thought was barren will bloom. What you thought was lost will return. The heart, cracked open, becomes a lantern—not in spite of its wounds, but because of them. And love, the true love that belongs to God, will fill every shadow with fire.

191
Broken Shells

So many broken people—like a dozen eggs hurled out of a 737 at twenty thousand feet, scrambled before they hit the ground.

The cracks run deep, shells busted wide open, yolks dripping down the sides of dreams they never had the chance to live.

We walk around in the mess, pretending the pieces don't stick. But they do—under our shoes, in our hair, the stink of broken lives clinging to us like old grease.

You look at them, look at yourself, and some days, it's hard to tell the difference. All of us scattered, smashed, waiting for some hand to clean us up or for gravity to finally finish the job.

But there's no cleaning this up, no putting it back together—just a slow slide from one cracked shell to the next.

192
Change is a Wild Animal

Grasping at it—it slips through like smoke, a thing too quick, too untamed to hold.

Change is a wild animal, not the kind you can tame with soft words or a leash. It snarls, it pulls, dragging you, kicking and cursing, through the mud and the mess, leaving you gasping, clinging to what little grip you have.

No sense in fighting it, no sense in trying to steer. It doesn't give a damn about your plans, your little schemes, the stories you tell yourself to keep things neat.

It just flows—relentless as hell. And you? You're stuck in the current, whether you like it or not.

193
Quiet Hum in the Storm

In the middle of the storm, when everything spins, cracks wide open, and the world stumbles, drunk on its own madness, I toss fear aside—not with grace, but like an old cigarette butt, flicked carelessly into the gutter, its ember snuffed by the rain.

God—yeah, maybe—a compass, a guide, something steady when I'm not. But I can't see it, can't hold it, can't name it. It's just there, a pulse beneath the chaos, a thread running through the dark.

Not loud, not demanding, but steady—a whisper I feel when the wind stops howling long enough. No sermons, no damn choir to drown me out. Just the quiet hum inside, the thing that doesn't quit, doesn't leave, even when I've got nothing left.

It keeps me moving, keeps me standing, while everything else falls. The storm doesn't ask for permission, it just comes, tearing through the weak places, testing the walls you thought would hold.

And God? God doesn't stop the storm, doesn't calm every wave. Sometimes, He just keeps you upright in it.

I don't need the thunder of angels, or a voice booming from the clouds. I need this—this quiet hum, this invisible anchor that keeps me from blowing away.

It's not about answers, not about rescue. It's about presence—about something that stays when nothing else will.

The storm rages, the world cracks, and sways, but the hum remains. A soundless song, a lifeline in the wind, a hand I can't see but know is there.

And somehow, that's enough.

194
Grace in the Dirt

In the end, we realize God's judgment isn't some hammer coming down, crushing us to dust.

It's more like a hand, outstretched, a quiet voice saying, you're not finished yet.

Not a damnation, but a chance—a second shot at this mess we call life. An invitation to change, to look in the mirror and see the cracks, the scars, and not turn away.

To embrace it all—the busted parts, the missteps, the nights you spent drowning in your own regrets.

It's all human. It's all part of the deal.

And forgiveness? It's not a free pass, but a slow walk down a road where you stumble, pick yourself up, stumble again. But with each step, there's grace in the dirt, humility in the fall.

In the end, it's not about being perfect. It's about facing the mess head-on and knowing that even in the wreckage, there's something worth saving.

195
Confession

Terrified. The confessional. Sister Agnes tapped my shoulder, like a countdown to a firing squad—three, two, one.

The moment had come, and I wasn't ready. I did my best to hold it—hold the breath, the guilt, the fear, everything pressed tight inside my chest, like it might explode.

The corridor stretched on, longer than it ever had before, lined with those old, stately pictures—peering popes with eyes that followed, watching me shuffle forward, a lamb on its way to slaughter.

Each step echoed louder, sharper, closer. To meet my Maker? No. To meet Monsignor Malone—the judge, the gatekeeper, the voice on the other side of a small sliding window.

I entered. My knees creaked on the wood; the smell of incense thick in the air—a choking fog that might drown me before I could confess a damn thing.

Silence. Then a rustle. The window slid open. My words tangled in my throat, caught there, as if they knew—I'd never say enough to be forgiven.

196
The Thread That Binds

In the dance of transformation, we find the essence of true faith, a harmonious blend of intellect and emotion, spirit and action intertwined, the essence of The Christ.

Drawing from diverse traditions, we weave a tapestry of belief, where evangelical fervor meets charismatic fire and ecumenical spirit embraces all.

Yet in this mosaic of faith, we find a common thread, a shared commitment to transformation in ourselves and in the world around us.

It is not about theological precision or political allegiance, but about the power of love to heal, to redeem, to restore.

In the radical middle, where theology meets practice, we discover the heart of Christianity, manifesting God's kingdom on earth.

Let us walk this path together, with open minds and open hearts, transforming ourselves and our world, in the light of Divine grace.

197
Filling the Cracks

Let's face the truth—the media spins its weary songs, and every morning, a baby cries.

Jesus is born again, wrapped in yesterday's newsprint, the world's heavy breath pressing down like smog.

Jesus walks to the Cross, carries the weight of a thousand sins—the broken bottles, the lost dreams, a parade of souls too weary to care, marching through the alleyways of despair.

Jesus is crucified every day—on the tongues of the angry, in the silence of the ignored, a crown of thorns woven from the harsh words of strangers, the indifference of friends.

Yet somehow, in the darkest hour—Jesus resurrects, is transformed.

He fills the cracks with light, a laugh echoing in the back of a bar, hope rising like the smoke from a cigarette, daring us to breathe deep.

And Jesus returns every day—in the laughter of children, in the hands that help the fallen, in the hearts that refuse to quit. He reminds us, amidst the chaos and the clatter, that love—that stubborn, reckless love—is the pulse beneath our skin, the promise whispered in the dark.

198
Winter, That Old Bastard

Winter, that old bastard, comes without warning—his breath a sharp slap, cutting through the layers I thought would keep me safe.

He's got no mercy, no patience for the weak. His fingers claw at my bones, digging in deep, reminding me how soft I've become.

The sun is a distant joke, a memory I can't quite hold, and warmth—just a fleeting ghost, laughing as it slips away, mocking me in its absence.

Comfort is a lie, told in the flicker of firelight. But winter knows better. He strips it all down, leaves me raw, shivering in the truth that no one is spared, not from him.

Winter, that old bastard, grins through the howling wind, and I take a bite of bitter chocolate like that's going to save me.

199
Fast Food God

God sitting at a fast-food joint eating a juicy burger—grease dripping down her fingers. And I'm standing there, hungry as hell, watching her chew, slow, deliberate.

She looks up, catches my stare. She doesn't say a word, just slides the tray over. Take a bite, she says, like she's offering me the universe between two sesame seed buns. I stare at the pickle.

And I take it—no hesitation. Because when God offers you a burger, you don't ask questions. You just bite in, taste the salt, the pickle too, the cheap ketchup, the limp lettuce. And for a second, everything makes sense.

It's all there in that first bite—the start, the end, life crawling out of the muck and back into it, round, and round, like the fries in the fryer, sizzling, burning, going cold.

What's the point? I asked her, mouth full of greasy beef. She shrugs, wipes her lips with a napkin. Who says there has to be one?

The truth is, life starts small—a cell, a spark, a flicker. Then it grows, crawls, climbs, builds cities, writes poems, blows itself to hell, then it starts again.

God laughs, bites into her burger. Intelligence? she says, it's overrated. We're all just waiting for the reset, waiting for the fries to cool, for the earth to burn up, for the stars to go out.

But until then, we're here, eating cold fries at McDonald's or Wendy's, staring at the pickle, sipping on sodas gone flat, wondering when the next bite comes and if it even matters.

God doesn't care. She just chews, wipes her mouth, hands me what's left of the burger. It's all yours, she says, until it's not.

And I sit there, silent, greasy, chewing on the universe.

200
Spirit and Soul

The spirit—it comes like smoke, slipping through cracks, the way a drunk stumbles out the back door of some sad bar, hands shaking like broken glass.

They say it's part of the soul, like your breath's part of the wind, like a dog's howl is part of the night. But hell, it feels like something else—something lighter, something always ready to slip away.

Sometimes they swear the soul is the big thing, the body of the ship, and the spirit just the sail, moving but never still, the thing that takes you somewhere—or nowhere at all.

But, just maybe, they're both parts of the same mess—the spirit and the soul, two thieves in the same getaway car, just trying to outrun the end in their own way.

And who am I to say where one ends and the other begins? I've got enough trouble keeping my feet on the ground while my head floats somewhere in between.

201
Wild Thing

Deep down, where the whisky burns slowly and the smoke curls up lazy, there's a hunger—not for the next drink or another warm body, but for something real, something raw, something that cuts right through.

They'll tell you it's the spirit, that thing we keep chasing like a dog after its own tail. But it's not out there—not in some church, some priest's words, or some book. No, it's buried in us, waiting, aching to crack open, to spill out into the dirty light of this busted-up world.

You can feel it, can't you? That pull, that call, like the night calling the day to come forward, to be real—to live like you mean it. No middlemen, no steps in between. Just you and the raw, damn truth of what you are and what you've been hiding.

It's there, deep in the bones, waiting for you to stop running, to dig deep and pull it out. That Divine thing, that wild thing, that's been sitting in the shadows for too long.

202
Where Nothing Else Fits

Stop chasing shadows. Stop filling the void with junk. Turn inward, to the place where it all starts, where the cracks hold the truth, and the noise finally dies.

Sit with the mess—the raw and the ugly. Feel the weight of it all without running, without hiding.

Listen closely. It's there in the silence—the stories you've missed, the details that matter, the life you've been drowning beneath all that junk.

Strip it down. Let it bleed, let it breathe—real, raw, and true. That's where you find yourself, in the quiet, where nothing else fits.

203
Hand of God

The hand of God reaches down, touches the faces of a million starving peasants. Cracked lips whisper prayers to a sky that never answers.

Their bellies rumble, like distant thunder, as the hand of God moves slow—too slow—while the world spins on, indifferent, cold.

They wait in the dirt, eyes hollow as empty bowls. The hand touches but does not feed, and they still bleed, still cry, still beg for a crumb that never comes.

The yolk is broken. God's hand lingers, but the hunger remains.

204
Pour the Light

In spite of the pain, in spite of the injustice, the darkness, the suffering—pour the light in. Pour it like cool water on a parched throat, pour it until it soothes, until it sinks deep, calming the places that never stop burning.

Into all things—every crack, every scar, every wound. The light of God, the universal Christ, filling up what's been emptied, what's been scorched. Softening the jagged edges of what's been broken because everything's broken in its own way.

Change comes like a storm, blowing through when you're not ready. It stirs in the air, an evil wind pulling at what you thought was yours. And here we stand, hands full of nothing, not knowing what to hold onto, not knowing what to let go.

So, pour the light in. The only thing we've got that works. Pour it like it's our last drink. Pour it until the world starts to glow.

Until the clouds finally lift, until all the dirt and grime don't seem so heavy anymore. Because love—love always wins its own dirty war.

205

Laugh of the Quantum Gods

The dice are loaded—nothing's left to chance. Every flip, every roll, every spark, scripted in the stars, hidden in the quarks, tucked in Planck's pocket long before you blink before you breathe.

The quantum gods laugh at your free will, your chaos theories, your universal theologies.

The bell rings, but it's a sound you'll never hear. It's all been whispered into the void before you had ears to listen.

Deterministic as the drone of a tired heart in a room you've never left, the future is sewn into the past. And every door you never opened was locked from the start.

Superdeterminism, they call it—like fate got drunk and spilled its guts. Nothing random, just a fixed game you thought you were playing.

But no matter how loud you shout, there's no moving the pieces. They've already moved. And all you've got left is to watch the universe unfold, like a rerun that never ends.

206

Chorus Blooms

Broken curses, mixed metaphors—top-of-the-line chorus girls blooming in full fragrance on city streets, their petals brushing grime, their beauty defiant in the dirt, in taverns behind the gas station, under rocks where the rats find shelter.

They're looking for solace, something soft in the brick walls, a sliver of grace between the neon flicker and the bartender's last laugh.

But it's all dust, and spit, and forgotten dreams.

Yet still, the chorus blooms again, pushing through the cracks of it all.

207
In the Stillness between Breaths

In the quiet places where rivers hum their secrets to the stones, We remember: "In Him we live and move and have our being." Not as a whisper from the sky, but as the pulse in our veins, the shiver of leaves when the wind stops pretending to be gentle.

We are small beneath the great weight of stars! Still, He is here immanent as breath, a flicker in the shadows we thought were empty. And yet, beyond the veil of all we can name, God hums a song galaxies cannot contain.

To say He is within and without is to speak of oceans while holding a single drop. But even this drop, glistening, trembling, knows the hymn of the sea that birthed it.

We walk through the world as wanderers between the immanence of now and the transcendence of forever. The Holy Spirit moves not above, not below—but through, ever through—the broken earth, the blooming rose, the fragile ache of every beating heart.

And somewhere, in the stillness between breaths, the infinite bends low and calls us beloved.

208
The Hour of Stillness

A sip of red wine—its warmth unfurls slowly, like a distant memory returning to settle in the mouth of the present. The glass holds the light, fragile as a vow not spoken. I wanted to pray, but silence came first.

The words waited at the edge of the tongue, then dissolved, as if the divine preferred the emptiness to the clamor of requests.

In the quiet, the world rearranges itself: the bare tree outside becomes a hymn to endurance, its branches etched against the sky like the ribs of something hollow, waiting to be filled.

And I—I become less solid, the taste of rebirth mingling with the bitterness, the sweetness. The hour is sacred because it passes.

209
Where the Current Leads

The river carries me forward, its song both wild and familiar. I lean in to listen, though the words shift and scatter, like leaves caught in wind-swirl patterns.

I asked for stillness once, but even the quiet is in motion. The sky shifts, the shadows wander. I sought a place to rest, but the resting place was never meant to stay.

Change flows as if knowing no destination, yet there is a pulse beneath the rush— a steady hum of something greater than drift or fall. What slips free may not be lost. What is carried away may be held in ways unseen.

So, I breathe with the current's rhythm, unfold my fingers, let the waves speak their mystery. Where it leads, I may not know— but in surrender, I sense the unbroken thread woven into chaos, running through the stream.

To drift is not to be forgotten. To be carried is not to disappear. The water sings to remind me— there is grace in being set free.

210
Foolishness of the Cross

The message of the cross is foolish—Paul said it first. What's grace got to do with the blood on the floor, with the streets filled with half-broken people crawling through their days?

Self-sacrifice, forgiveness, turn the other cheek—while the world burns and the rich laugh. Sounds insane, right?

God becomes a man, dies for the worst of us, rises like a myth we can't shake off.

They call it hope, but it's a mystery you can't swallow whole.

The mind screams for reason, but there's love in the cracks—love that doesn't make sense but holds you tight anyway. It's absurd, but it's real, when you stop trying to understand.

211
Ache of Dusk

Old gray hands folded, light dances on the water. Two birds on a branch, silent beneath a dim sky, no moon to guide them home.

The air hangs heavy, weighted with unspoken words, as twilight creeps in like a thief in the night, stealing time and leaving only shadows.

Time slips through fingers, while the shadows stretch and yawn. The world keeps spinning, but here, it's just stillness, a moment suspended.

Between what was and what might never be, lost in the quiet, adrift in the soft unraveling of the day.

The old know this dance—the aching beauty of dusk, waiting for a dawn that may never come.

212
Stranded

Stranded on a sandbar, sky too far to touch, arms outstretched like some madman reaching for something he can't even name.

The ocean beats like a heart, but not mine. It's bigger, older, pulsing thick and slow, dragging me along with it. My blood's turned to salt, my skin to sand, drifting away grain by grain every time the tide pulls back.

I've been here forever, caught in the middle of things—not ocean, not quite land, just stuck. The waves crash, the winds die, everything stops, then it starts again, like some cruel joke.

Nothing belongs to me anymore. Not the sea, not the sky, not even my own breath. But I've learned to live with it, learned to let the empty wrap around me like an old coat, familiar, worn, full of holes.

There's a strange peace here, in the stillness, when the world lets you go and you stop wanting, stop fighting. It's not happiness, but it's enough.

The sea keeps calling, but I don't answer. The wind tries to push me, but I don't move. I just stand there—salt in my veins, dust on my skin, waiting for nothing.

213
The Night's Slow Reckoning

With each passing night, the dark takes its share. We lie awake, thoughts slipping through the cracks like water through a broken jar. Sleeplessness is a thief, but its hand is gentle—it steals yet leaves behind something we cannot name.

Stripped bare, we confront what remains: truth, raw and unsparing, laid open like a wound. We press against it, hoping for numbness, but the ache persists, as if it knows we cannot be whole without it.

In the silence, the pieces of ourselves scatter across the floor. We pick them up, one by one, turning them over, searching for what fits and what does not. Torn but tender, we weave together what the night has unraveled.

The sky lightens—not suddenly, but slowly, as if to give us time to prepare for what's next. We rise, patched and imperfect, fragile but somehow unbroken.

The wounds, though tender, glow with the faintest warmth—a quiet promise that even pain has purpose.

And there, in the first light, a voice speaks—not loud, but steady as the dawn itself: "You are more than the pieces, more than the breaking. I am the thread that binds you, the hand that holds you whole."

We step forward, the night behind us, its lessons etched in shadow. What we lost, what we found—all of it carried, all of it blessed.

214
Weight of the Empty Chair

Real grief is the weight of the empty chair, the silence that fills the room with ghosts of laughter, a hollowness too loud to ignore.

When love slips through fingers, like smoke in the dark, let it break us—piece by fragile piece—shattering the illusions we once held so tightly.

The endless love that promised forever cracks open, and we bleed. Each drop is a reminder that nothing eternal can stay untouched by pain.

If we cling to the illusion of unbroken hearts, we drift—hollow shells caught in a current that leads nowhere.

Compassion wanes as the real fades, and the artificial glimmers, bright but cold, never warming the soul.

To feel the loss is to feel alive. To allow the ache to carve out space is to make room for truth—a raw, unyielding light that only grief can bring.

215
Quiet Song of Creation

In the beginning, God spoke into silence, and the formless became form.

Light separated from darkness, day from night, order from chaos—and it was good.

The sky stretched above, the waters gathered below, the earth rose to meet them, a dance of elements—and it was good.

The land brought forth life: trees, plants, seeds waiting in their time. The earth grew green with promise, vibrant, abundant—and it was good.

The sun ruled the day, its golden reign unchallenged. The moon kept watch at night, a quiet sentinel. Stars marked the rhythm of time, their flickering light eternal—and it was good.

The waters teemed with life, a chaos of motion and breath. Birds soared across the sky, their wings carving paths of wonder—and it was good.

The beasts walked the land, wild and free, each according to its kind, fierce and untamed—and it was good.

Then God breathed, and humankind stood. In the image of the Creator, male and female, called to live, to care, to be.

The world in its fullness—God saw, and it was very good. x Evening turned to morning, and creation sang its quiet song.

216
Whispers in the Ruins

The city may be broken, its streets crumbling like old prayers, forgotten in the wind. Its people wander, lost in the maze of their own longing, searching for meaning in shattered glass and fading neon lights.

But I walk among them with purpose, my feet firm on the ground of hope, my heart a vessel carrying belief that in every crack, every shadow, there is a seed of grace, a promise whispered through the dust.

Something more, something holy, calls from the depths of the unseen. In the ruins of despair, there lies the shape of redemption—not yet formed, but real, waiting to rise from the ash and breathe again.

217
Grace is a Troublemaker

He came back from the desert, sunburnt and empty-eyed, but full of something more. Walked straight into the synagogue, dust in his hair, cracks in his voice.

Takes the scroll like it's his birthright—or a dare—starts reading Isaiah like he means it. Good News for the poor, freedom for the caged, sight for the blind.

He read those words like a bartender, pouring sweet bourbon—no flourish, no trick, just a hard truth that stings your throat.

They sat there silent at first, like gamblers who knew the house always wins.

Then came the murmurs: Who the hell does he think he is? Joseph's boy, the carpenter's son. Get him out. Shut him up.

They dragged him out, tossed him toward the cliff—not for the blasphemy, no, but because he pulled the curtain back and showed them their own dirty laundry, hanging like condemned men.

They couldn't stand it, this messiah with rough hands, no fancy robes, or gold-threaded words—just promises for the broken, no salvation for the righteous.

And isn't that the way? They still do it. Open doors but slam hearts shut.

Preach grace from the pulpit but lace it with stones.

Good News is always a scandal. Churches like their messiahs clean, without calluses or scars. They want God in neat packages—without the sweat, without the blood.

But Jesus, He read the Good News like a punch to the gut—for the poor, the blind, the lost. And they threw him out, because grace is a troublemaker that doesn't leave anyone standing where they started.

218
God's Back Alley

Jesus, I'm crawling through this alley of busted stars, gravel biting my knees like tiny judgments, looking for your love in the cracks of the sidewalk, in the graffiti scrawled by the madman's hand.

The road twists, bends, curves—like the spine of a dead dream—down into the gutters of my soul, where shadows play games with the light, and the rats wear halos of cigarette smoke.

Jesus, I thought I'd find you in the holy hymns of saints, not in the sour breath of alleys. But here I am, on my belly, sniffing around for a scrap of your grace, while empty bottles roll like broken commandments, clinking a hymn that only the lonely understand.

I thought love would glow like neon promises, but it's more like a rusted streetlamp—flickering on and off, leaving me blind, then not blind, leaving me guessing at what's real.

This alley's full of ghosts, and my hands dig through trash piles of regrets, sifting through what's left of hope. But even in the stink and sweat of this dead-end world, something glimmers, something soft and broken—you, or just the last echo of a bruised wish.

Jesus, if you're hiding here, show me your face—behind dumpsters of despair, beneath the discarded sermons, where pain and laughter blur into something almost human.

I keep crawling, keep scraping—through dirt, shadow, and light—because what else is there but the search, the crawl, the endless reach for the small, soft hands of your love, buried somewhere in this alley.

219
The Furnace and the Flame

Suffering comes in the quiet moments, when the world leans heavy on your chest, and the sky splits, not with light, but with the dark ache of being alive. You curse it, you fight it, but it doesn't leave. It sits with you like an old friend you never wanted to call.

They say it refines you—that's what the preacher said, anyway, but what does he know of the furnace? Of fire licking at your edges, burning away the pieces you thought were you. Still, you sit in the heat, and, just maybe, you see the shape of something new.

There's grace in the breaking, though it doesn't feel holy. It feels like blood on your hands and salt in your wounds. But grace is stubborn. It finds you in the gutter, pulls you to your knees, and whispers, "This is not the end."

And you think about Him—the wood, the nails, the weight of it all. How He bore it, not because He had to, but because love always chooses to stay. You wonder if the cross wasn't just a symbol but a mirror. x You rise, patched and imperfect, not lighter, but stronger. The scars burn, but they teach. And in the distance, you see the faint glow of hope, not loud or blinding, but steady, like a flame that cannot die.

220
Seeking God

Crawling through alleys, searching for love in dark, reeking corners of myself.

Each breath a question, each sigh a prayer to nowhere—a flare lost in the night.

The road twists deeper, gutters of my soul spilling where griefs cling like leeches.

Shadows spar with light—silent, mocking sentinels. My spirit bows low.

I thought I'd find you in morning's bright, dew-washed fields, but you hide in dust.

Forgotten dreams creep, whispering through empty streets, hope clutching its chains.

Here light weds shadow, a marriage of brokenness, believing it heals.

In this darkened place, I trace the shape of absence—a blind man groping.

I know you are near—not a blaze, but the ember glowing in despair.

Not thunder or light, just a whisper in the wound—the knife's soft echo. x If I hold this space, where soul meets shadow and gasps, I might find your love—

Cradling my heart at the altar of ruins, where loss meets Divine.

221
Whisper in the Dark

In despair, we turn—grasping for that quiet thread, a frail tether to hope.

Grant us stillness now—not to endure, but to feel the weight of your silence.

You are here, they say, always near, yet unseen, hiding like the wind.

Where is courage found? In the heart of suffering? Or in the brittle lie that shadows always break to light?

We lean into silence, not for answers but escape, cradled by wordless truths that leave us empty.

Grant us the grace to rise—not above despair, but through it, dragging its chains.

A flame, yes—small, flickering, barely touching the darkness, its light swallowed whole.

Use us as peace? As love unending. No, like shattered mirrors, reflecting only fragments of the broken.

In the space where darkness shatters, where life and death collide—do we rest, or do we break?

222
The Secret Written

It is not in the temples, not in the creeds carved on stone or paper. No, it's deeper—a place we are afraid to look.

We are so busy building towers of words, stacking doctrine upon doctrine, reaching for the sky, that we forget the ground beneath us is holy.

You and I, we carry it already—this truth, this quiet, flowing thing. It whispers when we weep, it hums when we hold another's trembling hand.

Harmony will never come from agreeing on the shape of God. It will come when we see that the divine is shaped like each of us, woven into the soft breath of every living soul.

Speak to me from that place within you, the one where no lies live, where your heart beats raw and real. I will answer with mine.

Together, we might hear the song we've been chasing, the one written on the walls of our hearts before we even had words.

And then, finally, we will be whole.

223
Mile by Mile

Taylor's been driving—two decades of white lines stretched taut, the road a home and a cage, depending on the day.

Tonight, it's quiet. The hum of the engine beats steady as a pulse, and sermons crackle on an old radio. Jesus's voice, caught in static, whispers of love and justice, compassion stitched to broken airwaves.

Jesus kept it simple. But simplicity unraveled outside the glass. Billboards shouted above broken homes. Luxury cars flashed by, while men with cardboard signs stood still, silent mile markers of something gone wrong.

"Help the poor," Jesus said. Taylor saw poverty coast to coast—ghost towns of industry, factories yawning like graves, their workers scattered like autumn leaves. The preacher's voice spoke of a kingdom—radical, new, alive. Taylor squinted into the night, wondering if anyone else saw the same cracks in the asphalt.

"Empower women," they'd say, but always as a footnote, fleeting as an exit sign at 70 miles per hour. Taylor thought of Jenna—bright, fierce, aflame with dreams. Would the world stifle her fire or let it burn?

"Open your table," Jesus said. Taylor tried. He shared meals at truck stops, rides with hitchhikers, coffee with the weary stories spilled out like loose gravel. He welcomed, even when he felt unwelcome himself.

"Turn the other cheek." Hard words on asphalt. Anger was always a lane change away, but Taylor's hand stayed open, not clenched. He waved off the honks, let go of the slights. It wasn't weakness—it was strength, a freedom the clenched fists never knew.

"Don't be greedy." Taylor lived simply. Apps and gizmos promised relief, but he saved for what mattered: calls home to Jenna, a Bible stuffed in his glove box, the stars stretched out above—faith painted across the heavens.

"Heal wounds." Taylor wasn't a miracle worker, but he listened. A shared laugh, a lightened load—sometimes that was all someone needed. x Tonight, the stars burned bright, each mile soaked in their glow. Jesus's words weren't answers; they were directions, a way to steer through the dark.

Mile by mile, Taylor drove, not lost, but on the Way. Faith lived not in cathedrals but in sandwiches split at truck stops, in prayers whispered on the shoulder of the road. Out on that endless highway, Taylor carried the Gospel—not preached but lived.

224
The Becoming of All Things

We are not stones etched with commandments, but rivers—changing, winding, restless. Each sunrise pulls us further along, each failure carves something deeper within. Is this not the grace of becoming? To know that we are not yet complete, and neither is the world that breaks us.

We ache for permanence—a shelter against the storm of our doubts, yet God whispers not of walls, but of winds that teach us to bend. In every sorrow, every joy, He moves like a poet rewriting verses in real time—
Not distant, not still, but near and wild.

We are not puppets pulled by divine strings, nor are we aimless wanderers left to chance. We are co-creators of the sacred story, our choices stitching new patterns into the vast quilt of eternity. God leans close to our weary hearts, saying, "Let's make something beautiful from this mess."

If becoming is messy, let it be holy. If transformation takes time, let it be tender. The stars above may seem fixed, but we know the truth: Even the cosmos sways to an unseen rhythm.

So let us stumble forward, arms outstretched like children chasing fireflies. Let us weep when the journey wounds us and rejoice when the light finds us again. In this process—this wild unfolding— We are not alone, and perhaps that is the greatest miracle of all.

225
Quiet Tide

Kyle lived by the bay, a small-town man on Maryland's coast. Chesapeake whispers rolled softly; the sky wide, clear, too silent to trust.

Each morning, the sun creeping in, he'd shove his battered boat into the shallow waters. Bruised hands gripped rough wood; his eyes, lined and watchful, scanned the sea like a hunter.

Not one for words, his face held the stories—tides rising, falling, of oysters pulled, dreams sinking. Every wrinkle etched in saltwater ink.

To him, the water was more than a trade, more than a meal ticket. It was a mirror, vast and restless, its mysteries mocking his quiet soul.

His boat, beat to hell, splintered wood, frayed nets, seemed as tired as he was. Yet every dawn, he whispered a prayer—not for a bounty, but for strength to keep trying.

One morning, the tide whispered back, dawn ignited in flame-red fury. The air thick with some ancient hum, the sea's restless arms calling: Aspire, affirm, transform.

For a moment, he thought of Jesus—a fisher of men, walking on water, storms stilled with a word. And yet, irony—what fisherman catches hearts? What sea yields love?

Kyle cast his net, expecting nothing. And it came up as always: a starfish, a writhing crab, small fish gasping for air, their scales glinting like pieces of sky.

A modest haul by any measure. Yet his heart swelled—why? Gratitude bloomed for life's tangled mess: the gain and the loss, the joy wrapped in sorrow. Even failure, a hymn sung by the waves.

Sailing back to shore, his boat was heavier than it had ever been—not with fish, but with a strange and stubborn peace. On the water, in solitude, he found what had eluded him on land: every wave of a whisper, every gust a hymn, a call to love's endless redemption.

226
Primordial Truth

The truth never spoke the same language twice—not in the dusty tongues of prophets or the leather-bound growl of priests, not in the slick sermons of politicians or the metaphysical musings of old men in smoky coffee shops.

Hell, it never even knocked on your door. The primordial truth, that cracked, bleeding, raw-edged beast, would rather stay homeless than cozy up in some polished theology or clean white chapel.

It slips out in a stranger's laugh, in the way your mother looked when she thought you weren't watching. It crawls under your skin on nights when the wind rattles the windows and the dog barks at nothing.

Truth is a mute—part everything, part nothing, barking in a hundred accents. You never know if it's friendly or feral. We wanted truth to be neat, small enough to fit in our pockets, a universal all-access pass to God, to the stars, to ourselves. But truth—real truth—is the ache in your bones at thirty and again at fifty, different, but familiar.

It's the one word you can never translate, the smoke you try to catch with a net made of water. If truth had spoken the same idiom to everyone, we wouldn't have heard a thing. It'd be a song played at the wrong speed, a dance step you've never learned, or a garbled frequency on the radio in the desert, where every station is static.

That's why truth shatters itself—a million shards, each one stabbing us just enough to bleed. The mystic calls it an angel's voice. The scientist hears a

cosmic echo. The poet thinks it's the moon, spitting rhymes in the night. x
All of them right. All of them wrong.

It's the way your best friend dies young, and the sun rises the next day as if
nothing happened. It's the stray cat in the alleyway, surviving on scraps, but
never letting you get too close.

It's an idiom you can't quite grasp, words slipping into your coffee cup,
dissolving unnoticed. It's the hymn you hum without knowing the meaning,
the curses you shout when you realize the words are lost.

The primordial truth isn't a single voice; it's the scream in the hospital, the
laughter in the park, the way your lover sighs in their sleep, as if already
dreaming in another world. It's the bastard child of chaos and order, born into
a world that thinks in black and white, but dreams in color.

You'll never understand it. You'll only feel it brush past, like a ghost you
almost saw. It tangles itself into everything we don't quite know how to say,
or sing, or scream. The truth says everything, in every language, but ends up
saying nothing to everyone. It's the hum of a universe trying to talk to itself
when there's no one else around.

227
Neat Little Bottle of Truth

Stop trying to boil it down, some neat little bottle of truth that fits snug
on your shelf, like a dusty trophy no one remembers winning. Each one—
religions, philosophies, long-winded diatribes from people who swore they
saw God while washing the dishes or cursing their bad luck—all of them
splintered tongues, grabbing at clouds.

What you want is a single note from a song never sung, but it's always been
a symphony of mismatched instruments, out-of-tune players drunk on the
silence between the notes. Call it Absolute, if that makes you feel smart, but
don't dress it up in your little black words. Don't try to name it like some stray
dog you hope will come back.

Because the moment you call it One, you've already split it—knower and
known, observer and observed. You cut it in half just by looking too closely.
The Absolute slips right through—a ghost you almost saw, a shimmer at the
corner of your eye that fades when you turn. It's not about formlessness—
though that's part of it. It's that everything's a mask, trying to play dress-up,

trying to give the Uncarved Block some kind of shape so we can measure it and call it ours.

But shapes are lies, smoke rings in empty rooms. We keep cutting it up, dividing and subdividing, until we've got pieces we can pretend to understand. Look—it's not that it's indescribable because it's too vast. It's not like trying to cup the ocean with two small hands. It's because everything we say starts with this and that. Words are scissors, slicing through what they're meant to describe.

And what is, can't be cut. What is just is. There's no label for it, no pinning it down. It's like taking a knife to the wind and expecting to bleed.

Every verse in every holy book, every chant or whispered prayer, they're all just shadows tracing the outlines of something too bright to stare at head-on.

So, stop looking for a single thread that ties it all together, some common root from which all these tangled branches sprout. Because there isn't one. Every belief is just a reflection, a different cut of glass catching a sliver of light. But the light—the light's already broken into every color there is. And every color is still only half of something else.

Step back from it. Don't chase. Don't measure. Let it be what it is—unseen, unknown, ungraspable.

The Absolute has no preference for our need to understand it. We keep searching because we think that's what gives it shape. But the shape was always yours and mine, not its own. Put down the scissors. Let the silence speak for a while.

228
A Small Skinny Man

They found him curled up like an old leaf in an alley, next to a dumpster where no one looked twice. A small skinny man, the kind you forget is even there—until he isn't.

His ribs, sharp as broken glass, stuck out from a stained white shirt, a shirt that might have fit him twenty years ago. Time had whittled him down, bone by bone, until there was nothing left but edges.

Beside him, a half-empty pack of cigarettes—the last of his companions. And in his fist, a crumpled dollar bill, clutched like it still meant something. A miracle, a last bet at the racetrack.

No one knew his name, not even the liquor store guy who sold him cheap whiskey every Tuesday at 4 p.m. But once, he nodded at him—a silent exchange, a friendship forged in apathy, where words were just another burden.

His shoes, worn through, had soles like paper. Nothing was left to protect him from the concrete he walked every day, across a city that never cared if he made it to the next corner, let alone the next breath.

The paramedics came, zipping him into a bag like he was a problem to solve, a stain to scrub off the sidewalk. No one asked questions. No one paused. Just another quiet cleanup before the city moved on.

That's how it ends—no fanfare, no sob stories, no flowers laid gently in the gutter. Just a small skinny man, the kind you pass on the street without ever seeing.

He's gone now, and the alley stands empty. Even the wind, usually restless, can't be bothered to notice.

229
Chasing Smoke

They tell you nothing, babble, and nonsense advice about how to live. Words tumble out like marbles rolling off a crooked table—useless and lost.

No help from the morons. You're left to twist in the wind, arms flailing at shadows, grasping at words like smoke rings that vanish when you clutch tight.

You chase it—the truth, the meaning, until your shoes wear thin and your tongue's a dried-up leaf, cracked from shouting into empty rooms where only echoes answer.

And when you think you've got it—that shining thing, that final piece of it all—you scoop it up like sand only to watch it slip through every crack and crevice. All that's left is an empty bucket and a fistful of grit.

You stare at it, and you laugh—not because it's funny, but because you know the joke's on you. Hell, it's on all of us—digging up dirt, calling it gold, when there's nothing left but the wind and the sound of our own silent surrender.

230
Mad Men Wander Lost

Through streets paved with empty bottles and cigarette butts, mad men wander lost, where shadows stretch long like old regrets piled up at the corners.

They chase dreams that flicker like moths under dying streetlights, each step weighed down by all the chances they took and all the ones they missed.

You see them, leaning against brick walls, their hollowed-out eyes staring through time, their thin, trembling hands grasping at air, as if it might turn to gold if they just held on long enough.

They talk to ghosts no one else hears, arguing with echoes of voices that abandoned them long ago.

It's the fight that broke them—the grind against the world's edge, the way hope cuts deep then vanishes like a thief at dawn.

Now they stumble through alleys of what-might-have-been, each scar a line in a book no one wants to read, a story of trying and failing, of hunger and hurt, and the slow bleed of a soul when no one is left to see.

Mad men wander lost, picking at scraps of light in a city too dark to care. Still dreaming those impossible dreams, even as they fall apart, bit by bit, one last shadow against a world that's moved on.

231
No Sky

The world's a vile mess, like a bar at last call—spilled guts, empty glasses, and no one's leaving.

Too many cooks in the kitchen, all blind, burning the meat, chopping off fingers, blood seasoning the soup.

Rats gnaw through the trash, fat and bold, tails like needles piercing yesterday's paper. The headlines scream but say nothing, words as hollow as cans kicked down the street.

And there's no sky, just a lid clamped tight, a suffocating dome over this sorry pot.

Drink up. Choke it down. There's nothing else—just the rats, the filth, and that goddamn soup we're all still cooking.

232
Tyrants

They sit on thrones, with backs bent, spines brittle like promises made in war. Their laughter is a thin blade, cutting through the silence of the starving.

It echoes in marble halls, while children chew on the leather straps of history. They drink wine pressed from the blood of the meek, and wear crowns studded with the eyes of those who dared to look up.

Their words are bricks—each syllable another wall built to keep the world out, to keep themselves in. The air inside grows stale, but they call it sovereignty.

Once, they were men. Now, they are shadows, greedy fingers stretching across borders and graves. But even shadows eventually fade when the sun is brave enough to burn.

And the people—ah, the people—they learn to dance barefoot on the ruins of empires, to plant seeds in the ash of flags.

History never remembers the names of the tyrants. It only remembers the taste of freedom after they fall.

233
Even in Darkness

You clutch that stubborn hope, tight as a last cigarette, its ember trembling against the void.

Smoke curls upward—a fragile, flickering prayer rising, even as the rain falls.

"What a fool," they say, holding on when the world crumbles, its edges crinkling like burnt paper.

Still, you believe, in warmth that might return—a fool's dream, they scoff, but dreams are what build tomorrows.

Hell, why not hope? Even if it's just one match fighting the endless night.

The winds howl louder, tearing at the flame, mocking its defiance—but it burns, still burns.

Even in darkness, you hold the impossible, a fragile light in a world that forgot how to see.

234
God Comes

In the hush of dawn, God comes—on tiny feet, soft cries, milk-scented breath, new life unfolding.

He comes with each new child, eyes blinking at the light, small hands grasping at the air. A quiet entrance, not once, but over and over, like the sun rising without asking if we're ready.

He comes in suffering too—in the bent back of the farmer sweating beneath the sun's weight, in the woman with tear-streaked cheeks kneeling by a bedside, pleading in silence. He hangs there in every raw wound, every unspoken grief, each breaking heart.

The cross—not a one-time thing, but a daily surrender of breath, of blood, of hope that trembles on the edge of despair.

He dies, again and again, in the ones we lose: the child who breathes his last, the old man who drifts away, the friend who fades into the dark space of memory.

Each time, He is there—not leaving, not forgetting, but entering deeper into the pain, touching every tear with His own.

And then, resurrection. Not a grand fanfare, not a flash of glory, but a tender rebirth—in the first breath after the sobbing stops, in the way light spills through the crack of a closed door, in the whisper of forgiveness where we thought none was left.

He rises in the addict who wakes up one more day, choosing to stay. In the lover who opens their arms again after betrayal's bitter sting.

In the flower that pushes through hard ground, petals open to a world that crushed it once before.

Each new day, each small death, each quiet rising—He is there. A presence in the unfolding, a heartbeat in the letting go, a breath in the becoming.

God keeps coming back—not with thunder or lightning, but in the soft, steady way grass grows after fire, trees sprout from charred stumps, hearts mend, thread by thread.

He is the One who stays, the One who keeps dying, keeps rising, keeps arriving. In every moment, with us, always with us.

We stumble, we break, we bloom, and He is there—just as He was, just as He is, and always will be.

235
In Each Moment

He comes again— in the first breath of a newborn's cry, soft hands clinging to the air, as if to say, *Here I am.* Every child, a small gospel, whispering hope through the dawn's mist, fragile and fierce, a quiet revolution.

He suffers too— in the silent tears of the grieving mother, her hands trembling against the weight of absence. In the old man's sigh, soft as ash, as he lets go and slips quietly into the long night.

A cross planted in the soil of each heartache, pain shared, pain held, etched into the grooves of our restless lives.

But still, He rises— The Christ in every trembling step of one who dares to try again, in the quiet nod of forgiveness where wounds once bled, raw but healing.

Resurrection unfolds slowly, not in thunderclaps or glory, but like the petals of a flower timidly opening to the hesitant sun.

Each moment, a new coming. Each breath, a quiet gift. Each death, a doorway, swinging open into something we can't quite name.

God in the breeze, God in the falling leaf, God in the tender bloom that lifts its head after the frost.

Just this— Him in all things, The Christ returning, without fanfare, without end.

236
Woman

Who shaped her in secret places, wove flesh from dust, spirit from breath? Who traced the curve of her spine and planted fire in her bones? You crafted her with intention, her body a sanctuary, a sacred vessel of life—strength and grace woven in defiance of the void.

Her hands hold the memory of creation, her heartbeat the pulse of stars. Her skin carries the warmth of your light, yet the world would dim it. In her breath lingers the whisper of freedom, a freedom some would shatter.

She is not a possession to be owned, not a vessel to be claimed, though the grasping hands of history have tried. For You placed in her the power to choose—to say yes or no, to give or hold back, to offer or keep.

Her body is hers—a gift of Your love, to be honored, not diminished, celebrated, not shamed. Every curve, every scar, every line—a testament to the beauty of being, a rebuke to those who would deny it.

She walks this earth with the dignity of a queen, the fire of a prophet, the wisdom of a sage. Her steps are marked with the authority only You can bestow—and yet the world averts its gaze.

Teach us to see the holiness of her form. To know that when she stands, she stands beloved, crafted with care and intention, bearing Your image in every fiber.

Let her voice ring out, clear and unafraid, even as echoes of dismissal try to drown it. Let her words carry weight, her presence shape the world as You intended from the beginning.

For she is Yours, yet wholly her own—Your Divine creation, a sacred gift the world too often forgets.

When the Shadows Look Suspicious

You're just sitting there—coffee lukewarm, half gone, some old blues song playing too low on the radio. And then it creeps in, like a stray cat, rubbing its oily fur against your leg.

You glance up, and the cashier looks away—too fast. The guy at the next table shifts his eyes, like he knows something you don't. A woman walks past the window, and you're sure she's checking her reflection to see if you're still there.

You shrug it off, laugh it away. Everyone's a little paranoid, right? Maybe you didn't sleep enough. Maybe it's all the caffeine. Maybe it's just the weight of being alive.

But the cat keeps circling, tail twitching, eyes like two dark stones, watching your every move. And soon it's not just the cashier or the guy with shifty eyes—it's the postman who pauses a little too long, the driver in the car behind you, the voice on the other end of the line, the silence between words, the walls breathing.

Everything feels sharp, cutting through your skin, like the world's leaning in—closer, closer, trying to see what's inside your head.

You tell yourself it's nothing, just nerves, just stress. But the thoughts curl up like smoke, getting thicker, getting darker, until you're caught in a cloud of maybe-this-isn't-real, maybe-they're-all-in-on-it, maybe-they-know-something-I-don't.

And you're stuck, looking for answers in the patterns of Paint on the walls, in the folds of your bed sheets, searching for proof that you're not unraveling.

But hell, what do you do when even the shadows look suspicious? When you can't trust the mirror to show you who you are? When every sound, every flick of light, feels like a signal, like someone's flipping the switch just to watch you jump?

And before you know it, you're lost in the spaces between what's true and what's true enough to make you sweat—slipping through cracks like that damn stray cat, just beyond reach, just outside the corner of your eye. But you swear it's there, watching you, waiting.

238
Person Inside

I asked an old man once what it was like to be old.

He smiled, slow and tired, his eyes clouded but still sharp enough to cut through the question. "The person inside," he said, "has been the same age my whole life."

The voice in his head—never growing old, never changing. He was always the same, a child and a man, his mother's son, a boy chasing the horizon even as the years rolled by.

He waited to become an old man, watched his body betray him. His legs grew weak, his arms hung by his side, his mind slowed like a clock running out of time.
But the person within—that unyielding spark—never tired, never aged.

"Our spirits are eternal, our souls forever," he said, with the certainty of someone who'd lived long enough to know what endures.

"Next time you see an old man, an old woman, know they are still a child, just as you are still a child.

And children," he said, his voice breaking like a wave, "will always need God's love, care from others, purpose, and meaning."

239
Storms

Where are the storms? Where do they go when they're not ripping us apart, when they're biding time in dark corners, those crevices of our minds, waiting like old regrets, quiet, but never gone?

They say storms are born from grief, the sky's way of weeping, the earth's way of screaming. And they batter us, pummel us, grind us down until we're small, helpless.

These storms— they're more than wind and water. They're every lie we swallow, every betrayal lodged in our guts, the weight of dead dreams dragging us to the bottom where only the damned know how to breathe.

We drown in them, choke on the salt of our own bitterness. And they laugh—
the gods of the deep, the ocean demons, monsters made from the sum of our
misery.

They say tears fill rivers, wash over mountains, drown the fools who think
they can rise. We think we're climbing, but we're just sinking, slow and steady,
into a storm that never ends.

We wait for the day after, hoping for a little mercy, a little sun to dry us out,
to make us forget. But we know better.

These storms don't disappear. They slink back into the shadows,
curl up in the recesses, waiting for the next wound, the next cut deep enough
to let them out.

So, we light a cigarette, pour another drink, listen for the thunder, feel the air
tighten around us, and we wait.

Because the calm is a liar, and we're all just storm chasers, whether we like
it or not.

240

Missing

Each cold case, a black notice, like a post it note slapped on death's door. The
bureaucratic dance of the damned, where a body becomes a list of stats—
faceless fingerprints, DNA markers, a stack of bones turned into paperwork,
the color of ink bleeding over the lost.

Dental charts, clothing descriptions, the shape of a molar, the fit of a boot—
like piecing together a ghost from the scraps of a bad dream. A phantom
stitched from lab reports, and forensics that reek of formaldehyde and regret.

Each of these women had a story. They did once, before the world chewed
them up and spat them into unmarked graves.

Before their stories turned into unanswered questions, the kind that leave you
hollow and cold— like the steel drawers they lie in now.
Somewhere, there's a desk full of files, a graveyard for the forgotten. Detectives
sip stale coffee, their eyes glazed over, names fading like smoke. Each case a
distant echo, another woman nobody looked for, nobody cried for, a name
that never made the news.

Relatives deserve answers— yeah, maybe. But the dead don't talk back, no matter how many times you say sorry, no matter how many times you swear you'll find who did it. You won't. They disappear like whispers in the wind. Another black notice, another mark on the endless ledger.

And who's left holding the bag? A family that stopped waiting by the phone, a detective with bloodshot eyes, the black notices piling up. Stories that slipped through the cracks, drowned in the silence of a world too busy to care.

And that's the damn truth of it— the world moves on, forgetting faces and names, leaving only the cold, empty shells of the lost, filed away neatly, another set of stats, waiting for answers that'll never come.

241
Lies

He lies to himself— says he's happy, says he's strong, says the world's got no teeth. But deep down, he knows there's a dark pit inside, swallowing whatever's left of him, piece by piece.

You lie enough times; you start believing the bullshit.

He's painted his own prison walls a nice shade of denial, locked himself in with the stench of it. Because once you admit the truth, the whole rotten structure comes crashing down. He can't see the deceit in himself, so how the hell's he supposed to see it in others? No compass, no map, no north star— just a wandering ghost pretending to be a man.

And respect? Gone. First for himself, then for everyone else.

He starts thinking it's all a sad joke, people are walking mannequins, cardboard cutouts in a game he's made. He shoves the pieces around, burns the board if he wants, because why the hell not?

He's the liar. He's the king. But the king's got no kingdom— only a throne of empty promises and ashes of wasted days.

Without respect, there's no love. He can't love a world he can't even see. It's just a blur of twisted faces, and him, the beast in the center, snarling at shadows, hollowed out and angry, because there's nothing left inside.

Just the echoes of his own voice, bouncing off the walls, mocking him.

What does he do? He chases his impulses, swallows the dirt, stuffs his mouth with poison, indulges in quick fixes— sex and fleeting highs.

Like a dog licking his wounds, he takes the lowest pleasures, like a starving man eating trash until he's too numb to feel the hunger anymore.

But he never fills up, because there's no filling a void made of lies.
Just feeding it more emptiness until he becomes the beast he built— a creature that shambles through life, rotting from the inside out.

And it all started with a little lie. Just a whisper at first, that turned into a scream, until it drowned out everything— even the man he used to be.

242

Plutocracy Blues

They sit in their towers, golden teeth biting down on the world, their hands soft from never touching dirt, never planting seeds, never loving people, only digging graves.

Oligarchy— coming to a theater near you.

Just a fancy word for thieves who wear suits instead of masks, who call their heists "policy" and their greed "progress." They stuff their bellies with the sweat of the desperate, turn blood into dividends, misery into mansions.

They laugh at the rest of us, shuffling pennies for rent, selling hours for crumbs, turning democracy into vulgar farse.

Just a puppet show, strings pulled by the fat fingers of the rich.

Every ballot a blank check signed to the same grifter. They tell us to work harder, to dream bigger, but the game is rigged— a casino where they own the house, and we're just gamblers with empty pockets, betting our futures on a deck stacked with lies. And when we rise, they call it chaos. When we speak, they call it treason. But their silence is violence, their power a loaded gun pointed at the heart of everyone who's ever known hunger.

They think they'll rule forever, but towers crumble, and gold melts.
and even kings rot when buried beneath enough dirt. So let them have their day, their coins, and castles. The tide always comes in, and no amount of money can stop a sea of anger from swallowing them whole.

243

Old Man Sweeping Dust

A dawn's promise breaks— through shadowed and silent streets,
faint light clings to hope, weaving through cracks in stone,
whispering dreams yet to bloom.

A sparrow's faint chirp echoes through the empty lanes where old men once
spoke, sipping tea beneath tree shade, sharing stories with the wind.

A stray cat slinks by its tail brushing broken walls. Even the small things carry
the weight of stillness, each paw a soft prayer for warmth.

Bamboo bends in the breeze, leaves shiver against the light. Does the tree
know why it stretches its roots deeper, seeking something it cannot see?

Mist rises from roofs, wrapping the world in silence. Even the stones sigh,
their voices etched in cracks, memories of rain's caress.

What is the sun's wish as it climbs the pale sky's arc? Does it long to touch
each droplet on blades of grass, each fleeting dewdrop's sparkle?

The river murmurs— a song of ceaseless movement. Is it lost like us, wandering
toward the sea's arms, uncertain yet ever sure?

Dragonflies hover, brief flashes of red and gold. Do they envy us, anchored
by our heavy bones, or pity our endless chase?

Morning glories bloom, opening to light's embrace. Such fragile petals, yet
they break through bricks and stones, daring the world to see them.

An old man sweeps dust, his broom a whispering brush. Is he chasing time,
or simply letting it flow back into the earth's cradle?

The temple bell rings, vibrating through empty space. Does it dream of ears
to carry its bronze echoes, or is ringing its own joy?

The dawn continues— slipping through blind men's fingers. Each shadow
stretches, reaching for the touch of light, then folds back to dark again.

Is it hope that sings beneath the city's silence, or just acceptance?
A bow to the unknown path, a gift in each new breath.

Sparrows keep chirping— each note is a question mark. And yet somehow still, they sing without need for words, trusting dawn's slow unfolding.

244
Where Dreams Turn to Dust

We came in with hope, bright as morning, its edges soft with promise. The world seemed endless then— its roads unwinding forever, its skies wide enough to carry anything.

But the wind turned sharp, the clouds sank low, and the stars, once steady and sure, flickered and fell silent.

We left with only fading breaths, our footsteps heavy, dragging questions and goodbyes behind us— each one a farewell to something we couldn't keep.

Dreams turned to dust, scattered by hands we thought were kind. The ground remembers no mercy. It only takes. And takes. And takes.

The fields where we danced are barren now. The trees that once whispered our names are gone, their roots wrenched from the earth, their branches burned to warm nights that were not our own.

A crow watches from a fencepost, its gaze ancient, too knowing. It caws once and flies away, to where the shadows linger longest. Even the river forgot us. Its waters, once full and alive, run thin now, cutting through stone and memory, carving hollows into hearts we left behind.

We carry what we can, but it is never enough. Not for the night. Not for the road. Not for the empty hands we could not fill. Dusk stretches long, its fingers brushing the hills, its quiet, deeper than sorrow. And in that silence, we are smaller than even the dust.

245
Morning Coffee

Morning is for the birds. They sing while I curse— the damn coffee spilling again, hot on my leg, staining the table like a bruise.

The cat sits on the counter, doesn't even flinch, just watches me wipe up my mess with that blank, careless stare. It's a simple game:

I chase, the cat waits.
He dips his paw in the spilled cream, drags his tongue slow, each sip deliberate, like he's savoring the luxury of not giving a damn.

I think: What's it like to be a cat? To not scramble for meaning at the bottom of a cup? To not chase shadows of success? To just exist, content with a little spill.

The birds outside—still chirping. The sun rising, as it always does—indifferent. The cat looks at me, yawns, and walks away.

There's the lesson I never learn: Sit back, lap up the cream when it spills, and let the world spin without needing to win.

246
Let the Darkness Win

Broken wires, broken toaster—sparks! No light in the kitchen, no bulbs to fix anything. The fridge grinds like a dying dog.

The screwdriver's somewhere in the basement, lost in that dusty maze with all the ghosts of failed projects.

But hell, if I'm going down there— not tonight, not in this dark.

The cat sits in the middle of the room, perfectly content.

I swear I can see him smirking, even without the lights.

He's got it all figured out: watch me struggle, make a mess of myself, then top it off by pissing on the wall and leaping onto the made bed like some kind of victory lap.

What's a man to do? Go back to bed, I guess.

Let the wires stay frayed, the toast remain a dream. I'm no different from the cat, just scratching at problems in the dark, waiting for dawn to hand me an answer or burn it all down. Yeah, I'll stay in bed.

Let the shadows have the kitchen. Let the cat keep his smirk.

Some battles aren't worth fighting. The darkness? It can win tonight.

247
Woven into the Silence Between Words

Theopoetics—there's something deeper, a thread you didn't pull, but it's there, woven into the silence between words, a knowing before language, a truth that hums beneath the surface—like wind moving through trees, needing no name.

God exists there, in the spaces before speech, in the breath between thoughts, a quiet pulse we feel but can't describe—like the cat on the windowsill, watching the world, saying nothing.

Theopoetics knows this. It touches that silence, reminding us that before the first word, there was already connection, an understanding beyond letters and lines—like the way a flower bends toward light, without asking why.

We try to express it. Sometimes we stumble—use art, or poems, or songs. But the truth was always there, waiting to be felt, like an old friend you recognize without needing a name.

And that's the secret: not to capture God with words, but to feel the Divine in the quiet. To let existence speak before we open our mouths; to know we already have access to the holy—in the stillness before the noise.

248
Divine Poet

God is the poet of the universe, sitting in some cosmic café, half-drunk on stardust and broken dreams, scribbling on napkins made of galaxies—each word a burst of light, each line a river flowing through time. She doesn't shout or preach, just taps her pen, quiet and steady, letting the ink of existence spill across the blank page of the void. Watching stars burn out and new ones ignite, as if it's all part of some endless verse—no beginning, no end.

Sometimes the lines don't rhyme, sometimes the rhythm stumbles. But that's the point, isn't it? She lets it be rough, lets it breathe, lets the imperfections sing. Because perfection's a bore, and this world, with all its cracks, is a better poem for it. She writes us into the story, lets us stumble across the page, fall into dark corners, trip over lines. We're all part of the mess, part of the beauty, whether we like it or not. And that's why we keep going—because even in our clumsy steps, we're part of the poem, whether we make sense of it or not.

189

God doesn't explain the verses, doesn't hand out answers in neat little stanzas. She just watches us like a cat, perched on a windowsill, silent, knowing. Letting the wind move through the trees, letting the birds write their own songs, letting the rain splatter across the pavement like ink blotting out the words. And in those moments when we're quiet enough to listen, we can hear the heartbeat of the poem—a pulse that runs through everything: the stones, the stars, the dust on the kitchen table. It's all part of the same great poem, the one she's been writing since before time, the one she'll keep writing long after we're gone.

But here's the thing: God's not a perfectionist. She's not some grand architect with blueprints and straight lines. She's more like a jazz musician, improvising as she goes, leaning into the chaos, finding beauty in the broken chords, in the notes that don't quite fit. And that's why, when you look at the world, when you look at yourself, you see the smudges, the rough edges, the places where the ink ran. But it's all part of the song, part of the poem.

We don't need to understand every word; we just need to keep reading, keep walking through the lines, knowing that somewhere, somehow, there's a rhythm to it all, a meaning beyond the words, a beat that moves through everything.

God's the poet of the universe, and we're all just scribbles on her page. But what a poem it is—what a wild, messy, beautiful thing—this life, this world, this dance of dust and stars.

Sing your praises to the poet sitting in the corner, smiling at the mess we make, knowing that even in our chaos, we're part of something bigger, something more. We are the lines she writes, the ink that spills, the song that never ends.

249

Slow Down

Christ calls us—practice slowness. Grip the moment before you,
see it without hesitation. See the real, brilliant places right here in front of you.
Love your neighbor. Bless your enemy. Treat all creation with respect, because
each being— every leaf, every stone— is intentional, designed, crafted by
hands we can't always see.

There's a cat in the alley, watching the world go by. He doesn't rush; he doesn't need to. He knows what we forget— that the moment is enough, that slowness is the answer, if we only stop long enough to notice.

The world spins anyway, but we don't have to. We can stand still—
like trees rooted deep, like mountains untouched by time.
Christ whispers it softly— in the wind, in the quiet, in the space between breaths. *Slow down,* He says. Hold the moment like a fragile thing— because it is, because it's everything.

250

Becoming

We are more than flesh and fragile instinct—more than bones that bend beneath the weight of time. Within us flickers a strange and holy fire, a pulse of possibility, an ache for something greater than survival.

The world may call us accidents of dust, prisoners of fate, but listen—there is a voice in the wilderness of our hearts that whispers, *You are free.* Not free from pain, but free to rise beyond the narrow walls that fear and failure build.

What is this self-awareness, if not the mirror in which we glimpse the Divine reflection? To be made in the image of God ss not to be perfect, but to be endlessly becoming.

We are artists painting with both joy and suffering, sculptors carving purpose out of raw days. Our choices—small and staggering—shape the fragile arc of our lives, and each act of kindness, each refusal to bow to despair, is a prayer louder than words.

So, when the world says, "Stay in your place," We will say, "No—we were born for more than silence."
For dignity is not a gift the world gives; it is the birthright of all who breathe. To live is to dare, to fall and rise again. And in our rising, We become echoes of the Creator—co-authors of grace, bearers of light.

251
Artist

The artist stands— like a tree in the middle of it all, rooted yet swaying, branches reaching out, touching every being, whispering to the wind, awakening our sleepy hearts to the connections
we forgot were there.

We are not alone, the artist says. We are threads in a vast, tangled web, woven into each other and into the land, the sky, the water.
We breathe the same air. We share the same pulse— life in all its forms, singing the same ancient song.

And when we forget, when we fall into ourselves, lost in the noise of self-importance, the artist shakes us— a gentle tremor, like a pebble dropped in a still pond, disturbing the surface, forcing us to see what we've chosen to ignore.

A mirror held up— not to vanity but to truth. To the cracks in our care: for ourselves, for each other, for the earth that cradles us, and the creatures who walk beside us. Sometimes the artist disturbs— not with anger but with clarity, showing us the broken things, the places where we've failed. Not to shame, but to remind that we are more than this— that we can be more than this.

And then, like a breeze lifting fallen leaves, the artist motivates—
not with loud demands, but with a quiet invitation. *Come,* they whisper. Take care of what you are part of. Tend to your own soul,
and the souls of others. Tend to the world as you would tend to a garden— because everything grows when cared for with love.

The artist becomes philosopher— in the silent spaces between strokes of the brush, in the moments between notes of the song,
in the pauses between words on a page. They show us the deeper currents of being that flow through all things— the invisible roots
binding us to one another and to the larger web of life.

There is no separation here, only the illusion of it. And the artist, with quiet hands, peels back the veil, so we can feel our place in this great, trembling, living thing.

Through their work, the artist reminds us— we are not the center
but part of the whole, kin to the birds, the trees, the stars. We belong— to the soil beneath our feet, to the breath of the wind,
to the heartbeat of the earth itself.

And when the artist leaves the canvas, the stage, the page, they leave us— not with answers, but with a sense of belonging, a subtle knowing that we are part of something vast and sacred. And this belonging comes with responsibility— to care, to tend, to love this web of life that holds us all.

252
Patches of God

Where are those little patches of God— the ones that stitch the torn sky back together, whispering in the language of stardust?

They swirl in the darkness like wind-spun leaves over a forgotten river, turning fog into syrup— sweet and slow, the nectar of creation drips down the spine of the universe.

You want to see the face of God? It's there, pressed against the rim of the telescope, a cosmic fingerprint smudged in infinity. Not thunder, not fire— but the quiet revolution of atoms knowing their place.

Look closer— into the shadows between galaxies, hiding in the great voids where silence hums, like the breath of a waiting dawn.

The face of God isn't a face at all— it's the widening of your heart as the universe blooms like wildflowers across the fields of your desire.

253
Awakener

The artist is the awakener. She sits in quiet rooms or on busy streets, with a canvas, a guitar, or a notebook, her fingers stained with ink or paint, or the dust of this world. And he sees—oh yes, he sees— what we don't, or what we refuse to. Because it's easier that way, isn't it? To walk through life in a haze, thinking you're alone, thinking no one else understands.

But the artist— the artist knows better. She taps into that pulse, that heartbeat beneath the surface, that hum of connection between you, me, the wind in the trees, and the birds flying overhead.

He pulls the threads we ignore, lays them out bare, shows us how every line, every stroke, every word is part of the same web. And it doesn't matter if you're sitting in a café in Paris, or a diner in some dead-end town. It doesn't matter if you're rich or poor if your clothes are clean or dirty. The artist looks through it all, sees the thread that binds us— the one we pretend isn't there, because we're too busy looking down, staring at our feet, at our screens, too busy drowning in ourselves.

The artist wakes you up— not gently. No, there's nothing soft about it. He slaps you in the face with color, with sound, with words that make you sit up, that make you remember— you're alive. Yes, alive. And not just alive in your own little world, but part of something bigger, something that stretches beyond your skin, beyond your city, beyond your small, tired life.

You walk into a gallery, and there it is— the canvas staring back at you, shouting without a word: *Wake up. See this. Feel this.* You're not alone. You never were. And you feel it in your bones, that connection, that thread that runs through all things.

Or you hear a song— just a melody at first. But it creeps into you, makes its way into your bloodstream, until you're humming along without even knowing why. And suddenly, you're not just hearing it— you are part of it. Part of the rhythm, the beat, the thing that ties us all together.

The artist doesn't care if you're ready, doesn't care if you want to be awakened. He does it anyway. He pulls back the veil, makes you look— makes you see. That every face you pass on the street, every stranger you ignore, is part of the same fabric. And you can't unsee it now. You can't go back. Not once you've been awakened, not once the artist has shown you the web of life, the connections you've tried so hard to avoid.

The artist is the awakener. She tears down the walls we build between ourselves and the world. She reminds us— we are not islands. We are not separate. We are threads in the same tapestry, leaves on the same tree, waves in the same ocean.

And the artist— with his paint, or his song, or her words—
she makes us feel it. In our bones, in our blood, in the spaces between breaths.

254

Running Down to Mexico

A passion for sticky things— like honey dripping slowly off spoons, or her lips smudged red, running down to Mexico and back, loose pajamas sagging in the heat of the sun.

Too much powder on her face, like she's trying to hide from time. But time finds her anyway, etching itself into the corners of her smile. Her legs laugh at me—that kind of laugh that stabs right through the gut, leaving me dying in some cheap joy.

I wait at the bus stop, fresh tomatoes piled high— gifts from the earth, soft and ripe, too fragile for this world. The air thick with sweat, the weight of waiting heavy, and nothing but the sound of a far-off engine, whispering that it's such a wonderful day.

255
Cat's Dream

Goldfish stick to the side of the pool, quiet as the wind. The cat watches, then laughs—a sound that ripples the stillness—and dives headfirst into the deep, where a kissing octopus waits, her arms full of songs stolen from the sea's belly.

The cat drinks the joy of the waves, rides on the back of a slow turtle, through Neptune's secret maze. Past the sleeping coral and the dancing clams, she asks where the mermaids hide. But they are busy, weaving the night from threads of moonlight and tide.

Under the ocean's blanket, the cat curls into the soft current, her tail swaying with the rhythm of the deep, smiling as her dreams swirl like galaxies around her.

256
Incarnation

Incarnation, profound mystery transcending the limits of human understanding, yet touching the core of our being. The divine essence, in all its infinite and boundless love, choosing to manifest itself in human form, through the person of Jesus.

Convergence of the divine and the human, the eternal, and the temporal, the transcendent and the immanent.

The union of opposites, a merging of heaven and earth, spirit, and matter, speaking to the deepest longings of the soul.

God enters into the fullness of human experience, sharing in our joys and sorrows, our triumphs, and struggles.

Through The Christ, seeing God's unconditional love made flesh, reaching out to humanity with arms open wide, inviting us into relationship with intimacy and grace.

Revealing the inherent dignity and worth of every human being, for in becoming human,

God dignified human nature and affirmed its sacredness. We are not alone in our journey through life, God walks beside us, within us, experiencing human emotions and challenges.

The invitation to encounter the divine in the midst of the ordinary, to recognize the sacredness of every moment and every person.

Calling us to live with compassion, humility, and love, following the person who is Jesus, who embodies the essence of God's infinite mercy and grace.

257
Authentic Living

To live authentically is to walk unshod upon the sharp stones of truth, to refuse the easy lie that numbs the spirit. We are called to grow—not in power or wealth, but in the tender, fierce capacities of love, reason, and creation. To love without chains, to reason without fear, to create as if the world depends on the beauty we make—because it does.

This life is not a rehearsal for something else. It is the canvas where we spill our longings, the soil where our hands learn to sow and to heal. What we shape with our choices echoes across time—a whisper, a song, a monument of quiet courage.

Dignity is not a crown bestowed by kings nor a prize earned by virtue of perfection. It is the birthright of all who dare to be fully human. To live in respect for our own souls is to honor the fragile miracle of every life we touch.

Let us rise to meet the day as ourselves—unvarnished, uncertain, but real. Let our mistakes be honest, our joys unashamed, our kindness without cost. For to live authentically is not to avoid the struggle, but to embrace the raw, holy work of becoming—not someone else, but wholly, radiantly, ourselves.

258
Dying by Fly Paper

The great question of the ages— is it better to die by fly paper or quicksand? Or have some old bag lick you to death, her breath stale as last night's bourbon, teeth stained like old coffee cups you'd find in a greasy spoon.

Let's face it— death doesn't come like a clean bullet. It comes like a rusty '52 Studebaker, one headlight flickering, paint chipping, creeping down the road, looking for you. So, what do you do? You take to the street before death finds you hiding under that newspaper— the one soaked in fish guts and yesterday's lies.

You run. Run fast and don't forget the wallet, because even in the face of death, someone's always got their hand out.

And hell— bring the toilet paper too, because the mess politicians leave behind, you'll be mopping it up long after they're gone. But here's the kicker— you take the subway home, lock yourself in the closet, thinking you've outsmarted him. But death will find you there too, laughing his ass off, watching you cower, thinking you've won.

He's always one step behind— an old car sputtering. You hear it in the distance, that familiar grind of an engine that's seen better days,
but it keeps going, just like him, just like you.

259
That Sea of Black

Do all those good things in the dark, where no one can see your light.

Hide in your closet and pray. Talk to God when the walls press in— thick walls of clay, silent walls that hold you like the grave.

You sink down into the black sea, and you breathe there, like you've finally figured it out, like all that dark is what you needed.

You climb into your shell with your memories— the ones that bite, the ones that soothe. They wrap around you, tighter than skin, and you hum your blessings to a world so far away it'll never hear, won't ever care— some mountain, some planet, where no one's listening, not even the stars.

And then Jesus comes. He doesn't knock, just walks in, takes your hand like He's known you all along. He pulls you deeper into the cave, and it's cold, but you're burning.

He flips you inside out— like a coat that's been worn too long.
Shows you everything you never wanted to see, turns over every scar, every bruise. But somehow, you're still there, still breathing in that black sea.

And you're free— because He's there, and the walls are gone. And all that dark? It doesn't matter anymore.

260
Screams from Jabalya

The bulldozers crawl through Jabalya, ancient beasts with rusted teeth, turning streets into bones and dust.

Where children once ran, where mothers hung laundry, now there's nothing but rubble—broken dreams and torn tents. They set up homes in the scraps, laugh through cracked lips, ask themselves where to go now. There's nowhere, no direction but down.

Bombs hum like a lullaby for the damned. You hear it overhead, smell it in the air. Violence doesn't hide—it kisses every corner. And still they run, trying to outrun death's slow footsteps.

A man stands on the wreckage, looks to the sky, to the dirt, asks the only question that matters: Where will the people go when even the earth pushes them out, and the sky spits fire at their backs?

They try to leave, try to breathe, but the roads are closed, the exits sealed. The bulldozers grind forward, metal jaws chewing what's left of hope.

And God? If He's watching, sits there with His arms folded, while the world burns slow in His palm.

261
Somewhere in Gaza

Broken bones wash up on the shore of despair, dust from the crumbled city hanging like black sand in the wind.

The children roam the streets, hands bound, eyes crusted with blood. Their mothers lost to the wreckage, no one left to hold them.

They chew dirt to fill the silence, riding wild dogs through a nightmare that never ends.

The city's heart beats slow, its veins filled with terror. Roots of evil grow thick in the cracks. Another day breaks, but it brings no light.

And still the bones wash up, like memories no one wants. Still the dust chokes. And the children—GOD! The children— who will cry for them when the city forgets their names?

The wind doesn't care. The bones don't care. And yet, they keep coming.

262
Flesh and Spirit

We cling to painted faces, golden frames hung in dusty cathedrals, as though divinity could be held in the corners of our vision. But He is not there— not in the picture books, not in the quiet safety of our small, wooden prayers.

The Christ we often hold tight is smooth, unbroken. An icon we polish, a memory we tame. But the nails still pierce— and His body bleeds still, splinters of the cross wedged deep into the world.

Throw away this fragile Jesus, the one who fits neatly into your Sunday thoughts. Burn the paper versions where the flesh is missing, where the Spirit is caged.

Let Him rise instead, raw, and alive, both flame and ash, both wound and healer.

He is the hand that breaks bread and the hand that shatters the table. The eternal whisper and the shout that splits mountains.
The Christ who weeps in alleys and dances in burning fields. Do you dare to see Him there?

This is the God who breathes fire and water, who is both lamb and lion, both silence and song. To worship Him is not to hold, but to be held, to break your grip and let His blood run into your veins. Throw away the idols. Let the living Christ come— not soft, but real. Not still but moving. Not distant, but here, flesh and Spirit, touching the ground we fall upon.

263
Who Hears?

Who hears? you ask. But it isn't about you—not just you. You think it's your ears doing the work, but it's bigger than that.

Something larger— out there, in here— calls from deep inside your chest, begging to be heard. Not by your small self, but by that wide-open thing, the place where all the real stuff comes from.

And when you finally respond, it's not from the guy you think you are, but from somewhere bigger, somewhere truer— like breathing
for the first time.

264
The Sacred Mystery of Now

The mind, restless as a sparrow caught in a storm, fills the empty spaces with shadows—what could have been, what might be, what was lost and cannot be reclaimed. Yet beneath this noisy clamor, there is a stillness waiting like an old friend we've forgotten how to greet.

Compassion begins here—not with grand gestures or distant hopes, but with the courage to hold our own trembling heart and whisper, *"Be still."*
For we cannot offer peace to others if we have declared war on ourselves.
Yes, the ego loves its mirrors, its stories of triumph and disaster, its need to be someone, somewhere, something. But the truth moves quietly beneath it all—a vast, unshaken presence, the eternal hum of Being itself.

To transcend the self is not to vanish, but to return—to remember that we were never the stories we carried. We are not the broken clockwork of past regrets, nor the imagined futures that haunt our sleep. We are the breath, the now, the silent but powerful grace that holds all things together.

So, when fear presses in, when the mind builds its restless prisons, let us breathe and remember we are already whole. There is no distant horizon where we become worthy of peace. It is here closer than our next heartbeat.

And perhaps the greatest act of love is to remind each other, gently, that we belong to the quiet and to the sacred mystery of now.

265
Christ is a Force

Christ is a force—no question. He comes at you like a storm, sharp as a knife, cuts deep, twists, leaves you gasping.

And just when you need Him, He's there— a soft pat on the shoulder.

But don't get too comfortable. He'll turn His back, just to make you sweat.

Empty hands; he asks you if you see the jewel. Do you?

He's closer than breath, colder than space. He walks next to you,
teaches you how to walk those same cursed steps.
Takes you to the mountaintop, gives you the glory for a moment—
then hands you the Cross, and reminds you: you've got to bleed too.
And don't forget to scream to the sky, ask why, *Why the hell have you left me alone?*

But He won't answer. He'll just stand there—because He's both human and God, suffering and glory, the same gold coin, and you're stuck on both sides.

266
Hold the Truth Close

Hold the truth close; let it burn through your bones, feel it melt the chains, but let your spirit fly.

Christ waits in that deep, dark cloud. He strips you bare, empties you. And then suddenly—you're on the mountain, looking down with the eyes of God.

You see the world, its creatures blazing. And you gather them, one by one, place them in the ark— for future days, for future worlds, for all who cry and breathe fire. This is the truth. It's heavy— but it sings.

267
Unstoppable Light

Jesus walks back from the wilderness, dust clinging to his feet like an unspoken testimony. Forty days behind him, forty nights of hunger of wrestling with shadows that offered kingdoms and called it glory.

The wilderness is silent now, but its whispers linger— sand in his sandals, wind in his ears, truth in his chest. He steps into the synagogue on the Sabbath, the air thick with the ritual of centuries.

Elders nod, children squirm, scrolls wait in sacred stillness. He takes his place, his hands steady as they unroll Isaiah, each movement deliberate, as though cradling fire.

The words spill into the room— not soft, not gentle. They strike like thunder. *"The Spirit of the Lord is on me,"* he says, his voice cutting through the haze. *"I bring Good News to the poor."* The poor lean forward, hope trembling like a leaf. *"Freedom for the captives."* A murmur stirs, as though chains are rattling somewhere unseen.

"Sight for the blind." Eyes blink, searching for clarity, even as hearts begin to veil themselves. *"Release for the oppressed."* A breath catches. They will finally breathe. The words hang in the air, alive, electric, dangerous. *"Today,"* he says, his voice firm, his gaze sweeping the room, *"this scripture is fulfilled in your hearing."*

The pause is heavy. The moment could shatter the world. But they don't see it. They don't see the light breaking in, don't hear the chains snapping in unseen realms. Their hearts are locked, their eyes are clouded, their hands clutch the familiar, even as freedom knocks at the door.

Their awe curdles into anger. *Who is he, this carpenter, this nobody, to speak like a prophet, to wield Isaiah like a sword?* Their doubt hardens into rejection. They shove him out— not just from the synagogue, but from their town, their minds, their souls. The dust of Nazareth rises, his footprints pressed into the earth of a place that will not claim him. He walks away, the truth heavy in his chest, a burden carried in silence.

Their blindness is sharper than the desert sun, their chains tighter
than anything Rome could forge. He carries it all— their rejection,
their fear, their refusal to see the dawn rising in their midst.
The wilderness was harsh, but this is harsher: to bring light and be met with
shadow, to offer freedom and hear only the clink of chains.

Still, he walks. His path is not theirs to choose. The Spirit burns within him, the Good News is not silenced, the oppressed will breathe, and the captives will be free.

Even if they push him out, even if they bind themselves tighter, the truth will move forward, unstoppable as the rising sun.

268
Eyes Averted

Trained to look away, we turn from the suffering— eyes averted, closed like locked doors against the cries of the world.
The marks of the least ones are etched in the streets. Society turns its back, deaf to their silent pleas, numb to their unspoken despair.

"Nonpersons," they say— the homeless, the marginalized, fading into shadows as if their pain could vanish with the light.

We walk past their anguish, pretending not to notice, each step an act of betrayal against lives we leave behind.

Yet in each sad face, a story untold remains— a fragment of humanity we choose not to see.

Averting our gaze from the hurt of broken souls, we blind ourselves too, ignoring the truth that their pain is our own.

269
Flicker of Neon and Shadow

I'm stuck in the grind— caught between the peaks and the pits, a dance of joy and gut-punch sorrow, as the city hums its dark song.
Horns blare, sirens scream, and I walk through the alleys, a ghost among the broken, where shadows stretch and neon flickers like a dying star.

My face is a roadmap of it all— the highs, the lows, scars on my hands, weariness etched in my bones.

Each morning is a battle: coffee, smoke, pulling me through chains of bedsheets— another round in the fight.

The peaks are fleeting, golden light for a second: a lover's kiss, a laugh in the haze. But they slip away, sand through tired fingers.

The valleys are deeper, darker— a bottle's promise of relief. But at the bottom of every glass, I stare into my own hollow eyes.

I stumble. I rise. I fall again— a traveler on this endless road, looking for meaning in the mess, for beauty in the grime. The streets tell stories: graffiti on cracked walls, the poetry of the lost, the damned.

Each face I pass reflects mine. Each pair of eyes holds a bit of pain, a bit of hope. We're all stuck in this montage, each playing a part in this grand tragic play.

I write to bleed, to forget, to make sense of the senseless. Words pour like blood, staining the page with pain, with fleeting joy.

And in the silence, I face my demons— a war waged in the corners of my mind.

But there's grace in the grind, beauty in the fight. For in the dance of highs and lows, I see my own fragility, the thread that ties us all.

I'm a mosaic of broken pieces, a testament to resilience, walking this road paved in heartache and wonder.

In the end, it's the struggle that shapes us, the dance that gives it meaning. In the light, in the shadow, I find myself— a dance of joys and sorrows.

270
Paul's Pain

Pain is not the end, but a vessel, a refining fire, where the soul learns to shed its dross.

We are afflicted, pressed but not crushed, like olives beneath the press, yielding oil— pure, holy, enduring.

Thorns— a gift wrapped in agony, sharp enough to humble, to remind that grace is the marrow of strength.

Rejoice in suffering, for it births perseverance, and perseverance, character, and character, hope. Hope that does not falter, hope that anchors the soul when the waves crash and the winds howl.

Pain becomes the teacher, its lessons etched in the heart, its wisdom drawing us nearer to the One who bore the heaviest cross.

See the glory on the other side of pain—a weight of splendor
that outweighs it all, a crown forged in the fire.

Embraces it, not for its sting, but for what it promises: the unseen made visible, the eternal breaking into time, the hands of Christ
holding all things together.

271
Lunch Under the Tree

Under a tree, old as sin, Eve had lunch with God. God tossed a salad, His hands stained from making the universe—greens crisp, tomatoes red, cucumbers sliced like they had a purpose.

Eve, with that look—you know the one—reached for the fruit, shiny as every bad idea since time began. Her eyes were on it, the one that's been whispering since day one.

He knew what was coming. It was her call. Always was.

She bit into it—juice running down, like all the things you can't take back. And with that bite, the world shifted—like a hangover that won't quit.

God kept eating, unbothered, finding peace in a forkful of lettuce. No lectures, no hellfire.

They both knew this was how it had to go down. Curiosity's a bitch—but what else is there?

She swallowed, looked at Him, saw herself in those tired old eyes—all she was, all she'd be.

The garden held its breath, waiting for the punchline. God smiled a little sad, a little love. *Your choice.*

The fruit got heavy, another bite, sharper this time—reality setting in, clearer than she'd like. But that's the deal.

God finished His salad, set down the fork, said, *"Knowledge is its own Eden."*

She nodded, felt His words dig into her bones.

The garden—it's part of her now. The garden sighed, as if it finally understood the joke.

272

The Raw Quiet of Choice

Faith is not a candle handed to us in a quiet cathedral. It is the wild, flickering flame we must kindle ourselves In the vast dark of unknowing.
No priest or doctrine can walk this road for us. We stand alone beneath the sky—Heart bare, trembling, Waiting for an answer that may never come in words.

But it is here, in this solitude, that God leans close—not in thunder or command, but in the whisper of our deepest yearning. To believe is not to silence our doubts, but to hold them tenderly, to let faith and fear sit side by side like old companions on the same journey.

Rituals may shape the hour, dogma may teach the names of things—but neither can teach the ache of surrender, the quiet rebellion of saying *yes* When the world teaches only to grasp and retreat.

And so, we choose—not once, but daily—to trust in a love we cannot fully understand, to walk forward even when the path dissolves beneath our feet. Faith is not the absence of struggle; it is the courage to wrestle with angels and rise, limping but alive.

We are called to the intimacy of mystery, the wild hope that God meets us where we are—not where the world says we should be. So let us reach beyond the boundaries of fear and step into the holy unknown. For it is there, in the raw quiet of choice, that The Christ, the eternal Divine Spirit, waits, arms wide as the morning.

273

Shoes Left Behind

God slipped off His holy shoes, said He was tired of it all, going home for good. The crowd stood silent, eyes wide, burning questions stuck in their throats.

His voice cracked the sky: *"I'm leaving. You won't see me again, but I'll leave my shoes, so you'll remember."*

He placed them down—dusty, worn from wandering—holy symbols of the road He'd walked.

"Think of me often," He said, His eyes scanning the faces. But confusion hung thick, tears swelling, meaning slipping through fingers like sand.

"I'll send my Son to pick them up when you're ready." Then He turned, barefoot, lighter, as if the weight were gone.

The door shut but never locked—an invitation, a challenge, a promise.

The crowd stayed; the absence hit hard, like a fresh cut. Time dragged on, the garden shrank, memories and regrets filling every corner.

They drifted off, lost in Nod, chasing ghosts of answers, but Eve stayed.

Her tears fed the trees that bore no fruit, her sobs the only sound left.

The shoes sat still—a monument, echoes of the steps that once shook the ground.

She wept for what slipped away, for what she couldn't hold, for the silence where God's laughter used to live.

In Nod, they forgot—caught up in wars, in love, in dying.

But Eve remembered. She whispered to the shoes, *"Come back."* The door still shut but never locked.

Barefoot, she wandered, feeling the pain, the hope, the cycle of faith and doubt.

She waited—for the Son, for the day the shoes would be claimed, and the door would swing wide.

Eve wept, but she dreamed too—of a garden full again, of laughter, of love, of light.

274

God went to Coney Island

God spent a day on Coney Island, where madness and laughter mix, where the lights blink like broken promises, and the shadows hide in the cracks.

He walked the boardwalk, His steps slow, deliberate—like He knew something we didn't, like He could feel the weight of every step on that old creaking wood.

A man called into the fog, his voice rough, tired—not a prayer, not a plea, just a demand for something more than this carnival of light and shadow, this spinning wheel that never lets you off.

The clams heard the call, opened their shells, and took off into the sky—leaving behind their cold, wet graves, seeking freedom, seeking something, anything, away from this place.

The crabs, those scuttling bastards, felt the pull of the sea, became old men bent and weary, bowed their heads, and walked into the deep—back to the silence, back to the abyss, where the noise of the world couldn't reach them.

But the starfish? They just lay there, arms outstretched, unmoved by it all—not giving a damn about God's presence, not caring about names, titles, or roles.

God watched them—that sad, bittersweet smile. A creator's pride. A creator's regret. He saw the dance, the rise, the fall, the beauty, the tragedy, and He knew: this is life. This is all there is.

The boardwalk buzzed with life—kids laughing, vendors shouting, the smell of cheap food and salt air. All of it mixed with the Divine—a perfect, messy sauce of existence.

He walked on past the rides—the rollercoaster's scream, the lovers holding hands, the old couples walking slow, holding on to something fragile.

As the day faded, the sky bleeding gold and crimson, God turned—steps heavy with eternity, but light with the love of what He had made.

God walked back into the unknown, took the subway home, changed at 42nd Street, left behind a world that keeps spinning—a boardwalk of destiny, where the sacred and profane dance together, hand in hand.

275
Desert Night

In the desert at night, my mind expands, seeking the horizon—never found, never fixed.

Sky, sand, rocks—all merge into one fluid, forever in movement.

The crackling sounds of reptiles on cool stones—a symphony of the night. Each note a whisper, each whisper a secret of the endless desert.

Stone birds rush past, fooling and exciting the senses—a flash of feathers, a blur of motion, disappearing into the darkness. They leave me breathless, on the edge of something vast, something unknown.

Invisible creatures crawl beneath my feet—teasing, tickling, a reminder of life unseen but ever-present, in this vast expanse of silence and solitude.

Infinite broken mirrors hang from the ceiling of the galaxy, reflecting the light of a single blinking star. Each shard a fragment of a cosmic puzzle, each reflection a glimpse into the heart of the universe.

In this desert night, I am a speck, a whisper, a fleeting thought in the mind of the cosmos.

My soul stretches, reaches out, touches the edge of eternity—feeling the pulse of the infinite.

The cool breeze carries the scent of ancient sands, whispering tales of forgotten times, of lost civilizations, of dreams that once danced beneath this same star-filled sky.

I sit on a rock—smooth and cool, a throne in this kingdom of night and shadows. I let my mind wander, let it drift with the wind, across dunes and valleys, through time and space.

Here in the desert's embrace, I find a strange peace, a quiet understanding of my place in the grand scheme—a tiny flicker in the vast ocean of existence.

The single star blinks—a cosmic heartbeat, a reminder that even in the darkest night, there is light.

276
Held in a Breath

Spring flowers in a breath, a blinding burst of color, a meadow in a heartbeat.

I sit in green froth, planets swirling in my belly, a flock of stars taking flight like geese.

They vanish beyond the edge, leaving me a speck of foam, adrift in the infinite.

The air is thick with earth and bloom. My heart pounds—a drumbeat of being, echoing through the silence.

I breathe in the meadow, taste sunlight and petals, feel the warmth of life as it floods my veins.

Galaxies rise, migrate—wings of stars and dust climbing higher and higher, until they're gone.

Beyond sight, beyond thought, leaving only silence. In that stillness, I am a whisper, dust on the wind.

But even in this smallness, a quiet beauty holds—a thread to the cosmos, its endless dance of light and shadow.

I close my eyes. Colors fade. Everything melts into void, except the sun's gentle touch, the breeze on my skin—a single moment held in a breath.

277
A Glimpse of the Divine

Soft, calm bedspread of grass beneath my feet—a swirling black sky above. Eyes gaze to the zenith, hoping for comets, or better yet, a supernova, or a herd of black holes consuming galaxies.

Dissolve the ceiling, blow off the roof, send me to heaven to live with Andromeda.

The grass whispers secrets, each blade a green tongue, lapping at the edges of my consciousness.

The cool earth cradles me, a lover's embrace, drawing me deeper into the night.

Stars, like scattered diamonds, litter the canvas above. Each one a distant fire, burning through time and space, promising wonders beyond the reach of my imagination.

I lie there, a small, insignificant creature, hoping for a cosmic event—a spectacle to break the monotony of this terrestrial existence.

I want to see the sky torn apart, to witness the birth and death of stars—to feel the universe expand and contract in a violent dance of creation and destruction.

I want to be swallowed whole by the void—to become one with nothingness, to lose myself in the vast, unfathomable expanse of space.

A comet would suffice—its icy tail streaking through the blackness, a celestial messenger carrying tales from the edge of the known universe.

But a supernova—a cataclysmic explosion of light and energy, a cosmic phoenix rising from its own ashes—that would be quite a sight.

I want to feel the roof of my earthly prison shattered, to see the ceiling of my mind blown away—to be launched into the heavens, to float among the stars.

To live in the Oort Cloud, to be a part of the galactic ballet, to dance with the spirals and the clusters, to lose myself in the infinite.

The black sky swirls above me, a living, breathing entity—a vast, unknowable expanse. And I lie there, small, and still, hoping for a glimpse of the Divine.

278
The Body Speaks

I am a hospice chaplain, and I must speak of my body, along with my fragile soul and hopeful spirit.

To speak of my body is to tell a story many would rather not hear— not fit for dinner parties, board meetings, or polite company.

My body is a road map of scars, a library of aches— old injuries that never healed right, muscles knotted, a knee that creaks in the rain.

Each bruise a story, each wrinkle a chapter. A hidden text, no holy document— written in the shakes after too much coffee, the pounding heart on heavy nights, wondering how much longer I can carry it.

My body is proof that I've lived— survived more than I thought possible. It's a monument to every fall, bad decision, mistake, and triumph— a history of pain and pleasure, desire, and regret.

To speak of my body is to admit I'm still here, despite the odds, despite mornings when getting out of bed feels impossible. It speaks of resilience— how flesh heals but never the same, how bones break but bear the weight again.

My body is a reminder of love and loss, hands that once traced my skin, and the empty spaces they left behind. To speak of my body is to speak of hunger, of wanting too much, of quiet desperation.

It's about fear— how the heart races with both danger and love, how it sometimes can't tell the difference. That's the secret: there's no separation between pain and joy, between love and loss— it's all tangled together, woven into who we are.

And that's the text we're all trying to read— written in the way we move, touch, and are touched, in the stories carried in our flesh.

So, when you ask me about my body, its scars, and imperfections, you're really asking for the story of how I got here. And I'll tell you— if you're willing to listen, if you can bear to see the truth etched in every line and bruise.

Because my body isn't just a body— it's a book, written in pain, joy, loss, and survival. So here it is— take it or leave it, the secret text, hidden beneath the surface, waiting to be read if you're brave enough.

279
The Unbreakable Truth

How strange it is—this God who walks barefoot through the dust, whose hands are calloused by the same world that will nail Him to a tree. He laughs, He weeps, He thirsts—And yet, within Him, the infinite hums, wrapped in fragile skin. What else could love be but this?

We crave answers that settle like stones—yet He gives us a cross and calls it victory. What sense is there in suffering, in the silent sky above a dying man? But maybe the question is not *why*, But *how*: How do we stand in the shadow of death and still whisper, *"I believe in the dawn"?*

The resurrection does not erase the scars—it transforms them. Love does not promise escape from the absurdity of life; it promises presence in the midst of it. Christ does not rise unbroken—He rises holy because of His wounds.

And so, when despair drapes itself across our shoulders, when meaning seems to slip between our fingers like ash, we remember the paradox:
That to lose is to gain, that death is not the end, but the threshold of grace.

We are called to carry our own crosses—not in defeat, but in defiance. To love even when it costs everything. To trust even when the world laughs in its cynicism. For in this absurd, holy wager, we find something more eternal than answers: We find the unbreakable truth of a God who dies so that life might begin.

280
Faith, an Old Coat

Faith—an old coat, found when the chill bites deep, wraps around my bones, holding me upright.

I move through the streets, each step trusting something more—
a weight that won't break me, though the ruins press close.
Man among ruins, where dreams fall like dry leaves, and the wind whispers grace, soft as a mother's touch.

Faces of the lost reflect my own. Do they know of that hidden warmth, the quiet fire that still burns?

Streetlights flicker on. Men drown in cheap whiskey's lies. I lift a glass too, saluting the ache of this shared, fragile life.

In still, silent nights, grace lifts me—a soft presence, pushing me forward when my feet falter.

Beauty in despair— moonlight on alley shadows, stray dogs howling to stars, their cries a hymn to the vastness of it all.

Solace in knowing that in every crack and scar, there's a spark of light, a flicker of what could be.

I walk through the dark, faith a compass guiding me, pulling me closer to mercy, to home.

The city breaks down, its people wander but hope still breathes—
a faint pulse in each step.

Dawn breaks, shadows fade. Grace—more than a word or thought— a truth that carries us, a hand unseen that never lets go.

281
Thorn

Pain comes like a lightning bolt, sharp, bright, and unforgiving. It doesn't ask for permission, doesn't knock at the door— it kicks it in, a demon with a blade, jabbing, twisting, laughing in the night.

Some days, it's a rusty nail, buried in the ground, waiting for your step. You don't see it coming until it's too late— the wound festers, and the ache settles in, a tenant who never leaves.

Other nights, it's an insect with wings, a stinger full of venom, buzzing, relentless. You swat at the air, but it finds you anyway. it always finds you.

God, give me strength. There are days when the pain takes my breath, days when it whispers to leave my body behind, to escape the weight of bones and flesh that betray me.

But you say, "my grace is sufficient, my power made perfect in weakness." So I carry this thorn, this burden, this daily reminder that even in the breaking, there is beauty— even in the pain, there is you.

282
The Sacred Present

A sacred moment—true home in the present time. In this space, boundless and endless, miracles hide in simple acts—just being present on God's green earth.

It's in the flick of a match, the smell of fresh coffee, the way the sun hits the window at just the right angle, casting golden light on everyday sidewalks.

There's magic in the mundane—a quiet holiness in the clinking of glasses, the hum of city streets, the rustle of leaves in a forgotten park. Each sound a symphony, each sight a painting—life's sacred, quiet moments.

We search for meaning in grand gestures, in the extraordinary. But it's here—in the breath between words, in the pause before laughter, in the stillness of dawn—where the true magic lies.

Being present, truly here—not lost in yesterday's regrets or tomorrow's dreams, but in this heartbeat, this footstep, this fleeting touch.

On this God's green earth, we find our miracles in the simplest acts: a smile, a nod, a shared silence stretching out—boundless and endless, filling the sacred spaces between our breaths.

In the flicker of a match, the first sip of morning coffee, the warmth of the cup in hand, there's a sacredness that transcends the ordinary—a testament to the beauty of being alive, truly alive, in this very moment.

The streets hum with life, each person a universe, each step a story. And in the chaos, there's a calm—a center that holds together the sacredness of the present moment.

We find our sanctuary not in grand cathedrals or distant dreams, but here—in the simple, everyday acts—the unnoticed miracles that fill our lives with quiet wonder.

In the rustle of leaves, the laughter of children, the soft murmur of conversations, there's a holiness.

Being present, truly here, we touch the Divine—the face of God.

283
The Dialogue Where I meets Thou

We are not meant to live as shadows passing on distant roads, eyes averted, hearts walled in the small rooms of the self. To truly see another is to risk everything—to step into the fragile, holy space where *I* meets *Thou*, Where no masks can survive the light.

Here, in the quiet between words, we touch something eternal. It is not the grasping for control, but the surrender to presence—to the breath shared in silence, to the sacred weight of another's story unfolding before us.

The world teaches us to turn away, to flatten faces into labels, to replace encounter and dialogue with transaction. But God does not meet us in labels. He meets us in the gaze that does not flinch, in the hands that hold without asking for anything in return.

And when we stand in this vulnerable truth, We see the miracle of creation not in the stars alone, but in the trembling humanity before us—in the laughter, the tears, the questions no one dares to speak aloud. To meet the other is to hear the whisper of God saying, *"This, too, is my image. This, too, is beloved."*

We do not become whole by isolation, but by daring to reach across the chasm, by letting another's life press against our own. and when we meet the world in this way—open, unguarded, alive—we do not just find each other, we find the divine, breathing quietly in the space between souls.

284
Transformation

The professor speaks of proofs, angles sharp as cathedral spires, words thick as mortar, logic stacking brick upon brick— a fortress of intellect, solid, immovable, and as cold as stone.

The apologist comes with armor shining, each rebuttal a polished blade, answers as precise as clockwork, clicking and turning, tick, tock, time winding toward some grand truth. But the gears grind, the machine hums in an empty room.

People don't bleed for diagrams, don't weep over syllogisms. No one stands at the altar of rational analysis and finds the wounds in their soul healed.

What changes a man, a woman? Not equations scrawled in chalk, not debates that shine like glass but shatter with a single breath.

A hand extended, when the night is heaviest, a voice that doesn't argue but says simply, *I see you. I love you.*

Transformation isn't a storm but a seed— buried, hidden in the dirt, where the intellect would never look.

The mother who stays awake in the blue hours, praying for a child who spits anger like fire. The stranger who shares a crust of bread without asking your name.

These are the quiet fires, burning in the shadows, unseen by the debaters, ignored by the builders of towers.

A man turns not because he is convinced, but because he is loved.
Not because he loses the argument, but because he finds grace in the eyes of someone who refuses to turn away.

God did not come down with a chalkboard and a lecture. He came with dust on His feet, the grit of our streets in His voice, and hands that touched what others called unclean.

No apologetic method could weep at the tomb of a friend. No intellectual answer could kneel in the garden, sweating blood for a world that didn't understand.

People are transformed not by answers but by presence. By a heart that doesn't recoil, even when the darkness feels like it will swallow everything.

Let the fortress crumble. Let the blades rust. There is a simpler gospel, a truth that whispers, that breathes, that holds out its arms and says, *Come home.*

285
Lost in the Cosmos

Quarks belch from dying stars, a quasar flickers in some rough patch of the galaxy, and here I am, sitting on this spinning rock in the middle of the red shift, blowing kisses that loop around and smack me in the back of the head.

Galaxies scatter like freckles on an ever-expanding balloon. Supernovas burst, guts spilling into the void, and I'm just a damp dot on a damp speck, a tiny note in the cosmic symphony.

But damn if the stars don't sing, even in their final breath—blazing with a fire that lights up the sky before fading to black.

The quasar flickers, a cosmic lighthouse, sending out beams from when the universe was just a kid, dreaming big.

Here I am, lost in the shuffle, a grain of sand in this infinite desert, blowing kisses into the void, knowing they'll never reach—but sending them anyway.

Dots on a balloon, drifting further apart—each of us a lonely island in a sea of nothing.

And yet—there's beauty in the chaos, in the way stars explode like cosmic orgasms, in the way quarks spit out new beginnings even as the stars die.

I'm just a spark, a momentary flicker in the grand dance of the universe.

So, I blow my kisses—small acts of defiance—because what else can you do but keep sending out love into the dark?

I'm a part of this design, a tiny thread in the infinite tapestry. But I'm here, and in my own way, I matter.

I'll keep watching, keep writing, keep sending out my love until the dots connect, until the balloon bursts, and maybe then we'll see what this whole damn thing's been about.

Until that day, I'll sit here—a poet lost in the cosmos—because even the smallest acts hold a spark of hope that, just maybe, we'll find our way home.

286
Mask

Layer upon layer, the mask bites deep, tight. Fused to my skin, it clings like an old wound, a scar too proud to fade. I keep it there, gritting my teeth, daring no questions.

Sometimes I wonder—who am I beneath it all? But questions like that have sharp edges. Better to keep moving, step after step, through this twisting maze, fog thick as regret.

No hand reaches out, no voice cuts the silence. It's just me, the stillness, and a half-hidden truth—its edges always slipping away.

And yet I keep walking, haunted by a whisper: that beneath the weight of it all, beneath the mask, something waits.

287
Come Higher

We search for God in the stars, in the equations that resonate beneath the surface of being. But look closer—in the quiet evolution of our own hearts, God's fingerprints are there too. We are not static beings, But seeds unfolding toward the sun, called to grow beyond what we once thought was possible. Awareness does not arrive like a thunderclap. It blooms slowly—a widening of vision, a soft unraveling of ego's tight grasp. To know ourselves as more than flesh Is to awaken to a deeper call—To see that life itself is holy motion.

We carry the imprint of something vast, Yet we are not bound by that alone. We are builders of meaning, painters of possibility. To rise in love, in truth, in grace, is not to escape the world—but to weave something luminous within it.

Our moral responsibility is not a burden; It is an invitation—to reach higher, to be wiser, to see the divine not as a distant judge, but as the sacred hum beneath all becoming.

Whether in prayer or science, in silence or wonder, the truth is there: we are both the question and the answer, the travelers and the path. And as we climb, faltering and relentless, We glimpse something eternal in the ascent itself—the Creator whispering through the climb, *"Come higher still."*

288
Blossoms from Pain

What blossoms from pain holds the sunlight in its veins, but it doesn't come easy. The storm tears at it, rips it open—petals bleeding, roots clawing into the dirt like an old man holding on to his last breath.

Even in shadows, where the light doesn't bother to go, you'll see it—petals pushing through cracked pavement, finding air in the weight of a fist, the way a sigh sneaks out when you thought you were done crying.

Suffering whispers secrets—dirty, sharp-edged truths to the waiting earth. It doesn't ask for permission. It just plants itself like a seed in your gut and starts to grow.

Pain is the gardener. It doesn't wear gloves, doesn't care if it cuts its hands on the thorns. It works all night, tending the fields of loss while you're lying in bed, staring at the ceiling, waiting for the morning to save you.

And when the first bloom comes, you don't recognize it. It's too raw, too ugly, too real.

But it holds the sunlight in its veins. And if you look long enough, you'll see it glow—not like salvation, but like survival.

289
Let the Mirror Crack

It's hard to find something broken in a world built out of cracked glass and duct tape, where everything's already in pieces, and you're just trying not to step on the sharp bits.

But you've got to try. Start with the mirror. Look for the cracks—the ones in your smile, the ones around your eyes, the ones you swear weren't there yesterday.

Grab that reflection before it turns its back on you, before it shrugs and disappears into its own little world, where everything looks fine, but nothing really works.

You won't find glue strong enough for this kind of breakage. Not the industrial stuff, not even the miracle epoxy they sell on late-night TV (Guaranteed to fix anything! Yeah, right).

This kind of brokenness needs the big guns—the loving arms of Christ, carpenter by trade, fixer of hearts by Divine appointment. He's been patching up the mess since the beginning, and let's face it—He's got His work cut out for Him.

But sometimes, being broken is the best thing that can happen to you. It lets the light in—big, wide cracks that bleed sunshine into the darkest corners of your soul.

And there He is, God with His flashlight, shining it on all the busted parts, pointing out what's worth keeping—"Look at this! Still good!"—and what's got to go. ("This? Yeah, no. Toss it.")

You'd think He'd give up by now. So many humans, so much junk to sort through, so many mirrors smashed out of frustration or just plain clumsiness.

But He's there, patient as hell, chipping away at the plaster you slapped over the cracks, holding your shaking hands while you try to put yourself back together with scotch tape and hope.

And that's the punchline: the idea that someone would care enough to keep fixing what you keep breaking, even when you pretend you don't need it, even when you think you're fine.

So let the mirror crack. Let the light pour in. Let Him find you in the mess and laugh with you at the irony that all this chaos was the plan all along.

290
The Tree of Knowledge

What if the fruit of the Tree of the Knowledge of Good and Evil wasn't some ripe, glistening apple? What if it was a bitter turnip—wrinkled, tough, and biting with regret? Would Eve have even bothered? Would she have stood there, eyeing that gnarled excuse for a vegetable, and thought, *Yeah, let's risk eternal damnation for this.*

And what if the tree—the whole tree—was planted upside down? Roots in the air, leaves in the dirt. God was having a laugh. He hangs a few eggplants up there, a couple of dried-out rutabagas swaying like forgotten Christmas ornaments.

Do you think Eve would've been tempted then? Maybe not. She wasn't even hungry. Maybe she was bored, staring at Adam as he scratched his head and tried to name the 8,000th bird, calling it something brilliant like *a blue flyer.*

Maybe she wanted to find the Tree of Stupidity instead. Now that's a tree! Dangling with dung balls, carefully rolled, and hung there by some enthusiastic beetle who thought, *This'll really mess with them.*

Eve might have laughed, but she'd still pick one, just to see what happens. Maybe stupidity tasted sweeter than knowledge, or maybe it didn't taste at all, but she'd have bitten anyway, just for the thrill of doing what she wasn't supposed to do.

And Adam? He'd have stayed clueless. Wouldn't know he was naked. Wouldn't care. He'd look in the pond, see his reflection, and think about the color of his sneakers—if they even existed, or if they should exist, or why they'd exist at all.

The snake might've thrown in the towel. *What's the point?* it'd hiss. *These idiots don't need my help to screw things up.* And God? He'd shake His head, watching them from the clouds, thinking, *they managed to ruin paradise without even tasting the fruit. What a species.*

And the fall? Oh, it still would've happened. It always does. But instead of shame, there'd just be confusion. No fig leaves, no curses—just Adam and Eve wandering around the garden, arguing over whether dung balls should be eaten or framed.

And maybe that's the joke. Not the fruit, not the tree, not even the beetle. The joke's us—standing there, staring at something ridiculous, and deciding it's worth everything to reach for it anyway.

291
At the Temple

The High Priest smirks from his marble throne, robe dragging the dust of crushed starlight and the blood of a thousand sacrificed lambs—his fingers pointing like crooked arrows at the God Most High, bringer of law, justice, and wisdom. Purveyor of cosmic creations given to a humanity that is tripping over its own shoelaces.

Love? Oh, love's a bone in a doctor's dream—a dislocated heart, fractured promises, all waiting for the High Priest to step out of the Holy of Holies, where he's just finished raising the dead, his robe still buzzing with leftover power, the kind that makes you think, *Is this really covered by my insurance?*

And there she is—that woman who bled for decades, invisible to everyone except the young man connected to a dusty garment. She reaches out, grabs it, and bam—the High Priest knows. But does anyone else? The Scribes? No, they're busy writing another rule about why laughter is a sin.

Jesus, meanwhile, munches on sardines fresh from Peter's net, talking about his next big event—a cookout in the middle of the Sea of Galilee. *BYOB,* he says, *but only if you can walk on water without soaking your sandals.*

Peter's broke again, shelling out for another wedding because Jesus can't stop making wine—fine Cabernet from dirty foot water. Paul pockets the change, writes another letter to the Corinthians, telling them to get their act together and stop asking for refunds.

They all sit around, searching for the Holy Grail, but no one realizes she's right there, the girl from Magdala, elbows on the table, rolling her eyes at their cluelessness.

Even Judas doesn't see her. He clutches his silver—rotten, stinking silver—thinking it's worth more than what's slipping through his fingers.

Peter, bless his soul, is back at it with the sword, lopping off the ears of Roman servants like he's pruning hedges. Malchus ends up in the emergency room, asking for holy implants and a strong cup of tea.

And the High Priest? Oh, he's laughing now, but not for the reasons you'd think. He's turned the whole thing into a lucrative sideshow, charging admission at the temple gates, selling forgiveness by the pound while the God Most High, bringer of the eternal stern look, stands in the wings, waiting for someone to overturn the tables of the money changers.

292
The Night Jacob Became Israel

Jacob couldn't sleep—insomnia, a curse left over from the flood—not with the stars leaning too close, whispering secrets only lunatics could decipher. The desert hummed, the sand shifted like a restless body, and the goats bleated their complaints into the void. God, watching from His usual perch, shrugged, and tossed Jacob a rock. *Rest your head on this,* He said, like it was the answer to everything.

Jacob, desperate for relief, thought it was some kind of celestial sleeping pill. He tried to swallow it with a glass of goat's milk, choking, sputtering, his throat aching like the promises he'd made and couldn't keep.

God laughed—not the gentle kind, but the booming laugh of a universe that doesn't care if you understand the joke. *You won't sleep that way,* He said, *but here's an idea: I'll dislocate your leg. When the pain turns to screams, you'll pass out. See? I work in mysterious ways.*

Jacob groaned—not just from the hip grinding out of place, but from the weight of it all—the wives, the sons, the promises piled high as mountains, all of it cracking his spine like a bundle of wet sticks.

And then, out of nowhere, the stranger appeared—not walking, not crawling, but just there, like an idea Jacob didn't want to have. They wrestled. The moon held its breath. The stars pressed closer, their edges cutting into the sky like shards of broken glass.

Jacob's muscles screamed; his hip twisted into a question mark. But he wouldn't let go, not until the stranger blessed him. Not until the stranger admitted that Jacob was something more than a tired man in the dirt.

When it was over, the stranger said, *Your name is Israel now. You wrestled with God, saw His face, and you're still standing. Well, limping, but close enough.*

Jacob sat there, his chest heaving, his name transformed into a nation. He thought about his wives—their laughter and tears, their sharp words cutting like knives, and their hands pulling him back from the edge. He thought about his sons—a tangle of dreams and jealousies, each one a piece of his heart walking around outside his body.

And Jacob—no, Israel now—felt the pain of his people before they even existed. The weight of a nation unborn sat on his shoulders, pressing him into the earth, but he didn't mind.

He had seen God's face and lived to tell the tale. He had been blessed by a stranger in the night, his hip screaming a hymn he didn't know he could sing. The stars finally backed away, giving him space. The rock beneath his head felt softer now, or maybe he was just too tired to care.

Jacob—Israel—closed his eyes, and the desert held him like a promise it didn't plan to break.

293
Moses's Chisel

Moses squinted at the stone tablets, his face still glowing like a bad sunburn from that last Divine encounter. *So, uh, are you sure there are only ten?* he asked, watching God carve with cosmic precision. *I mean,* Moses continued, *back at the burning bush, You made it sound like there were at least fifteen, maybe twenty. Or was I too busy not being consumed to take proper notes?*

God didn't look up, just kept etching away, sparks flying off the tablet like He was welding together the universe. *Maybe the guys down there with the Golden Calf have the rest of the list,* Moses said, half-joking, half-hoping. *Let's be honest—they've already rewritten half of it.*

The top of Moses's head started to itch. Rays of light were shooting out like bad plumbing. *Is this really necessary?* he muttered, scratching at the Divine glow. *I mean, I get it—I've been in Your presence. But this is going to make dinner conversations awkward.* God finally looked up. *Do you have a problem with these commandments?*

Well, Moses said, his voice cracking just a little, *I'm not sure about this one about saying Your name in vain. I mean, let's be real—we've been doing that for years. Shouting Your name every time a goat wandered off, or when we stubbed a toe on some desert rock. You haven't smited us yet. What gives?* God sighed, the kind of sigh that comes from knowing you're dealing with the most stubborn leader of the most stubborn people.

You'll understand that one when you get to Mt. Nebo, God said. *Until then, just trust Me. Right,* Moses said, his mouth twitching in that way it always did when he knew he wasn't getting a straight answer. He glanced down at the tablets again. *Honor your father and mother? I mean, sure, but have You met mine? They'd have opinions about this whole prophet gig.*

God went back to carving, and Moses let the silence stretch, his mind wandering to the people at the base of the mountain. They were still dancing, half-drunk on calf worship, their golden idol gleaming in the firelight. *I bet they'd appreciate a commandment about not throwing wild parties when your leader is gone,* Moses said. God ignored him. Finally, the tablets were done. *Take these down,* God said. *And remember these are blessings, not burdens.*

Moses raised an eyebrow. *Blessings? You're telling me "Don't covet your neighbor's ox" is a blessing? Half the people down there don't even have oxen.* God smiled, a slow, knowing smile. *You'll see,* He said. *It's not about the ox.*

Moses turned to leave, the tablets cutting into his arms, his glow lighting up the rocky path. Behind him, God called out, *And Moses? Don't lose these. You're not getting another set.* Moses rolled his eyes, but he smiled too. *Yeah, yeah,* he said under his breath. *Just don't ask me to carry fifteen next time.*

The mountain echoed with laughter, holy and human, as Moses descended, ready to face the chaos below.

294
The Drift

Grasping, it slips free—like sand through fingers, like love you never deserved, like that dog you couldn't keep—the one who looked at you as if you could save her.

Change flows like untamed currents, the kind that drag you out past safety, past shorelines, past any place you can scream for help. You're carried—not like a king in procession, but like driftwood, splintered, half-drowned.

Shifting like shadows, life moves and mocks. Each step forward feels like a dance, but the music keeps changing, waltz to punk, jazz to silence. And yet, in the still depths, somewhere below all the noise, you know it's not about the rhythm. It's about staying upright when the floor tilts.

Existence flows on, with or without you—like a train barreling toward nowhere in particular. You can hop on, hang from the side, or get flattened on the tracks—the train doesn't care.

Eyes fixed on bright skies, we march forward, faith like a flag in the wind—bloodied, half-tattered, half-bold. We call it mercy because to call it anything else would break us.

With faith in mercy, I stride—not confidently, but enough to get by. The blessings are there, sure, but they come with splinters—a warm meal laced with guilt, a sunrise you only see because you haven't slept.

Unburdened by fear? That's the biggest lie of all. But we tell it anyway—to ourselves, to each other—because what's the alternative? To admit the tragedy? That everything beautiful is borrowed, that every laugh is chased by silence, that every stride forward brings us closer to the last step?

And yet, the current carries on. It pulls us toward light, toward shadow, toward everything in between.

And, just maybe, in the shifting, the splintering, the laughter and the silence, there's something worth holding.

Even if it slips free.

295
The Breath Between Worlds

Creation hums beneath our feet, in the restless dust and the murmuring stars. It is the rhythm of things becoming atoms assembling like pilgrims seeking their form. In the endless pulse of time, galaxies are spun like fragile glass and just as easily shattered.

The immanent God, hidden yet everywhere, whispers in the language of energy, binding worlds together even as they dissolve. Creation and destruction—an inhale, an exhale—the universe breathing through the lungs of eternity.

In this vast machinery of birth and ruin, we glimpse something beyond mercy or wrath—a presence in the quiet burn of supernovas and the decay of fallen leaves. Not the tender shepherd with arms outstretched, but the architect of fire and collapse.

The God of entropy and new light, whose love is not absence but transformation, whose touch leaves nothing unchanged. In every heartbeat, a death; in every death, a beginning.

And here we stand, trembling sparks within the inferno, trying to name what cannot be named. Yet even as we fall into the unmaking, we rise again—our ashes seeded with possibility, our ruin stitched into the lattice of something wholly new. This is not the end. It is the same beginning. Again. And again.

296
The Roots Beneath Us

Helplessness is an old, bent tree in a wind too strong for kindness. We cling to its roots, shouting at the sky, cursing the rain, as if blame could calm the storm.

Anger is the language of the frightened heart. It barks, it snaps, it builds a cage of its own making. We think it shields us, but it only presses the walls closer.

Look around—the air is thick with uncertainty, the ground trembles with it. We are children, all of us, reaching for the first hand we see, even if that hand is a fist.

And oh, the voices. They rise in chaos, offering certainty like cheap bread. *Trust me,* they say, their eyes hard as iron, their promises sharp as knives. We reach anyway. How human we are, to mistake steel for solace.

But somewhere, far from the noise, there is a quieter truth. It hums in the spaces where no one shouts, in the cracks where the light slips in. It says: *not every hand can save you, not every certainty will hold.*

Yet still we long, and still we reach, and still, we pray—not for the storm to end, but for the courage to stand beneath its weight.

And when the wind bends the tree, when the rain stings our skin, we will not curse. We will kneel. And in the earth beneath our hands, we will find the roots.

297
The Shape of Meaning

Meaning is not something we find—like an old coin buried in the sand, nor a map with dotted lines leading to some gilded chest. It is something we make—a crude sculpture from scraps of broken glass and discarded wood, sharp and splintered in the hands.

The puzzle pieces are often the fragments of our shattered hopes. A dream of love, broken like a cheap porcelain vase, its shards too delicate to touch but too jagged to ignore. We sit cross-legged on the floor, trying to fit them together, but the edges never align. The picture we make isn't the one on the box.

And here comes irony, swaggering like a drunk at the last call, spilling its laughter all over the bar. *You wanted meaning?* Here it is a desk job, a mortgage, a half-eaten sandwich on a Wednesday afternoon. Here it is the sound of your own breath at 3 a.m., when the world feels like an empty stage and you've forgotten your lines.

You search for a Divine message, but the letters in the sky are just clouds—shapeless and drifting. You want the universe to whisper, but it only hums—a low, indifferent tone that sounds like silence.

Still, we keep going. We press the pieces together with glue that barely holds. We carve out meaning from the stone of disappointment, grind it smoothly with tears. And when we stand back, we see it—not a masterpiece, but something ours.

The joke, perhaps, is that meaning was never hidden. It was always in the act of searching, of shaping, of cutting ourselves on the shards and daring to call it art.

And if the final piece doesn't fit, if the edges still show the cracks—so be it. Even a broken mirror can reflect the sun.

Meaning isn't the answer. It's the question, the attempt, the struggle to build a life worth living from a pile of rubble.

298
Contemplating the Machine

Contemplating the meaning of life—am I moving like a smooth gear, humming with purpose, teeth locking perfectly in the churning metallic symphony?

Am I well-oiled, my edges slick and shining, turning with quiet grace toward some distant, unseen goal? Or am I a worn-out bushing, aching with friction, grinding to finality with every labored turn, begging to be extracted from this terrifyingly noisy machine?

The machine doesn't stop, doesn't care. It groans and howls—a blind beast of its own momentum. We're all in here somewhere—gears and levers, pulleys, and pins, working in tandem or falling apart.

And I wonder: who built this thing? Who dreamed of endless motion and called it progress? Did they imagine a purpose, or just a noise to drown out the silence?

Sometimes, I wish for rust. For the slow, inevitable decay—a final protest against the screaming cogs. To crumble to nothing, fall free from the teeth that bite too hard, and let the machine figure it out without me.

But then—in the stillest moments, when the grinding fades, I think it's not the machine that terrifies me, but the thought of not being a part of it at all.

299
Clown and Mirror

The clown, face painted bright as sorrow, sits cross-legged on the floor of a dim room, trying to tape a shattered mirror together. The glass bites back, each shard a razor's edge reflecting a face that is not their own.

He holds one piece up to the light—a woman's face, soft and pale, eyes like clouds about to storm. She is crying, but the tears aren't his. The clown wipes his cheek, just to make sure.

Another shard shows a man, grinning too wide, teeth sharp as knives. The clown laughs nervously, but the sound dies in the hollow room, a balloon deflating in a silence too heavy to lift.

Piece by piece, he puzzles it together—a child with a freckled nose, a soldier with a scarred brow, a woman with lips painted red like a wound that won't heal. Each fragment is a stranger. Each reflection a question.

The tape sticks poorly, curling at the edges, its adhesive losing faith. The clown whispers, *this will hold. It has to hold.* But the cracks remain, spiderwebbing outwards, impossible to erase. He steps back to see what he's made—a mosaic of faces—none of them his. All of them strangers. The clown tilts his head, searching for recognition in the fractured gallery.

What is a face, after all, but a mask worn too long? The greasepaint smears, the lines blur, and even mirrors forget what they were meant to hold.

The clown kneels, presses his palms to the glass, ignoring the sting of splinters. *Who am I?* he whispers. The mirror answers with silence and a hundred stolen gazes.

In the corner of the room, a balloon floats listlessly, its string tethered to nothing. The clown reaches for it, but his hand stops short. Sometimes, even air is too heavy to lift.

Outside, the world calls—a child's laughter, a dog barking, a train grinding along its tracks. Life moves on, indifferent to rooms full of shards and clowns without faces.

The clown stands, his knees cracking like glass. He leaves the mirror, taped but not whole, and steps into the world with painted lips and hollow eyes.

Someone laughs at the sight of him—a bright, careless sound. The clown smiles back, the curve of his mouth a masterful lie. After all, what's another mask when your face was never yours to begin with?

300
Neon Truth

The city at dusk, a patchwork of broken promises and flickering lights, leans against the horizon like a tired boxer. Its skyline hums with the faint glow of ambition, windows reflecting windows, each one a little lie about how much living is going on inside. Down on the street, there's a single neon sign burning its message into the twilight: *OPEN*. The letters buzz faintly, a hymn to commerce, or a eulogy.

Beneath it, the store is shuttered tight. The gate, rusted and curled like the lip of someone who doesn't want to talk to you, hasn't moved in years. The sign lies, or maybe it hopes. Hard to tell in a place like this. Cars roll by their headlights sweeping shadows onto the cracked asphalt. No one looks at the sign. No one wonders who it's for.

Above, a window opens, and a woman leans out, lighting a cigarette like she's done it a thousand times. Her face catches the neon glow—*OPEN,* it says, but her eyes are closed. The street has its usual symphony: a dog barking somewhere unseen, a bottle smashing two alleys over, a man shouting at someone—or no one. You could walk this block a thousand times and still not know its secrets.

A boy on a skateboard clatters past, his wheels sparking against the pavement. He doesn't slow. He doesn't stop. His backpack hangs loose, like he's waiting for it to fall. The sign catches him for a moment—*OPEN*—and he's gone. Inside the store that isn't a store, there's nothing left. Empty shelves. Dust settling in places no one will clean. A cash register still sits there, its drawer frozen open, its mouth stuck mid-sentence. But no one will ever know. The gate is rusted, remember? The hinges scream louder than the city.

And yet, the sign burns on. It doesn't flicker. Doesn't falter. It declares its truth into the gathering dark. It is *OPEN*. Somewhere in the city, a man on a rooftop looks at the horizon, a beer in one hand, his phone in the other. He doesn't see the sign. He doesn't see the store. But he feels the same thing they do something that should be there, something that should be alive, but isn't.

The night deepens. The sign doesn't care. The streets grow quieter, the distant sound of a subway rumbling underground. The city settles into its skin, each building exhaling softly. The neon buzzes.
By midnight, only the drunks and the desperate wander beneath it. They stumble past, their shadows falling just short of the gate. No one looks up. No one dares. The sign still says *OPEN*, though nothing is, though no one is. It hums louder now, like it knows the truth. It isn't for the living, after all.

Dawn comes slow, and the sign finally dies. Its glow fades into the gray light, its promise evaporating like the mist. The city stretches awake, the street emptier than before. But somewhere, a new sign flickers on. It hums its own tune, declares its own lie. And the city listens. And the city believes.

301
Ode to Bill Evans

The piano is the color of rain-swollen wood, keys bruised with a hundred confessions. Evans sits in the half-light, a shadow pretending to be a man— or a man pretending to be a shadow.

The apartment hums with absence— no power, no phone, just the steady pulse of withdrawal ticking inside his skull. The city outside doesn't knock, doesn't ask. It just keeps moving, a river of strangers carrying umbrellas against nothing but the weight of the sky.

"You don't understand," he says, to no one, to the cigarette smoke coiling by the window. "It's death first—then transfiguration." Every note he plays is a funeral for something he never had but always wanted. The notes rise like moths fluttering toward a dying bulb. Borrowed money, borrowed time— both spent faster than memory.

When the pain lifts— it's like being born into another mistake, but for a moment, for the width of a single chord, it's light. Pure and blinding as forgiveness. Then comes the fall— a slow descent, stitched with silence. The keys go quiet. And somewhere beneath the city, a train moves like a hymn without words.

The day resets itself, waiting for the score, the small salvation in the needle's whisper. His fingers ache for the piano, but all they find is air.

302
Patchwork Bird

A bird made of patchwork fabric takes flight into the stitched-together sky. Its wings are a mosaic of memories—scraps of old dresses, maps with routes no one dares to take, and photographs so faded their faces have turned to ghosts.

Each feather hums with a story, a threadbare lullaby from a forgotten life. Here, a square of gingham whispers of a girl running barefoot in a summer field. There, a torn atlas murmurs of cities that never existed, roads that lead nowhere but dreams.

The bird flutters, its seams straining against the wind. The sky doesn't care for fragility—it pulls and tears, it demands strength or nothing at all. But the bird keeps climbing, higher than anyone expects. Its wings creak, the stitches groan, but they hold. They were made for this.

Below, the earth is a patchwork, too—fields stitched together by fences, rivers winding like loose threads through mountains frayed with time. The bird looks down, and for a moment, it sees itself mirrored in the world, a reflection pieced together from what was left behind.

It soars over a city where no one looks up. The streets are too loud, the people too busy sewing their own stories into the fabric of survival. But somewhere, a child sees it, points to the sky, and laughs like a bell ringing through a forgotten church.

The bird dips its patchwork wing in salute. The wind catches a corner of fabric—a strip of faded green that once belonged to a soldier's jacket. It flutters away, carried off into the horizon.

What is lost isn't really lost, the bird seems to say, its wings flapping like a chorus of hands waving goodbye. *What is broken can still fly, can still catch the light, can still be seen.*

And so, the bird keeps going, its fabric fraying with each mile, its patches growing looser, until, piece by piece, it becomes the wind itself—a breath stitched into the world, a reminder that even scraps can rise.

303
The Uninvited Miracles

Miracles that slither under closed doors—slick, serpentine, unwelcome. You didn't ask for them. You didn't light the candle or whisper the prayer. But here they are, curling at your feet like shadows you can't escape.

Miracles that drop from the sky like dead flies—silent, brittle, absurd. You look up, expecting wings, halos, a flash of light—but all you see is the emptiness they left behind.

Silent miracles, the kind with no business with you. They perch on the edge of your day, half-glimpsed in the corner of your eye. They do not knock. They do not ask. But they linger, like a forgotten thought you almost remember.

And then, the box of miracles—hidden away, sealed with ribbons of gold and locks forged from riddles. It sits in the dark, waiting for its moment, its singular purpose. You know it is there, but the key was lost long ago.

Only when it snows on the moon, the box says, its voice the creak of old wood. *Only when the impossible makes a fool of the real.*

So, you wait—not for the snow, not for the moon, but for the slither, the drop, the silent weight of miracles that have no business with you but are there anyway.

304
The Omega Point

We are not wanderers lost in an indifferent universe. We are threads in a vast tapestry, spun by the hands of a Creator who dreams in stars and seas. To live is to take part in this unfolding, this slow, deliberate becoming. We rise not alone, but as a chorus—called forward by the quiet voice of Christ, singing through the currents of time.

The earth turns, and so do we. Our bones remember the dust from which we came, yet our souls ache for the heavens. Teilhard saw it—the sacred spiral of life, the pulse of creation reaching toward its final crescendo. We are more than matter; we are the fire within the clay, the breath behind the beating heart.

This journey is not just biological—it is love, awakening in the marrow of the world. Christ is not a distant figure on a golden throne—He is the force binding atoms, the whisper urging cells toward complexity, the light within the labyrinth of consciousness.

And what is the "Omega Point" if not the home we have always longed for? Not the end, but the fullness of all things drawn into divine embrace. We are not falling apart—we are being gathered in, layer by layer, dream by dream, until the infinite breathes in us fully.

So, when the road feels endless and the weight unbearable, remember we are co-creators of this holy ascent. Each small act of love adds to the rising. Each cry of hope echoes through the stars. We are not alone on this path to union. Christ walks with us—The Alpha, the Omega, and every step in between.

305
The Cost of Grace

Grace was never meant to be easy. It is not a coin we slip into the hands of heaven for safe passage through this world. It is a fire—beautiful, consuming, unrelenting. To accept it is to be changed, To walk not away from the world's suffering, But into it, with open hands and steady feet.

Bonhoeffer knew this: Faith without sacrifice is not faith at all. To follow Christ is to bear the burden of others, To stand in the breach when justice is crushed beneath the heel of power. Costly grace does not ask, "What will I gain?" It whispers, "What must I give?"

And in that giving, we lose the comfort of religion as a ritual, as a refuge from the chaos outside. Religion-less Christianity—Faith stripped down to its bones. Faith as a radical, defiant love. Faith as action when the world demands silence.

To believe is not to hide behind hymns and sermons. It is to speak truth to tyrants, to lift the fallen, to be a shield for the vulnerable even when it costs everything.

Grace is costly because love is costly. But Bonhoeffer showed us that it is worth the price. For in every small act of courage, in every refusal to bow to injustice, Christ's face appears again—not in the safety of temples, but in the wreckage of this weary world, calling us still: *"Come, follow Me."*

306
Stones and the Dust

As Jesus came out of the temple, one of his disciples said to him: *Look, Teacher, what large stones, what magnificent buildings,* their arches sweeping like prayers to a God we can almost touch.

And Jesus, with the calm of someone who has seen too much and knows better, replied: *They will be gone soon enough. Every stone will be unstacked, every room blown to the sky, and the dust will rain down like sour water for nearly an eternity.*

The disciples stared at him; their hearts heavy with fear. For wasn't this the temple, the sacred place, the home of all they held holy?

What do we do then, they asked, *when the walls crumble, when the sky turns to ash?*

Jesus sighed, the kind of sigh that knows the weight of their worry but cannot take it from them.

God is always here, not in stones or walls, not in gilded rooms or golden light. He is here— and he touched his chest—*in your heart, in your mind, in your soul.*

The temple of spirit, he told them, *cannot be destroyed. Bring on the earthquakes, the floods, the fires. Let the ground split open and the heavens roar. Let time gnaw at every pillar until even memory forgets what once stood here.*

Just make sure, he said, *that no one leads you astray. They will come—smooth-tongued, carrying promises like lanterns that lead only into darkness. Keep your eyes open, your heart steady. Do not trade the eternal for what you can touch.*

And as the sun dipped low, casting long shadows across the stones, the disciples turned and followed him.

But one lingered, looking back at the temple, at the towering walls that seemed too strong to fall. In the silence, he could almost hear the stones whisper, their voices dry and brittle: *We are not forever.*

The years rolled on, and the temple fell, its great stones scattered like seeds across the earth. Dust rose, clouded the sky, and rained down on the people until they forgot what it was, they were mourning.

But somewhere, in the hearts of those who listened, the temple still stood—unshaken, undimmed. Its doors open to every soul willing to walk within.

And when the floods came, and the fires raged, and the earthquakes broke the bones of the earth, those who remembered felt no fear.

For they carried their temples with them—untouchable, undestroyable, eternal.

307
Hollow Room

There is a room inside us, hollow, echoing, filled with the whispers of what we've lost. We paint the walls with worry, nail up the portraits of things we can't forget, things we never had.

The Holy Spirit stands at the door, knocking—not loudly, but with a rhythm so steady it shakes the bones of the soul.

And yet, we do not answer. Instead, we fill the hollow with fragile things: a song that falters halfway through, a dream that crumbles under daylight, a love that leaves more than it gives.

We build towers of thought to keep the silence at bay, but they sway—precarious—on foundations made of fear.

Behind every tremor in the mind, every brittle nerve, every sleepless night, is the great separation—a soul adrift, its anchor cut loose from the eternal wind that once carried it.

And still, the Spirit waits—its power not in thunder or flame, but in the soft breath of presence, in the gentle weight that holds us when the walls begin to crack.

What is this reality we flee? It is not cruel, but it is relentless. It does not barter, but it gives freely. It asks only that we stop, turn, and see that the door was open all along.

In that moment, the hollow becomes a cathedral, and the echoes sing instead of haunt.

The Spirit, long denied, floods the room with light—a light that does not leave, even when the shadows return.

308
Breath and the Blade

There is a weight in the air, not the weight of mountains or storms, but something sharper—a blade, a whisper, a shadow that cuts without sound. The powers of evil do not knock; they slip through cracks, through wounds left untended, through the quiet corners of the heart where doubt breeds like a fever.

And yet—there is another breath, a wind that does not steal but fills. It does not creep but roars with the sound of life, of fire igniting the marrow, of light carving its way through the darkness.

To be touched by both is to stand between two rivers—one black and silent, one golden and alive. And they fight in your blood, pulling, tearing, each demanding the throne of your soul.

The Holy Spirit does not take by force. It waits, patient as a gardener with winter soil, knowing the seeds planted in faith and tears will one day bloom.

But the powers of evil—they claw and grasp, promising kingdoms, delivering ruins. They thrive in silence, in the absence of yes or no, in the gray fog where surrender feels like peace.

One's being is a battleground, a holy altar, a fragile thing of clay and breath. To stand in this space is to ache with the weight of eternity, to tremble at the hand that touches next.

Yet, the Spirit speaks: "I am here. I was always here. Let me breathe, let me burn, let me fill the void with something unbreakable."

And so, the choice—to let the light in or to let the shadow reign. A trembling heart with the power to say yes, or to say no, or to say nothing at all.

309
The Space They Leave

When did your mother pass away? When did Frank die? I didn't know Becky expired. Did you see her body in the casket? Didn't she look great—like a wax doll at a yard sale, painted up to seem less dead?

I don't go to funerals anymore. Everybody's strange there. Some laugh too loud, some cry just enough to look real, but most hover in that awkward limbo, their faces frozen in polite despair.

Funerals are like bad dinner parties: cheap wine, stale sandwiches, and everybody pretending they loved the guest of honor.

Not sure about cremation, though. Feels like rushing the end—as if the fire gets to finish what life barely started. And besides, I don't smoke.

The dead keep piling up, but I don't feel smaller without them. If anything, their absence takes up more space, like the way silence grows louder in an empty room.

I don't need a graveyard tour, don't need to see their names etched in stone, don't need the folded flag or the priest's monotone promises.

Death isn't something you visit. It's just there—like bad weather, like a slow song you can't get out of your head.

So don't ask me if I saw her one last time. I'd rather remember Becky laughing, Frank drunk and telling lies, Sam with his stupid jokes, and your mother back when her hands still smelled like fresh-baked bread.

310
Small Song of the World

The wind steps lightly through the grass, carrying no shadow, leaving no debt. It asks no name of the leaves and receives no answer.

A bird folds its wings mid-flight—not falling but becoming the fall itself. Its song is the edge of silence, where the world breathes and does not breathe.

A stone rests by the river, its roundness older than the stars' first light. It remembers nothing. It holds everything.

And here I am, a traveler with too many bags, watching the wind, hearing the bird, touching the stone.

I am none of these things, but they are all of me.

311
Ash and Echoes

The ashtray spills over, gray dust on a table of cracked Formica. I've been here too long, and the coffee tastes like the bottom of someone else's cup.

She left last week. Or maybe it was a year ago—time folds up in these walls.

The bartender talks about the Dodgers, but his words scatter like broken pool cues across the felt.

Outside, the moon's a nickel tossed into a gutter. I light a cigarette with a match from a bar I'll never go back to.

The edge of the counter bites my arm, a reminder I'm still here.

Tomorrow? Maybe I'll write something better. Or not.

There's always another night to sit here, listening to the clatter of bones in someone else's game.

312
The Quiet of Love

In the stillness of the forest, where shadows and light dance in silence, the trees do not seek to surpass one another. Each stands as it is—rooted, whole, its presence enough to complete the song.

The mountain does not disdain the valley, nor does the valley envy the height of the peak. They are companions in their difference, a quiet harmony that holds the earth together.

Love is this quiet. It is not the loud clamor of the self but the gentle giving of breath to the world.

It is the falling of the leaf—not in defeat, but in surrender to the seasons, to the great rhythm of all things.

When you meet another, bring no weapons of judgment, carry no banners of pride.

Instead, offer the stillness of love, the peace that listens and does not demand, the kindness that seeks no reward.

For in this quiet, in this intimacy with love, you will find no enemy, no other, only the unbroken circle of being.

313
Fried Eggs and Smoke

Emily's at the stove again, cigarette dangling from her lips, ash curling into the grease pan. She's swaying, not with the rhythm of life, but the rhythm of gin—cheap stuff, bottom shelf, the kind that tastes like regret.

The eggs crack like tiny explosions, each yolk a sun too fragile for this kitchen. She laughs, her voice rough, a cackle sharp as broken glass, like the bottles she used to toss into the alley behind the bar.

"Life's a fried egg," she says, and I don't ask her what she means. I just watch the whites spread thin, bubbling like secrets no one tells.

She flips them with a fork, jabbing like a boxer past her prime, fighting an opponent only she can see. Her hair's a mess, her housecoat stained with yesterday's spills.

The radio hums some sad country tune, but she's not listening. She's humming her own song—a hymn to lost lovers, missed trains, and the God who stopped answering her calls.

"Eat up," she says, sliding the eggs onto a chipped plate. The yolks run like rivers of gold trying to escape. I take a bite, and it tastes like smoke, like failure, like something you shouldn't love but do anyway.

She pours herself another drink, whiskey this time, as if the gin's betrayed her. "To hell with it," she says, raising the glass like a saint blessing the chaos.

And for a moment, I think she's the bravest person I've ever known. The pan still sizzles, a lonely applause for a life that never learned to sit still.

And Emily, drunk as ever, smiles like she's figured it all out—or she hasn't, but doesn't care anymore. She lights another cigarette, leans against the counter, and watches the smoke spiral toward the ceiling.

"You're too young to understand," she says, but I'm not. I'm old enough to know that fried eggs and drunken girlfriends are sometimes the best things you'll ever have.

314
Already Here

Jesus is already here. Stop searching the clouds for some divine hand to carve a message into the sky. The heavens have spoken in the language of rain and stars for ages, but you were waiting for something louder, weren't you?

What are you waiting for? The choir of angels has already sung in the laughter of children and the quiet breathing of the weary. The sign you crave is in the trembling hands of the broken, in the unspoken prayers of the lost.

Stop looking up for miracles painted in lightning. Bend low instead—to lift, to carry, to heal. In the simple kindness of a shared meal, in the stubborn mercy of forgiveness, Christ is made flesh again and again.

Go help your suffering brother, your lonely sister, the stranger whose story you do not yet know. Love like the sun that warms the forgotten corners of the world without asking who is worthy.

Manifest the love of Christ, and you will find God not hidden in the sky, but right here—in the space between heartbeats, in the silence that breathes after the storm, in the trembling moment when you choose love over fear.

Open your eyes. Jesus was never far. He was always in the reaching hand, the offered cup, the mended wound. He is here, and so is your chance to see.

315
Out of the Chaos

The heart trembles, a storm churns beneath the ribs, wild winds of fear and hope, grief and joy entwined. Yet even in the chaos, a voice speaks:

"Do not fear, for I have redeemed you; I have summoned you by name; you are mine."

Emotions collide, like waves against the shore, breaking apart what once felt whole. But in the shards of yesterday, His hands are at work, gathering fragments, whispering, "I make all things new."

Out of disorder, He shapes harmony. From the ache of uncertainty, He calls forth purpose.

"For we are His workmanship, created in Christ Jesus to do good works."

The tension stretches the soul, a bowstring pulled taut. And in the release, a song is born—a melody of grace, a rhythm of hope.

"Weeping may last through the night, but joy comes with the morning."

Chaos within becomes the spark, igniting the fire of creation. For He who calms the storm also commands the light to shine, even in the darkest places.

"And God said, 'Let there be light,' and there was light."

So let the chaos come, let it stir the deep, for even in the tempest, He reigns. And from the fertile ground of struggle, He will bring forth beauty, for His glory and our good.

316

Glass Amnesia

Glass amnesia blocks the rays of the sun but only when lovers lock tongues, dancing in the shadows, trying to forget the world. The streets are full of echoes—ghosts in suits and dresses, their feet moving but going nowhere as the world spins on an axis of rusted nails under the weight of forgotten promises.

Happy children with little feet—bare and tender—caress their only mother's lips, soft against weary cheeks, kissing them farewell as they march off into the twilight of urban decay. Tiny soldiers in a war they don't understand, their laughter swallowed by the roar of distant bombs, the sky opening up to swallow them whole, lifting them into oblivion where memories are just dreams that refuse to die.

The city hums with a low, feverish buzz—like a dying insect trapped under glass, its wings twitching, struggling to remember what it means to fly. The buildings lean forward, moaning, waiting for the final collapse, for the streets to fill with the blood of forgotten wars, the rivers running red with the tears of mothers whose children never returned from the playground.

Death strolls down the boulevard, a cigarette hanging from her lips, smoke curling into the shape of lost souls—twisting, turning—before fading into the blue-gray sky.

The soulless politician tips his hat to the beggar on the corner, a nod to the soldier lying in the gutter, a wink to the lovers dancing on the edge of oblivion, their tongues tied together in a knot of desperation, forgetting that the world is burning, that the night is creeping in, that the end is always just around the corner.

War lingers in the alleys—a shadow with an assault weapon, a whisper in the ear of every man, every woman who still believes that there's something worth fighting for. It waits patiently for the moment when the last flicker of hope is snuffed out by the cold, indifferent wind.

The trains roll by—empty but for the memories, the screams that no one hears, the faces pressed against the glass, eyes wide with the knowledge that the end is closer than they thought, that the world is just an incinerator, and they are the actors who have forgotten their lines.

Glass amnesia blocks the rays of the sun, but only when the world stops spinning, when the dancers fall silent, their feet tangled in the threads of a dream they can't escape.

317

Pebble in My Shoe

She looks at you with disdain, then scratches her arm as if to say you're nothing but a mosquito.

And then the dog comes, following her like she's the Queen of Sheba on her way to her coronation.

I take the shoe off, fiddle with my sock, and sure enough, there's that little pebble—looks like it chipped off from the side of a tombstone.

Hard as granite with sharp edges, stained with the blood of an old foot that's stuffed into a beat-up old Oxford that lawyers used to wear to court, but now just a cast-off, soleless article purchased at the Goodwill store.

Think I'll take the stone back home and throw it in the fish tank along with the plastic diver and the skull. Should have stayed home.

Home where the wine bottles wait, and the computer mocks, and the cat curls up on the windowsill, staring out at the rain like he's waiting for Godot—or just another hot day.

I light my pipe and watch the smoke curl and dance, wonder if it's all worth it—this stumbling through life, collecting stones in my shoes, and dreams in my head, and regrets in my heart.

The blonde's gone now, didn't even notice me or the way I limped off that bench, stone in hand. And the dog—he's off sniffing some other corner of the world, living in a way I can't quite understand.

I sit at my desk and stare at the screen. The words don't come—not tonight, not with the stone sitting in the fish tank, mocking me like everything else in this distorted world.

Living is like walking on a hot sidewalk with gravel in your shoes. Sometimes you don't know how that damned little stone got there, but you keep walking—because what else is there to do?

318
I Embrace My Faith Like a Dog with a Bone

I embrace my faith like a dog with a bone, clinging to it—my anchor in life's rough seas where the waves crash and howl, and the night swallows the stars.

Patience by my side like an old friend—we've walked these streets together through the rain and the grime, the bars, and the broken dreams.

We share drinks and stories, laugh at the absurdity of it all, knowing the world doesn't owe us a thing.

In the tempests of trouble's storm, when the world spins out of control, I cast off fear like an empty bottle. God guides my heart—a compass in the chaos, steady and sure.

I find my way, stumbling sometimes, but always forward, always reaching for that sliver of light, that promise of dawn in a city that never awakens from its deep sleep, where hope hides in the cracks and faith dances in the shadows.

The streets are a labyrinth full of lost souls and forgotten dreams, but I walk them with purpose—head held high, eyes on the horizon, heart beating with the rhythm of something bigger, something unseen.

I pass the drifters and the dreamers, the ones who have given up and the ones who still fight, and I nod to them—a silent salute, a shared understanding that life is a brutal dance but one worth dancing.

In the quiet moments, when the chaos recedes and the world is still, I feel it—that divine grace, lifting me, pushing me forward, reminding me I am not alone.

The city hums with a low, constant murmur—a discordant melody of lives intertwined, each note a story, each chord a struggle. But in the cacophony, there's a harmony, a sense of something greater, something holy.

I embrace faith strongly, like a dog with a bone, clinging to it—my anchor in life's rough seas where the waves crash and howl.

Patience by my side like an old friend—we walk these streets together through the rain and the grime, the bars, and the broken dreams.

319
The Emergency Department

Emergency Department—where lights are too bright and the air too cold, we lay bare, suctioned, sealed, but still we bleed, ending in silence.

Doctors with gloved hands, nurses with tired eyes, do their part—but in the end, it's just us facing the void, a final curtain call, no applause, no encore.

The flickering fluorescence, the antiseptic scent, the beeping of machines—a symphony of dread where humanity is stripped to raw nerves and naked flesh, where hope is a fragile whisper lost in the clamor.

The ER doc's mask hides more than just a face—it conceals the distance, the dispassionate gaze, the mechanical precision that slices through hope, dissects our fears.

In this cold emergency room, we are more than patients—we are silent actors in an unfeeling play, scripts unwritten, endings unknown, each breath a gamble, each heartbeat a prayer.

The walls witness our silent pleas, the floors remember our silent falls, and in the shadows, our ghosts linger—the ones who couldn't hold on, the ones who slipped into the void, their whispers mingling with the hum of machines and the shuffle of feet.

We enter with our lives in balance, our souls on the line, laying ourselves bare to cold steel and colder hands, hoping for miracles in a land where certainty is an illusion.

In this place, where dreams dissolve and truths are sharper than knives, we find ourselves stripped, vulnerable, exposed—clinging to the frayed edges of faith and fear as the lights burn too bright and the air turns too cold.

We walk out—those of us who can—carrying the scars, the stories, the silence etched deep into our bones, a testament to survival, a mark of our dance with death.

320
Autopsy of Love

This autopsy of love, where we lay ourselves bare, hoping for some kind of redemption, some salvation in the slicing, but finding only emptiness and the stark, sterile silence of a love gone cold.

Your eyes dissect me, cutting me into tiny pieces to be frozen and examined at your leisure on your psychic surgery table.

Always probing and piercing those soft areas of pale white skin—the delicate underbelly dragging on the sharp rocks.

Suctioning, suturing, and sealing the wounds—they still bleed, and we both wind up dead in the operating theater under the cold, indifferent lights.

You take your scalpel eyes and carve into my memories, peeling back the layers, exposing the nerves—raw and screaming—each incision a reminder of the pain we thought we'd buried.

We dissect the past—every argument, every lie—laid out like specimens on a tray glistening under a fluorescent glare, each one a testament to our failures, our missteps.

The bedroom echoes with the sounds of our dissection—the whispers of lost moments, the echoes of broken promises—a symphony of sorrow played out in the sterile confines of our examination.

We hoped for healing, for a miracle in the mess, for some divine intervention, for God to step into the laboratory with us, to stitch us back together, to close the wounds and stop the bleeding.

We were surgeons of our own demise, cutting too deep, too often, until there was nothing left but the empty shell of what we once were—two bodies on a table, lifeless and cold under the indifferent lights.

This autopsy of love, where we lay ourselves bare, hoping for some kind of redemption, some salvation in the slicing, but finding only emptiness and the stark, sterile silence of a love gone cold.

Where once there was passion, now only the cold, clinical aftermath of hearts that dared to love—and died in the process.

321
When Your Presence Fades

When your presence fades and your voice is a distant echo, adrift and uncertain, we seek solace in our minds, our cloudy thoughts—in constructs of our own making, patching the holes in our hearts with dreams and fleeting memories.

It's a hard road when the light goes dim, when the comfort of your touch is just a memory, and we are left alone in the hollow silence—where once there was laughter, now only shadows remain.

We build our walls, our little fortresses, fill them with shadows and whispers, trying to recreate the warmth, the safety we once knew. In the darkness of our doubts, we huddle in our self-made sanctuaries, seeking refuge from the cold.

Adrift in this sea of thoughts, we cling to whatever floats—the fragile remnants of belief, the shards of hope we find in the wreckage of our faith— holding tight to the pieces, trying to make sense of the fragments.

We seek comfort in our minds, in the fantasies we spin—trying to mend the cracks, to fill the empty spaces with dreams and illusions—leaving us more lost, more adrift in the harsh light of reality.

But still we reach, we search for something real, something to hold on to when your presence fades.

We listen for your murmurs in the quiet moments, in the spaces between breaths, hoping to catch a glimpse, a fleeting sign of the connection we once had—the bond that time cannot sever.

In the darkness, we light candles—small flickers of hope to guide us through the night, to lead us back to ourselves, to the core of our being, where your essence still lingers—a silent witness to our struggles, a beacon in our despair.

We journey inward, through the labyrinth of our minds, seeking relief in the memories, in the remnants of your love—piecing together the fragments, building a mosaic of our pain and our resilience.

For in the echoes of our souls, in the silence that surrounds us, we find a glimmer of truth, a spark of understanding—that we are not alone, that your presence, though faded, still guides us, still holds us in the cradle of its light.

322
Ukraine Spring

Tell me it's spring when a daffodil punches through brown grass its yellow head a tiny defiance in my blurry vision. Ukrainian yellow I think a good name for a new color.

But then a tank crushes the flower only in my twisted thoughts.

I imagine daffodils still push up into the Ukrainian sky children with yellow bouquets on a train to somewhere safe. In Russia daffodils rise too beneath a cold sky while children play unaware of distant guns and bombs.

A ballet dancer left the Bolshoi dances in Poland now she's like a daffodil slender persistent.

In spring there's hope even when the dance floors are empty
and the theaters are gone.

We cling to these fragile signs— daffodils dancers, children who still run and laugh as tanks roll over everything else.

Tell me it's spring because in destruction's heart we need to remember life continues flowers will bloom and dancers will find new stages. We need to believe in the yellow in the hope that somewhere life is still beautiful and worth fighting for.

Tell me it's spring because even when winter grips the heart the daffodils push through defying the cold a testament to resilience, to life's relentless return.

We need these reminders of these small miracles to guide us through the darkness to show us that beauty persists and hope endures.

Tell me it's spring and let the daffodils be our guide symbols of survival emblems of hope.

323
At the End of the City's Guts

At the end of the city's guts where asphalt chokes on river brine, friends huddle in a bar that smells like yesterday's regrets.

The neon flickers tired and worn, casting shadows on their faces etched with lines of laughter and sorrow, every drink a toast to what once was.

The bartender knows their names, their stories, their lies, pours another round of solace in chipped glasses, cheap and strong.

The jukebox plays a mournful tune, a soundtrack to their shared defeat, but there's comfort in the company, in slurred confessions and drunken truths.

They talk of dreams long buried, lovers lost, chances missed, the weight of what-ifs heavy on their shoulders, dragging them down.

But for a moment in the haze, they find a spark of something real, a connection forged in the ruins of broken promises and faded hopes.

The night wears on relentlessly, the outside world a blur, but inside they cling to each other, finding strength in their collective fall.

The dawn breaks with weary light, casting long shadows on their retreat, the city awakening indifferent to the lives spent in its grip.

They rise slowly and deliberately, shuffling back to their routines, each step a testament to resilience forged in fire.

The memories linger like smoke in the quiet corners of their minds, but they march stoically, holding onto the fragments of solace.

In the stillness of their hearts, compassion weaves its thread, bright and pure, a silent strength binding them through the years.

Old men battered by the grind, yet unbroken, unbowed, they continue with quiet dignity in a world that often forgets.

And the game continues, the bar remains a sanctuary, a place where time slows just enough for old men to find themselves and each other once again.

324
The Circus of Time

Circus dancers spin, billowing clouds grace the sky—life's elusive show, a spectacle of fleeting time, where moments dance and then fade away.

Under the big top of existence, we twirl and leap, a frenzy of motion, trying to capture the ephemeral, to hold onto something real in this carnival of chaos.

The clouds roll by, indifferent, painting the sky with their transient art, while below, we perform our acts—desperate clowns and daring acrobats—each moment a fragile masterpiece.

We juggle dreams and broken promises, tightrope-walk the edge of sanity, hoping for applause, for recognition, in this grand, uncaring theater where the spotlight fades as quickly as it appears.

Time, the relentless ringmaster, cracks its whip, drives us forward through rings of fire and shadows deep, until the music stops, the lights dim, and we're left with nothing but echoes.

Moments dance then fade away—like whispers on the wind, like smoke from the cigarette burning down to its final ember—a reminder that all we have is this fleeting performance, this brief, beautiful act before the curtain falls.

We are the circus—the dancers, the clowns—spinning in the twilight, gracing the sky with our struggles, our joys, our sorrows, knowing that in the end, we all vanish into the night.

325
Subway Refrain

The train rattles—a beast in the dark, graffiti and grime its cloak, faces blurred, stories untold, all lost in the underground's choke.

In the murky depths of the soul's subway, your voice crackles through the wires—a haunting melody in the cacophony, echoing through the tunnels of my mind.

Your words cut through the noise—a sweet song in the mechanical roar, bringing memories of forgotten joys, of nights spent dreaming, wanting more.

Each stop a jolt back to reality, but your melody lingers, soft and low—a siren's call in the city's brutality, reminding me of places only we know.

The lights flicker, shadows dance—ghosts of moments we left behind. In this metal labyrinth, a trance—your voice a balm to my fractured mind.

We're all seeking something down here, in the belly of the urban beast. But your song brings me near to the love that is now dead.

I ride these tracks night after night, chasing the echoes of your refrain through the endless tunnels, the dim light—finding solace in the subway's pain.

I surrender to the steel rhythm, to the city's relentless drive. In this subterranean prism, your song keeps my love alive.

326
Labyrinth of Words

These wires coil around my soul, burning and branding me with their touch, transforming me into a quivering mass, lost in the labyrinth of your words.

Each syllable a searing flame, each sentence a chain that binds. I am scorched by the heat of your voice, your whisper a dagger that twists and winds.

I can't escape your electric grip, the way your language ensnares. I am a prisoner to the rhythm, to the cadence of your despairs.

You weave your spell relentlessly, drawing me deeper into your maze. I stumble through your twisted paths, lost in the haze of your verbal blaze.

My mind is a battlefield, a war zone—your words the weapons that strike, cutting through my defenses, leaving scars bleeding into the night.

I try to break free, to find my ground, but your voice is a drug I crave. In the torment, I find a strange solace—in your words, I become a slave.

These wires coil around my soul, tightening with each breath you take, branding me with the fire of your presence until there's nothing left to break.

Lost in the labyrinth of your words, I surrender to the pain and the pleasure, for in this tangled web we weave, I find a piece of forever.

327
The Circus of All We Have

It's all a circus of strange dances and billowing clouds.

I turn on the light switch—vestal virgins, princes, and saints stand around me and sing hymns of glory.

The two-minute egg is finished in the pot, my heart is ripped to pieces, and the dying child with cancer is suddenly caressed by a wave of boundless love.

A robin sucks up a worm in the backyard, and I wonder at the absurdity of it all—this wild, chaotic ballet of joy and pain, of the mundane and the divine.

The saints with their hollow eyes, the virgins with their false purity—they sing their hymns, and I can only laugh—a bitter chuckle in the face of it all.

Life's a mad dance, a circus of hopes and despair, where the sacred and the profane twist and turn, hand in hand.

The egg boils, simple and true—a small act of normalcy in this carnival of existence where love and suffering are two sides of the same coin.

The child's eyes, wide with fear, soften in the touch of that boundless love, and for a moment—just a moment—there's peace in the chaos, a brief respite from the endless storm.

Outside, the robin does what robins do—no fanfare, no song, just the act of survival—a reminder that life goes on in all its brutal simplicity.

I stand, light switch in hand, watching the strange dance, the billowing clouds, the sacred hymns, and shattered hearts, knowing that this circus—this beautiful, twisted circus—is all we have.

328
The Broken Egg

The egg is broken—the hand of God touches the face of a million suffering, starving peasants.

I leave the house one more time and close the door, the creak of the hinges a whisper of farewell.

The world outside is the same—gray and unforgiving—but inside, something has shifted—a crack, a fracture where the light seeps in.

God's touch, they say—gentle, divine—but it feels like a punch, a jolt of reality that leaves you reeling.

The broken egg on the counter—a simple mess, a symbol of everything that falls apart, everything we can't control.

I step out into the world, the cold biting at my skin, the weight of a million cries hanging in the air—a chorus of despair that echoes in my mind.

The door closes behind me, a finality in its thud, and I walk forward—each step a battle, each breath a testament to the struggle, the fight, the relentless march of existence.

The hand of God is everywhere, in everything, but all I see are the broken pieces, the fragments of dreams, the faces of those who suffer.

And yet I keep moving, one foot in front of the other, through the gray, the cold, the endless night—hoping that somewhere, somehow, there's a crack, a light, a glimmer of something more.

The egg is broken, the world is vast and cruel, but I walk on—closing doors behind me, searching for the hand of God amid it all.

329
The World of Clowns

The world is full of clowns—a few are funny, but most are simply sad, and some are outright ugly and evil. If you look, you will find happy ones at the end of a subway car holding a zucchini or scratching their noses with a toothbrush.

A yellow squash will do nicely—not so sure about the one over there on the sidewalk with his pants down. Clowns come in all shapes and sizes. Some work in circuses, some at carnivals. Some sing in operas and kill their lovers.

Some sell hamburgers or electrical appliances on TV. There are as many clowns in the universe as there are red dwarf stars.

Some strangle and eat little children, then pose with First Ladies. Some live off the public dole, taking up space in government buildings.

They spout nonsense and lies, and we ensconce them with riches and ritual power—and we laugh at their foibles. Some even dress up as holy men and make great-sounding pronouncements about truth and God.

There are clowns who paint their faces and hide behind thick layers of mud and makeup because it hurts too much to be seen. A red nose and black eyes—useful tools in the arsenal of silence. Some squirt seltzer water, but they are long gone.

Orange hair is popular these days, along with a big bright red hat and a tablecloth necktie. There are secret pockets in their overcoats where they hide their weapons of mass delusion.

My father was a clown—a nice Jewish clown. He didn't need any makeup, didn't work in the circus, but he could make people laugh just by walking into a room. If it was dark, he brought his own light—and isn't that what it means to be a true clown?

He wasn't famous, didn't sell you a damn thing, but he had the gift—the rare and precious ability to turn the mundane into magic, the ordinary into extraordinary.

Here's to the real clowns—the unsung heroes of humor, the ones who brighten our days without the need for a stage, without the need for a mask. They are the light in the darkness, the laughter in the silence, the truth behind the makeup, the heart beneath the costume.

330
Sailing Toward Ararat

Like Noah, I feel like I'm drowning in a sea of grief, tears, and exhaustion. I pray for the end of the plague, the release of all the animals inside of me, and a place to rest on top of some solid mountain peak.

Each of us lives within our own sacred ark, tossed in a wild and tumultuous sea. Ararat, here I come!

The waves crash relentlessly, the storm rages on, and I am adrift clinging to the hope that somewhere, somehow, there's a break in the clouds, a glimpse of land, a promise of solid ground.

The animals inside me roar and claw—a menagerie of fears and desires, a chaotic, restless zoo begging for release, for peace.

I've built this ark from fragments, from pieces of dreams and shattered hopes—a makeshift vessel to carry me through the flood, to keep me afloat in this endless expanse of sorrow.

The sea is unforgiving, the horizon ever distant, but I hold on—guided by a faith that beneath the tempest there lies a place of calm, a sanctuary where I can finally breathe.

Ararat, here I come—a cry into the void, a plea for salvation, for a place to lay down my burdens, to let the waters recede and find the shore.

Each of us, our own Noah, sails through the storm, searching for that sacred mountain where we can rest our weary souls, where the animals within can roam free, and we can stand tall on solid ground.

I sail on through the tears and the grief, through the nights of endless rain— hoping, believing that somewhere out there, Ararat waits—a beacon of hope, a promise of peace.

331
The Keys to the Door

I'm not a locksmith, but what if death wasn't laced with the dust of long-forgotten dreams? Why is it that death creeps around the corner like a small, sulking child with a bad temper? Not sure if anybody knows.

I saw death a few weeks ago when I opened a can of cat food. It looked fine to me, but then it said I'd find the key to death when I saw my next patient.

What an auspicious occasion—several keys were lying on the bed next to my patient, but he was too weak to lift any of them. So, I helped him lift the third key, and he was dead in five minutes, with a bright smile on his face.

I told his wife I wasn't a locksmith, but she smiled and thanked me anyway. Death—a sly trickster, lurking in the commonplace, in the opening of a can, in the lifting of a key.

It doesn't come with a grand flourish—just a whimper, a suggestion, a subtle nudge in the quiet corners of our lives.

What if death was something different—not a dark shadow, not a lurking fear, but a gentle transition, a passage through a doorway we all must eventually find?

The patient's smile was serene, as if he'd found some hidden truth, something we all search for in the chambers of our hearts, in the corners of our minds, in the spaces between our thoughts.

His wife—her gratitude—a strange comfort in the face of finality, in the acceptance of the inevitable, in the understanding that sometimes we must help each other find the keys to our own release.

What if death was like that? A moment of clarity, a fleeting understanding that there's more beyond this life—a step into the unknown, guided by the keys we find in our final hours, in the simplest acts, in the touch of a hand, the opening of a door.

I saw death, and it wasn't a monster, wasn't a terror—just a quiet presence, a necessary end, a new beginning, waiting patiently.

Death—we fear it, we run from it—but in the end, we all must face it, lift the key, open the door, and walk through into whatever comes next.

332
Transparent

In the quiet of a world that hums its dissonance, we walk unseen until love bursts forth—a brilliance, not our own, but passed hand to hand like a candle lit at midnight. To project love is not to embellish the self but to dissolve it into something greater. Each gesture of kindness, each pause to listen, is an alchemy of spirit, drawing Christ into the room, barefoot, gentle-eyed, waiting for hearts to unbolt their doors.

To love is to become transparent, where grace passes through unfiltered and lands, trembling, upon the world. We do not preach Him into being; we manifest Him in the simple geometry of care—an unspoken prayer when you lift someone who is too tired to rise on their own. This is how the Second Coming arrives, quietly, unmistakably, not in thunder but in touch. Christ wears every human face touched by mercy.

And when you kneel, not in ritual alone, but in the dirt of someone else's despair, the true miracle blooms: that we, cracked vessels of dust, can carry the infinite. Love is never invisible—it is the very shape of resurrection in our midst. And those who see it will say, "He is here. He has come again."

333
Fragments

The large fat man on the gurney—two nipples on a giant marshmallow. No beach, no ocean, no sand for toes—trauma bay D.

Beer cans to the ceiling, a roach motel, a homeless man snores on his cot.

A feather falls from the sky—the cat leaps—a flock of Canada geese flies overhead.

A slice of cheese on a plate—a swift swipe of a paw—the cat claims his prize.

The priest and his rosary arrive none too soon. A little plastic cross—Mary to the rescue.

A wildly sunny day—the flowers are screaming at me.

Only in my dreams—standing beside a woman in pain—she bleats like a lamb bound for the slaughter. I stare at her feet.

Family members at the side of the bed—grief beyond words—I am a stone statue.

Two old geezers, his friends—old butterfly tattoo—return to the caterpillar.

A single raindrop on a flower petal—a ray of sunshine—a day without drama.

A blue sky, a bright white sun—if only I could enjoy the day.

334
Loose Change

Loose change falling from gaping holes in my tattered jacket—a cacophony of small metal clinks, each coin a testament to broken dreams and nights spent chasing shadows.

Pennies, nickels, dimes—they scatter on the pavement, echoes of a life stitched together with frayed threads and whispered promises.

The jacket, once proud, now a map of wear and tear—a rag of missteps and stumbles, each rip, each hole, a story I'd rather not tell.

I walk these streets, a ghost in the morning fog, hoping to find enough pieces to make it through another day, another night, another endless stretch of time.

The coins roll away, escaping my grasp like moments I've let slip by, like chances I've missed, like the dreams I've abandoned.

People pass, eyes averted, unwilling to see the man whose life is measured in the clink of loose change, in the weight of worn fabric.

But in those coins, in that scattered silver and copper, there's a truth—a raw honesty, a reflection of a world that's as fragmented as my jacket, as lost as the change that falls from it.

So, I gather what I can, pocket the remnants of my worth, and keep moving—always moving—through the gaping holes in my tattered life, hoping for a patch, a stitch, a mend, something to hold it all together if only for a little while longer.

335
Bald Spots

Mowing the bald spots on the lawn, hoping to see grass—a fool's errand—but we've all got our dreams.

The sun beats down, a relentless taskmaster. I push the mower, sweat dripping, shirt sticking, wondering if today's the day the green will finally show.

Excited chickens in the neighbor's yard, scratching the dirt, clucking like prospectors—they've found gold, the treasure of Sierra Madre in the damn dust.

They've got it figured out, those chickens—simple pleasures, simple minds— digging for scraps, bits of life, while I wrestle with the mower, the bald spots staring back, mocking me.

Life's a lot like this patch of dirt—a broken, dry dream. Sometimes you've got to laugh, find the humor in the futility, in the chickens' joy, in the absurdity of it all.

336
The Orange Peel

The orange peel soaks up the light of the sun on the back porch—a simple thing, a small miracle in the mundane of life.

It sits inert, curled and drying, turning the sun's rays into something tangible, something warm and real in a world that often feels too cold.

The porch creaks beneath my feet—a tired sigh of old wood—and I watch the orange peel bask in the afternoon light, a quiet moment of stillness in the chaos of existence.

The sun beats down, relentless and uncaring, but the orange peel doesn't mind. It absorbs the heat, turns it into a memory of summer, a taste of brightness in the bitterness.

Sometimes it's the small things, the forgotten things, that hold the most beauty, the most meaning.

An orange peel on the back porc¹, soaking up the sun, reminds me of childhood—of simple pleasures, of moments when the world made sense.

I sit down, the chair groans u ¹er my weight, the warmth washes over me. I think of nothing, letting the quiet seep into my bones.

The orange peel glows—a tiny beacon of light, a reminder that life goes on, that there's still beauty to be found, even in the smallest, most overlooked corners.

I sit. I watch. I let the sun do its work—on the orange peel, on the porch, on me.

337

The Memory of Fireflies

Taking the pizza box to the trash in the morning, thinking about last night's fireflies.

The dawn light is thin, a pale wash over the tired streets. I shuffle in my slippers, the box flopping under my arm—grease stains and crumbs, witnesses to another empty evening.

Yes, the fireflies—small flickering miracles in the stale night, tiny beacons of hope in Brownian movement against the backdrop of despair.

I stand on the porch, beer in hand, watching them dance—their light fragile but persistent—a reminder that even in the darkest moments, there is light. Thus, sayeth the Lord.

The pizza is cold, limp—not fit for a Brooklynite. The laughter long gone, just the sound of a late-night taxi and fireflies blinking their silent message.

Now the morning comes, and the magic fades, replaced by the ordinary—the routine of taking out the trash, of facing another day.

But the memory of fireflies lingers—a whisper of something more, a hint of possibility in the tedium.

The trash can lid clanks shut, the pizza box discarded, but the light of last night's fireflies stays with me—a small, stubborn flame in the gray dawn.

338
The Window He Left Open

She sits in the dark, the curtains drawn tight like mourning veils, the only light the faint glow of the stereo, where Chet Baker breathes life into the silence, each note rising soft and fragile like a ghost refusing to rest, and she listens because that's all she can do now—listen and ache and try to feel the edges of him in the horn's lonely cry.

Her son loved this sound, this melancholic drift, this bittersweet ache that seemed to know him better than words ever could, and now she sits in the place where he used to sit, surrounded by his absence, drowning in the quiet that comes after everything you've loved has slipped through your fingers like smoke from a dying candle.

He was more than a son; he was an artist who left pieces of himself everywhere—a canvas smeared with the frantic colors of dreams he didn't finish, a guitar resting in the corner, strings still vibrating with his last touch, notebooks filled with half-written poems and sketches of faces he saw in passing but never knew. And now she is left with these fragments that don't speak but scream in silence.

She keeps staring at the window he left open, the one he chose, and she wonders why the night was kinder than she could ever be, why the stars above offered more comfort than her open arms, and the question fills her heart like lead, searing through her soul with the heat of unanswered prayers and broken promises.

She presses her hand to her chest as though she can hold the pieces of herself together, but the music keeps playing, keeps bleeding out into the room, Chet's horn bending and breaking like her, rising into something beautiful only because it is unbearably sad.

She doesn't know how to stop replaying his last moments—wondering if he felt free when he let go, or if he regretted the leap halfway down, but she knows this much: grief is a song with no end, and it rewinds and repeats, every chorus dragging her back to the place where she wasn't enough to keep him here.

The world outside goes on, indifferent and loud, but here in this room where shadows gather, she waits for something that will never return, while the horn plays on and on, not knowing that the person it was meant to reach is gone, not knowing that she is all that's left, sitting in the dark, listening, breaking, holding on to a song that sounds too much like goodbye.

339
Egg and Sink

The boiled egg in the sink, badly peeled like the pock-marked face of a plague survivor—sitting rejected, stinking, and alone—gazing at the tyrant drain.

A casualty of morning clumsiness cracked and broken, bits of membrane clinging stubbornly, refusing to let go.

I look at the sullen, shriveled white orb, this sad misshapen thing—a small failure in a thread of larger ones.

It stinks like disappointment, a reminder that even the simplest tasks can go awry, and that even the Creator's perfect creation isn't fit for human consumption.

It's just an egg, for God's sake—but it feels like more—a symbol of the dreadful day already slipping away, of the small defeats that pile up until they're too heavy to carry out of the kitchen.

I turn on the tap, water rushing over a partially premature oozing yolk, trying to wash away the sin, my shame, my guilt.

But the stink remains—the stubborn clinging of fragmented shell, a witness to imperfection, my evils, my failures.

The sink, a stage for this tiny tragedy, reflects back the harsh light of morning's unforgiving glare, and I can't help but laugh—a bitter chuckle in the quiet kitchen.

The egg lies on its aluminum slab—alone and beaten—a monument to all the things that go wrong, the utter failure of man's plan for the universe, and God's turning away in grief and despair.

I leave the corpse in the sink and walk away—a man parboiled in his own mind and ready for fast food in the Land of Nod.

340
Blood and Breakfast

Blood on the Edmund Pettus Bridge drips into my cereal, coats the scrambled egg on the plate.

Morning news blares, history's shadow casting long over breakfast's mundane ritual, reminding me that some stains never wash out.

Each spoonful a bitter taste, each bite a reminder that the past is never just the past—it bleeds into the present, colors every waking moment.

The bridge—a monument to pain, to courage, to the fight for something better.

But here in my kitchen, it's just blood in the cereal, a heavy weight on the day.

The egg yolk, broken, stares back from the plate—a symbol of something fragile, something lost under the weight of all that history, all that blood.

We carry it with us—these ghosts, these echoes—in every bite, every breath, the struggle of those who came before, fighting still in the quiet of our mornings.

It's a hard thing to swallow—this mix of past and present, of blood and breakfast—a reminder that the fight is never over, that we are still breaking eggs, still breaking heads, still bleeding on bridges, still trying to make something whole out of something so broken.

341
A Blue Sky, A Bright White Sun

A blue sky, a bright white sun— if only I could enjoy the day.

The world outside is perfect, clear, and clean, not a cloud in sight,
but here I am, trapped in my own mind, lost in the shadows that cling to the edges of my soul.

The sun shines, mocking my misery, casting light on the cracks in my facade, exposing the wounds I try so hard to hide.

People laugh, they smile, they move through the day with a lightness I ~~n't touch, a joy I can't reach.

If only I could join them, step out of this darkness, breathe in the bright air, let the warmth seep into my bones.

But the weight is heavy, the thoughts are dark, and no matter how bright the sun is, it can't pierce through the fog that wraps around my heart.

I sit, watching the world move on, a spectator in my own life, yearning for a taste of that light, that brightness, that ease.

A blue sky, a bright white sun— if only I could enjoy the day, if only I could find a way to break free from the prison of my mind, to step into the light, to feel the sun on my face, to live just for a moment without the shadow of this endless night.

342
Old Butterfly Tattoo

Two old geezers sit on a bench, watching the world stumble by, their laughter a rasp like dry leaves caught in the wind. One rolls up his sleeve, revealing an old butterfly tattoo—ink faded, wings crinkled by years that bit and tore—a relic of wild nights and restless days.

That butterfly, once a symbol of flight, is now just a ghost on wrinkled skin, a quiet reminder of when dreams were painted in bright, impossible colors and nights stretched endlessly, unbroken by regret.

They've seen it all—the rise and fall of hope, the slow grind of years wearing dreams to dust, turning wild flights of fancy into cautious steps on worn paths.

Return to the caterpillar, to the inevitable crawl, the slow descent back to earth, where the ground holds more truth than the sky ever promised.

The park is quiet, the world moves on, but they sit rooted in their history— two old men with stories etched deep in their bones, their silence a testament to battles fought and lost to victories too small to celebrate.

The butterfly tattoo, a mark of freedom's fleeting touch, now becomes a symbol of return to simpler times, to the earthbound reality that waits for us all.

Return to the caterpillar, to the endless cycle where we crawl, we fly, and, in the end, we come back down—grounded by the weight of years, finding peace in the dust, in the quiet return to where it all began.

343
A Woman in Pain

Standing beside a woman in pain, she moans like a cow, guttural and raw, and I stare at her feet—bare, twisted, planted on the cold tile floor as if the pain roots her there, holds her captive.

The room is dim, filled with the sterile scent of antiseptic and despair, her cries bouncing off the walls in a symphony of suffering that shatters the quiet, each note a jagged edge that scrapes at my nerves.

She writhes; caught in the grip of whatever demon claws at her insides, and all I can do is stand there, a useless witness, feeling the weight of her agony press down on my shoulders like an unseen chain.

Her feet—calloused and cracked—speak of a life worn down by endless steps, each one a testament to the journey that brought her here, to this moment of raw, naked pain.

I stare at those feet, unable to meet her eyes, unable to bear the full force of her suffering, so I fixate on the details—the chipped nail polish, the way the veins thread beneath the thin skin like rivers on an old map.

Her moans fill the room, a relentless soundtrack to helplessness, and I am rooted in place, a spectator to her torment, wishing for the words, the touch, the magic that could ease her pain.

But there is nothing—only the silent prayer that this too shall pass, that relief will come, that her cries will fade into the quiet of exhaustion.

Standing beside a woman in pain, I stare at her feet and feel the impotence of my presence, the sharp reality of her suffering carving itself into my soul, one more scar in the endless landscape of human pain.

344
Where the Path Leads

Where does the path lead, and does it really matter? The trees lean close as though they've been listening for centuries. Their branches brush the sky like the forgotten prayers of the earth. Is Christ there, walking ahead of us, or is He only a mist that rises and fades? But mist can touch your skin, unseen yet present. Maybe He is the very breath that clings to the morning air—the quiet that comes when you stop asking what comes next.

If there is no path, can there be justice? Or is justice what we make as we move, step after step, choosing the uneven stones over the easy plains? Faith doesn't always need the straight road. Sometimes it takes the narrow one inside you, the path you didn't know you were already on. The one that twists through doubt and sorrow until you arrive at a clearing wide enough for forgiveness to sit down.

What about hope? And love—especially love? Do they need a compass? Or do they find you when you're lost enough to see that every crooked turn carries you closer to your own heart? Does the path always lead to love? I hope so. I certainly hope so. For at the end of love's longest road, Christ is waiting—not far away, but near, with a cup of water and the same old wounds, saying: *Here you are at last.*

345
Immersed in the Scorching Embrace

Immersed in the scorching embrace of the desert sun, where the horizon blurs and the path ahead remains veiled in uncertainty, I am standing on the precipice of faith.

It's a journey fraught with doubt, a pilgrimage of the spirit guided by the flickering flame of hope. The heat beats down, a relentless force stripping away pretense and illusion, leaving only the raw, naked truth of my existence. The sands shift beneath my feet, each step an act of faith, each movement forward a surrender to the unknown, where certainty dissolves and the soul's true quest begins.

In this vast, desolate expanse, I confront my fears—the shadows that dance at the edges of my vision, taunting me with their whispers of despair, challenging me to find the strength within. The horizon, a wavering line, calls me onward, a distant promise of revelation, a beacon of light amid the void. It's here, in the crucible of the desert, that I face the depths of my being—the doubts that gnaw at my heart, the questions that refuse easy answers.

But amid the doubt, there is a spark, a flickering flame of hope guiding me through the darkness, illuminating the path with its gentle glow. This pilgrimage of the spirit is a journey into the unknown, a venture into the depths of faith where the mind surrenders, and the heart takes the lead.

In the scorching embrace of the sun, I find the courage to press on, to embrace the uncertainty, to trust in the unseen hand that guides me through the desert's trials. It's a journey of transformation where the soul is purified, the spirit refined, and the essence of faith revealed in the silent, unwavering light of hope.

Immersed in the scorching embrace of the desert sun, where the horizon blurs and the path ahead remains veiled in uncertainty, I find myself standing on the precipice of faith.

346
1959 Cadillac Bone Yard Blues

1959 Cadillac bone yard blues, where the steel giants go to die—a graveyard of chrome dreams, rust eating away like a slow disease, biting through tired metal bones. Is it a car that passes gas and sniffs its own demise, or just the slow rot, the engine cranky and wheezing, pistons slick with old grease, fins still horny, poking the air, searching for a soulmate from a time long past—a relic from when dreams were gasoline and chrome?

She sits, grass growing through her guts, nature reclaiming what we left behind, a monument to forgotten roads, lost highways that used to go somewhere. The paint, once pink and proud, now just a faded gray joke, peeling like old skin on an old bag baking in the sun.

Each scratch a scar, each dent a ghost whispering tales of what she used to be, when her ashtray was clean, and her white walls were white. I walk through this boneyard, a place where metal dreams die slowly, and I shout "Pinky!"— for what was, and for what never will be again.

The windshield's cracked and clouded, a smeared window to the past, reflecting a sky that doesn't give a damn while I stand, the last mourner in this cathedral of rust. Tires, once gripping the road like a lover, now flat, sinking into the dirt—anchors to memories of joyrides, of moonlit nights when the world was wide open.

Leather seats, stiff and torn, used to cradle lovers, held their laughter, soaked up life in every thread—condoms in the backseat, arguments, secrets—now just dried up and forgotten.

I can see her in her prime, a big pink steel baby rolling down the boulevard, radio blaring, tail fins cutting the air like a knife—a goddess on wheels.

But now she's just a hollow shell. Time has had its way with her, and all I can do is mourn what was once beautiful, what's now turned to dust.

1959 Cadillac bone yard blues—a symphony of decay, a dirge for the days when cars had souls, when Pinky was queen.

347
From the Backseat of a '52 Plymouth

My father's '52 Plymouth, a gray hunk of metal, dumpy like an old grandmother, but it was mine. No seat belts, no rules, just a kid in the back, locked in his own world.

Dad spat out the window, yelled at jerks on the road, cigarette smoke swirling, phlegm flying at 40 miles an hour. Mom called it disgusting, but I thought it was art—the kind that stuck to windshields.

One night, some bastard ripped out the radio, leaving a hole—a festering wound. I cried over that empty dashboard, my first love violated, broken like rotten teeth. Dad cursed and lit another cigarette.

He brought home a new '55 Ford, but the Plymouth stayed with me—that busted, stinking beast, the spirit of Grandma riding shotgun.

You never forget your first love, even if it was just a car.

348
The No-Legged Man

The no-legged man paddles down the sidewalk, tweed hat cocked low, hiding half his world. Stumps set on a dolly, like a tree trunk on wheels, legs buried somewhere deep—maybe in the dirt, maybe in dreams.

He's got a few pencils, red erasers chewed to the nub, a cigar box for pennies—his own little cash register. He scoots to the next corner, selling shoelaces or maybe just hope.

An old woman with a bucket kisses him on the cheek, and I watch as he rolls into a doorway, disappearing like smoke. Maybe just to grow legs.

349
Cold Hotdog

Cold hot dog in a stale bun, sweet sauerkraut sliding off, flat soda with no fizz—this is the feast, the half-hearted meal, the reflection of a life that never quite hits the mark.

Under the dim streetlight, the city hums, an indifferent sound. A drunk man stumbles, cursing the pavement, blaming the ground for his own lack of balance.

The moon, pale and distant, hangs like a forgotten promise, like it's given up on us all, just watching the madness below.

Somewhere, a siren wails, cutting through the night—a lonely cry in a sea of whispers.

The alleyways tell secrets—lovers quarrel in hushed tones, their anger absorbed by brick and mortar.

A cat slinks, eyes gleaming—a silent witness to our little tragedies.

This is our canvas—we paint it with despair, with fleeting joy, with small victories, and the endless grind.

A half-eaten hot dog, sauerkraut slipping away—a metaphor for dreams that never quite stay in place.

The neon lights flicker, promising escape but delivering none.

The bartender wipes down the counter, eyes glazed over—another shift, another dollar, another night of listening to the sorrows of strangers.

Life is just a series of moments—some beautiful, most mundane.

We chase the extraordinary but settle for crumbs—a cold hot dog, a flat soda, tokens of our resigned acceptance.

Yet in all this chaos, in the mess we call life, there's a strange comfort—the predictability of disappointment, the familiarity of failure. We laugh, we cry, we cling to our small comforts while the world spins on, oblivious to our plight.

We celebrate the nights spent under indifferent moons, the silent cats, the weary bartenders, the lovers' quarrels.

There's the beautiful struggle—the endless search for meaning in all this madness—and that, perhaps, is enough.

350
Eight-Year-Old Methuselah

Old before his time, an eight-year-old Methuselah, ashen-faced, a spent life already burned out, sitting on the front stoop, waiting for his universe to crumble around him—or just his snow cone to melt in his hand.

On summer nights, when he hears the sheep in the far-off hills, he dreams of a good night's sleep and his mother's soft eyes. Soft eyes he rarely sees these days, or a firm, caring hand on his shoulder.

No summer nights, no sheep on far-off hills, no soft eyes, no firm hands. Just the sound of the subway and cherry juice dripping down his sleeve.

The city breathes its heavy sighs, the streets whisper tales of despair and broken dreams. Children grow up too fast here, their innocence traded for survival in alleys and on cracked sidewalks.

His small shoulders bear the weight of years unspent, of dreams deferred, of a future written in graffiti on the walls of tenements. He sits and listens to the city, its heartbeat a monotonous hum, the subway cars clattering like a broken symphony, each station a note in a song of endless routine.

He watches the people pass—faces lined with worry; eyes cast down—moving through life like ghosts in a machine.

He knows their stories without hearing a word, their silent screams echo in his mind, their burdens mirror his own, and he wonders if there's a way out, if there's a place where the sheep still graze in distant fields, where nights are filled with stars and not the cold glare of streetlights.

His snow cone drips, forgotten—a small river of red on the concrete, a testament to fleeting pleasures, to the transience of joy.

He dreams of a world beyond this stoop, beyond the reach of the subway's roar, where a child's laughter is more than a rare echo in an urban canyon, where a mother's eyes are soft, and a hand on the shoulder is more than a memory.

But for now, he sits—an old soul in a young body—waiting for the day to end, for the night to bring its empty promise, for the city to finally sleep, if only for a moment.

And in that brief silence, he finds a sliver of hope, a glimpse of a future where cherry juice and sheep and soft eyes are more than distant fantasies.

351
The Long Stringy Waitress

The long, stringy waitress comes down to collect her pocket pittance, scrounging greasy-fingered around the plates, fondling nickels, and pennies, wishing they were something else—anything besides gumball machine food.

She wants to kill the chef or just eat his liver and freeze the rest, savoring the dark, rich flavor of revenge. She remembers the good old days of Fred's Greasy Spoon Diner—she was bad, and that was good. The all-night, eat-all-you-can parties, sacrifices, and sins under the moonlight—a life lived with purpose, a wicked sort of joy.

She delights in spoons, forks, and knives—piercing gaping holes in roast chickens or other formerly living organisms—her own form of ritual, a sacrifice to the gods of survival.

She fries endless strips of bacon, making faces with the eggs, smiling at the absurdity of it all, finding a twisted comfort in the sizzle and pop of grease.

She dreams of dying a million times in scalding hot coffee—a slow, painful end that feels like justice, an escape from the endless repetition.

She plays with the stove, setting herself on fire. But the thrill is gone, the flames a pale imitation of the passion she once knew—now just a dull burn in a kitchen filled with ghosts.

The patrons come and go, faces blending into one long, monotonous line of empty stares and hollow voices. They don't see her, don't notice the rage simmering just beneath the surface, the pain etched into every movement.

She scrapes the plates clean—a ritual of futility—and counts the change with fingers stained by grease and time, each coin a reminder of what was lost, each tip a mockery of her worth. The long, stringy waitress longs for the nights of fire and blood, the dance of chaos under the stars. But now, it's just another shift, another round of meaningless tasks, another day in a life that feels like a sentence.

She watches the clock, counting down the minutes to the end, but knowing that the end is just another beginning—another round of the same old song. She dreams of a way out, a door to another world where the grease and the pain and the endless plates don't exist, where she can be more than a tired waitress with a pocket full of pennies.

But for now, the long, stringy waitress scrounges and scrapes, wishing for more, remembering the fire, and dreaming of dying a million times in scalding hot coffee.

352
Jesus Walks the Streets of Gaza

Jesus walks the streets of Gaza, his feet bloodied, his skin as gray as the dust. There are no Muslims in Gaza, there are no Jews in Gaza, there are no Christians in Gaza—only the shattered hearts of mothers and children.

Jesus lifts broken stones and broken bodies. He has lost track of the dead, but he knows how many tears have fallen. He picks up each drop of blood and places it into his cup. The blind beasts who hide in holes guard their prey. The tanks in the streets, driven by blind men with dubious intentions, crawl like leviathans. Each tank is a cross, and on each cross hang the bodies of ten thousand children.

There is no more room for crying mothers, and for each caring soul holding an I.V. bag, there are ten thousand bombs and a million bullets. There are hostages embedded in concrete, and politicians embedded in lies and deceit. For every lie told, there are ten thousand more children who will die.

The streets are silent except for the whispers of pain, echoes of laughter that will never return. And Jesus, with his bloodied feet, walks through the rubble, his hands touching the lifeless, his heart breaking with each step.

He feels every wound, every shattered bone, the weight of despair hanging heavy. He knows the names of every soul, the dreams extinguished, the futures erased. The smoke rises—a gray veil over the city—and Jesus walks, his eyes fixed on the ground where every stone tells a story, every corner holds a memory.

He looks toward Jerusalem but knows that his work is here—in Rafah, in Khan Yunis. He sees the beasts on both sides of hell, their eyes cold, their hearts hardened by war. And he weeps for them too—for the humanity they've lost, for the love they've forsaken.

He sees the tanks, the metal monsters that roam the streets, their treads crushing the remnants of life. Each one a cross, and he feels the weight of each life taken, each innocent breath silenced. There's no solace here in Gaza, no peace in the cries of mothers, the silent screams of fathers, the haunted eyes of the survivors. And Jesus, with his bloodied feet, walks on.

He kneels in the dust among the ruins. He prays to His Father in Heaven for the broken, the lost, the innocent lives caught in the crossfire, and he weeps—his tears mixing with the blood-soaked earth.

He knows the pain of each child, the fear in their eyes, the last moments of their lives. And he gathers each tear, each drop of blood, and holds them close—a testament to the suffering, a cry for mercy.

353
In the Soft Surreal Night

Kiss my mother's thumbs in the garden where clocks grow and shadows hum lullabies to forgotten stars. The moon wears a hat of whispers, and the roses dance in pairs while the trees tell secrets to the wind who listens with care. In this place of dreams and echoes, kiss my mother's thumbs and let the world spin backward in the soft surreal night.

I love the roundness of your face, your front tooth with the crack, the way you eat onions with a spoon. Tell me more, my sweet—why so many birds cry at your window and why the cereal boxes spell out your name. Let's take a long fling to Bangkok or a vacation in Peru, among the pyramids in Arkansas and the deep rivers of the North Country.

Forget the children, take the cats. Meet me with my mother on the side of the road and kiss her thumbs. Let us enjoy this second of paradise before the world ends.

Your face, a moon in the twilight—your cracked tooth, a story untold. The way you savor onions with a spoon, a ritual, a dance in the mundane.

Birds gather at your window, lamenting the dawn, their cries a symphony, a serenade to your waking. Cereal boxes line the shelves, letters dancing in unison, spelling out your name—a secret code of the morning.

We dream of Bangkok, the colors, the chaos, the markets alive with whispers. Or Peru, where the air is thin and the pyramids rise from the Arkansas soil, ancient, misplaced, a riddle to unravel.

The rivers of the North Country call, deep and cold, carrying the secrets of forgotten lands. We will navigate their currents, cats in tow, children left behind, ghosts of a life unlived.

On the roadside, my mother waits, her thumbs ready for your kiss—a blessing, a binding, a moment stolen from time. In this second of paradise, we find our solace before the world unravels, before the stars fall from the sky, and the birds' cries fade to silence.

Love me in the surreal light, where faces are moons, teeth are tales, and onions are feasts. Let us grasp this fleeting dream, hold it close, let it be ours—as the world spins madly on and we, mere dreamers, find our place in the chaos.

354
Fried Fish in the Air

Fried fish in the air, a stinking clam, spilled milk's scent, dog laps at the mess. The kitchen's a battlefield, grease splattering like shrapnel, the clam reeking like forgotten dreams, milk pooling on the linoleum, a slow river of regret.

The dog, oblivious to the chaos, laps it up with a lazy tongue, his world simple, uncomplicated—no worries beyond the next bite, no dreams beyond the next meal.

I sit at the table, beer in hand, cigarette burning low, watching the mess unfold, feeling the weight of years, the dull ache of existence.
Fried fish in the air, a reminder of dinners past, meals shared in better times, when laughter was easy, and love wasn't a ghost.

The clam, stinking like failure, a testament to the rot beneath the surface, the milk a symbol of innocence lost, spilled out, wasted, like so many of our dreams. The dog—he doesn't care. He just licks and licks, happy in his simple way, ignorant of the complexities, the heartaches, the endless grind.

I take a drag, feel the burn, watch the smoke curl and fade, thinking about the roads not taken, the choices made and unmade, the life that slipped through my fingers.

Fried fish in the air, a stinking clam, spilled milk's scent, dog laps at the mess. It's all there, laid out like a map—the past, the present, the future, wrapped up in the smell of fish, the sight of a dog's tongue lapping up the last drops of hope.

In this moment, it's all clear—the absurdity, the beauty, the pain, and the pleasure—all wrapped up in the scent of fried fish and spilled milk.

The dog looks up, tail wagging, as if to say, "This is life, this is all there is—so lap it up, take it in, find the joy in the mess, the peace in the chaos."

I take another swig, another drag, watch the world turn, knowing it's all fleeting, all temporary, but for now, in this kitchen, with the stink and the mess, there's a strange kind of peace, a quiet acceptance, a dog's simple wisdom.

Fried fish in the air, a stinking clam, spilled milk's scent, dog laps at the mess, and for a moment, it's enough.

355
A Bag of Old Bones

A bag of old bones shuffling on the street, gray wisps dancing in sunlight.

She moves like a ghost, a shadow in the city's glare, footsteps slow, deliberate, each one a testament to survival, to the passage of too many years.

The sun casts long shadows, highlighting the cracks in the pavement, the cracks in her face, wrinkles deep as memories, stories etched in skin.

Gray wisps, her hair, caught by the breeze, a dance of tired strands whispering tales of youth, of days long gone.

In her hands, a bag heavy with the weight of time, filled with the remnants of a life, old bones and faded dreams clinking together like lost hopes.

The city rushes by—young and vibrant, too busy to notice the old woman, the ghost, the shuffling reminder of mortality.

She stops to rest, leaning against a wall, the bag settling at her feet, a sigh escaping her lips, a sigh that speaks of years, of battles fought and lost, of loves and losses.

People pass, eyes averted, avoiding the specter of their future, the inevitability of decline, but she stands there, a silent testament to the persistence of life, to the stubbornness of existence.

Gray wisps dancing in sunlight, a brief, beautiful rebellion against the creeping shadows, against the march of time.

She shoulders the bag again—a bag of old bones—and continues her shuffle, each step a defiance, each breath a victory in a world that moves too fast for an old woman with a bag filled with the ghosts of yesterday.

The street stretches on, a river of concrete and dreams, and she moves through it—a solitary figure wrapped in the cloak of years—a bag of old bones clinking softly in the sun.

Shuffling on the street, gray wisps dancing in sunlight, a bag of old bones—a life carried forward, one step at a time.

356
Magritte and Dali Share a Urinal

Magritte and Dali shared a urinal. "This is not a pipe," said René, and Salvador just looked at his watch, melting like the time it couldn't keep.

Poor Vincent couldn't hear the water in the sink, his ear lost to the madness of the stars, while Pablo turned a blind eye, angular visions splitting the tiles.

They all left the bathroom at the same time but did not close the door, letting the scent of true art waft into the crowded café beyond.

Mona Lisa stirred her coffee, smiling enigmatically at the scene, while Frida's eyebrows tangled with the steam rising from her cup.

Outside, a train emerged from a fireplace, whistling a tune only the mad could hear, and in the sky, clocks hung like fruit from the branches of an invisible tree.

The urinal stood alone, a monument to the absurd, echoes of their laughter bouncing off the porcelain walls. René lit a cigarette, the smoke forming question marks, while Salvador sketched dreams on the napkins stained with wine.

Vincent gazed at the sunflowers growing out of the ceiling tiles, their yellow heads nodding in a silent symphony of color.

Pablo's blind eye saw more than the sighted ever could, his vision a kaleidoscope of angles, each turn a revelation.

The door swung gently, an invitation to the unreal, where reality was but a suggestion and madness was the muse.

They shared more than a urinal, those men of broken visions; they shared a world untethered, where pipes were never just pipes and time melted into pools of possibility.

Magritte's bowler hat floated above the scene, a silent witness, while Dali's mustache twitched with every tick of the dreamer's clock.

Vincent hummed a starry tune, his brushstrokes lingering in the air, and Pablo sculpted shadows with a glance, a gesture, a sigh.

The bathroom door remained open, a portal to the unknown, where artists danced with madness and urinals spoke in tongues.

357
Wish It Could All Stay in Vegas

Wish it could all stay in Vegas—sixty years of crazy marriage. The smoking, the drinking, the gambling, sleeping drunk and naked on the couch—a man with a wayward mind, somewhere on a street in Vegas.

The love of Tina's life still, but strokes kill the soul sometimes, take the heart out of a man's straining desire. Just ninety pounds now—a bag of bones and a catheter in a hospital bed. No more talk, no more walk. The bottle is dry, but not his diaper.

Tina nurses him like he was a tiny, screaming infant, except he isn't screaming. He barely opens his eyes these days, but she feeds him with a small spoon, wiping his chin as he slobbers his pureed baby food.

Jake sleeps twenty hours a day—he used to gamble twenty hours a day. And so, they both wait—Jake and Tina—on the cusp of eternity, another throw of the dice, another drink, another diaper changed.

Wish it could all stay in Vegas—the neon, the noise, the promise of another hand, another chance. But life has a way of cashing in, calling time on the long shots.

Jake with his crooked grin, his reckless charm, now just a memory in the lines of Tina's face. She remembers the way he would dance on the edge of everything.

Now the days are long shadows, the nights silent prayers. She watches him breathe—a slow, steady rhythm—as if time itself is hesitant to take the final step.

The love that burned bright, a flame that defied the wind, now a quiet ember. She whispers to him stories of their past, of wild nights and stolen kisses, hoping he hears, hoping he remembers—her voice a lifeline to the man he once was, the man she still sees beneath the frail shell.

Another spoonful, another wipe, another moment stolen from the void. Jake and Tina—a love story written in the margins, in the spaces between life and death.

They wait together, two souls intertwined, holding on to the fragments of a life that was never ordinary, never dull.

And so, they wait in a small room that smells of crap and faded dreams. Another day, another hour, another diaper changed, another breath taken.

Wishing somehow it could all stay in Vegas, where the stakes were high, and every roll of the dice promised a taste of eternity.

358
Drink Up

I've aged like a fine wine—or more like a not-so-fine cheese—a little stinky and with a brown moldy rind, sitting atop a cracker on a small table, on a broken dish.

The aches in the back and the sagging in the middle and the flaccid things that used to pound with virility and power—the dried-up stuff everywhere.

Those bulbous things on the skin and the odors coming out of holes you never noticed before.

Looking through the lenses of old age is like peering through a concrete slab and hearing the sounds of your liver and not hearing your wife too well anymore.

Don't know what kind of wine I am—not a fine Cabernet, but a mediocre Merlot—drink up anyway.

The days pass in slow motion—a reel of creaking joints and thinning hair—I wake up and stretch, feel the pull of time in every muscle—gravity, my relentless companion, pulling everything south toward the inevitable end.

The mirror shows a face I don't quite recognize—a roadmap of years, every line a story, every wrinkle a scar—the spark in the eyes dimmer now but still there—a testament to the life lived, the battles fought, the victories, and the countless defeats.

There's a wisdom that comes with age, but I find it's more like a reluctant acceptance—a knowing that the body will fail, the mind will falter—but the spirit, ah, the spirit—it fights on.

I sit with a glass in hand, swirling the liquid, watching the light catch the hues.

Not a fine Cabernet—but a mediocre Merlot.

Drink up anyway.

359
A Feast

Three cooks in the kitchen, stirring the pot— a dozen eggs waiting for the crack, the sizzle, green tomatoes in a bag, their future uncertain.

Garlic wafts through the air, simmering somewhere, finding refuge near the ceiling, lingering like an old lover hidden in a pantry filled with cat food and Hungarian macaroni.

A pan flute plays a tune, soft and haunting, whistling its way to the bank— a mocking serenade, grabbing a few more TV dinners and a pack of Lucky Strikes, preparing for the evening's spectacle—a dinner for the fancy folk and politicians from up north, twelve judges with toothpicks dangling from their mouths and sour mash to boot, their judgment heavy in the air.

We wait for the Lucius One, the star of the night, to descend the long flight of stairs— each step a prelude, a bourbon cocktail in hand, a cherry poised between her lips— the room holds its breath, expectant.

The dozen eggs stare at me, becoming an omelet— their fate sealed in the flick of a wrist, while the tomatoes dream of Coney Island, riding the Cyclone, free from this culinary destiny.

In the pantry, I sit with Harold the dog, sharing a meal of cat food— the absurdity not lost, as garlic continues its dance above, and the cooks keep stirring, creating a feast for the indifferent—
a tableau of chaos and flavor, life distilled in a simmering pot.

Here in this moment, everything converges— the garlic, the eggs, the tomatoes, the judges, the Lucius One, the dog, and me— an unholy communion in a kitchen's heat, whistling all the way to the bank or perhaps to oblivion, with the pan flute's melody and a pack of Lucky Strikes. This is going to be some dinner after all.

360
Alchemy

When a man loves a woman, there's a strange alchemy that unfolds—a quiet transformation in the mundane. The wash will be done, not out of duty, but with devotion.

He stands before the laundry basket, filled with a week's worth of life—shirts stained with coffee, jeans that have seen too many miles, and a dress she wore on that Sunday afternoon when the sun set their world on fire. He takes each piece with a reverence unknown to the gods of old, sorting whites from colors, delicates from the rough and tumble—his hands moving with a tender precision. When a man loves a woman, he finds poetry in the spin cycle, a rhythm in the rinse, a symphony in the soft hum of the dryer. He watches as the stains of the day fade into the ether, leaving behind a canvas ready for tomorrow's brushstrokes.

There's a beauty in the banal, a sanctity in the simple acts— the folding of her favorite blouse, the pairing of socks once lost and found.

He breathes in the scent of clean cotton— a promise of mornings yet to come, where love is woven into the fabric of their everyday existence.

When a man loves a woman, he becomes an alchemist— turning drudgery into devotion, tasks into tokens of tenderness, each cycle a testament to a love that refuses to fade, that endures the wear and tear of time and tide.

In the stillness of the laundry room, he stands—a solitary figure.
But in his heart, a universe unfolds— a testament to the truth that love is found in the smallest gestures, in the quiet moments where nothing and everything converge. When the wash is done, he is once again simply a man who loves a woman.

361

Motel Moon

Two miles east of Sam's candy store and gas station, just below Uranus in a crater left by the great meteor of 1348, lie the remains of Motel Moon.

Tattered and despised, yet still standing, its walls echo with the ghosts of con men, whores, and politicians with bright, fat faces and orange hair.

The last time I stayed there, a 1957 Ford Thunderbird awaited me— its chrome glinting in the dim light, pink skin smooth, windows rolled down as if expecting a girl on roller skates
bringing a hot dog and a Coke. She smiled, threw me a kiss, and I invited her in.

We watched *Gunsmoke* until the sun disappeared, and she transformed into an old hag— brown teeth, breath like decay.

We spent the night together— I in the bathtub, she hanging from the chandelier, while Matt Dillon popped in for a drink, and Miss Kitty cleaned the litter box.

Walking to the office to grab a pack of Chesterfields, I found my mother with another man, and then another, and yet another—each encounter a punch to the gut.

Returning to my room, the hag had turned back into a beautiful young thing. We made love in the back of the Thunderbird, under the flickering neon lights of Motel Moon. Think I'll come back next week, fall into another crater, find a new love on the dark side— where dreams decay and the past is a ghost that never leaves.

362
Quantum Entanglement

Quantum entanglement—a particle vibrating in resonance with a sound coming out of my head will instantaneously affect an atom inside a star in the Andromeda Galaxy, which is 2.5 million light years from Earth.

The greatest illusion of this effect is the notion of separation—So says my ancient Jewish grandmother as she turns off the TV, caresses my innocent face, and offers me a hardboiled egg sandwich. A simple eternal truth in her wrinkled hands.

I look at her with compassion and whine, *Grandma, but I want to watch Howdy Doody. I don't have time for quantum physics. My heart yearns for dear Clarabell and Buffalo Bob. Can't you just talk to Uncle Albert or Cousin Max about your quantum conundrum? I have my own difficult entanglements to deal with."*

Grandpa tells me about the God who loves me but won't give me the skills to catch flyballs in the outfield. He tells me to look handsome and see the writing on the wall, but I'm so nearsighted
and can't see the blackboard.

Grandma, I'm just a child and girls won't even look at me with desire. They ridicule my scrawny body and laugh behind my back. And I know that their giggles are heard in the Andromeda Galaxy— a cosmic joke at my expense."

Grandma just smiles, turns Howdy Doody back on the TV, and gives me another hardboiled egg sandwich— as if to say some truths are simpler than you think.

In that small living room, with the flickering screen casting shadows, I ponder the mysteries of quantum entanglement—
how my voice, my very being, could touch the stars while struggling with the here and now, the awkwardness of growing up,
the distant, untouchable allure of girls who giggle, and the Divine indifference to my outfield troubles.

But Grandma's smile, her silent wisdom, her belief in connections unseen, offers me a strange comfort as Howdy Doody fills the room, and the egg's simple solidity grounds me in the paradox of existence, where the universe's vastness meets the intimate space of a grandmother's love.

In that very moment, I realize that quantum entanglement isn't just a curiosity, but the fabric of our lives, the invisible threads that bind us to each other, to the stars, to the laughter, and to the struggles of the Divine and the mundane.

363
Ulysses Got Lost on the Subway

Why did Ulysses get lost on the subway? Could he not read the map? Were his ears stuffed with the wax of denial, or was he just stuck on some deserted island in the middle of the Mediterranean?

Did he not feed his men with wine and song? Did he not promise them glory, only to find himself adrift in the urban maze— the metal serpent that coils beneath the city, a labyrinth of steel and grime, where the Minotaur is time itself, and the hero's journey is reduced to a daily commute?

He searched for the sirens' song in the echoes of the tunnel, their voices now a distant memory, lost in the clatter and screech, the hum of fluorescent lights, the indifferent faces of fellow travelers, all sleepwalking through the haze of routine.

He sought the wisdom of old seers in the graffiti on the walls— the cryptic messages left by modern prophets, the poets of the underground— their words a blend of rage and despair, hope and defiance, a mirror to his own fractured soul.

Or did he simply yearn for the sea— the salt air and the boundless horizon— a longing that the subway's dark corridors could never satisfy, a reminder that even heroes can be tamed by the mundane, their epic quests reduced to finding the right stop, the right transfer, the right path through the urban sprawl.

But in the end, Ulysses is just a man, caught between the myth and the mundane— a wanderer in a world that has forgotten its own stories, lost in a city that never sleeps, but dreams in shades of gray, where the only monsters are the ones within, and the only journey is the one we take every day in search of something more, something real— something that reminds us of why we keep moving, why we keep hoping, why we keep fighting against the tide of time.

So why did Ulysses get lost on the subway? Was it the map, the wax, the island— or something deeper? A question that echoes through the tunnels of our own lives— a reminder that even the greatest heroes can lose their way, but they never stop searching, never stop believing in the possibility of finding their way back home.

364
Emaciated Time

Time, time, emaciated time, strung out like a junkie on the last shot, worn thin like the soles of old shoes, drawn out in silent tubes running under rivers, dripping slow and bitter—splinters and shards of what once was, scattered on desolate landscapes, grains of sand lost in a windstorm.

We wait for beams to cut through the fog, for dolphins to leap out of the hazy air like they've got something to prove, for the sun to finally get its act together and say hello to the edge of the sky like an old friend it's been avoiding for too many lifetimes.

Time cloaked in wondering, stumbling drunk down dark alleys, searching for the stairs where dappled dogs perch on parapet walls, howling at the moon— or just watching the mess down below.

Time's looking for those endless beaches, with sand black as the heart of the city, where the waves don't crash—they slink up, slow, slick, and oily, like they've got secrets to pour for anyone drunk enough to listen.

But the stairs—they're just a rumor, the kind of thing you hear about from a guy three seats down the bar.

And the dogs—they're long gone, chasing whatever dogs chase in the middle of the night.

Time, time, it's all slipping through your fingers, like dirty dishwater, like smoke from a dying cigarette, like that last shot at something real before the lights go out.

365

Letting Go

Grasping, it slips free— like water through trembling fingers, shaped by no hand, owned by no heart. Change flows as untamed currents, rivers with names forgotten in their rush, coursing through moments, carrying me on— further than I dared to dream, further than I feared to fall.

I reach out again— for permanence, for solace, for something known. Yet the sky shifts its hue before I can name the shade of its stillness.

The wind turns another page before my thoughts can trace the last whisper. Is there a way to hold what flees? A way to anchor oneself when time itself sheds its skin like a serpent in the wild?

Perhaps not—perhaps the gift is in the letting go— the surrender to a greater sea, each wave an unseen hand pressing me forward into an unknown grace, into another beginning.

Carried, always carried, not by the strength of my grasp but by the whisper of something divine— calling through the chaos, a steady murmur beneath the rush. So, I drift, not lost but loosened, fingers uncurled from the illusion of control.

The currents may be untamed, but there is a riverbed beneath— deeper than change, firmer than fear. To be carried is not to be abandoned.

Grasping—yes, still I try— but when it slips free, I remember: the current itself belongs to the maker of the tides. And in this drift, I find a peace beyond the shore.

Printed in the United States
by Baker & Taylor Publisher Services